TANZANIA IN MAPS: Graphic Perspectives of a Developing Country

TANZANIA IN MAPS: Graphic Perspectives of a Developing Country

edited by
L. Berry PH.D
formerly Professor of Geography
University of Dar es Salaam
Tanzania

AFRICANA PUBLISHING CORPORATION · NEW YORK

Published
in the United States of America 1972
by Africana Publishing Corporation
101 Fifth Avenue
New York, N.Y. 10003

Library of Congress Catalog Card No. 70-654258
ISBN 0-8419-0076-0

Printed in Great Britain

CONTENTS

5

LIST OF TABLES

CONTRIBUTORS

ROGER ALDRIDGE *Lecturer in Education, University of Dar es Salaam*

JOAN BATTERSBY *Formerly Lecturer in Education, University of Dar es Salaam*

EILEEN BERRY and LEN BERRY *Professor of Geography, University of Dar es Salaam*

LIONEL CLIFFE *Lecturer in Political Science, University of Dar es Salaam*

BASHIR DATOO *Lecturer in Geography, University of Dar es Salaam*

SALIM HAMEER *Formerly Assistant Research Fellow, Bureau of Resource Assessment and Land Use Planning, University of Dar es Salaam*

TOM HANKINS *Research Fellow, Rural Research Project, University of Dar es Salaam*

JOOP HEIJNEN *Research Fellow, Bureau of Resource Assessment and Land Use Planning, University of Dar es Salaam*

ARNE LARSEN *Research Fellow, Interdisciplinary Rural Research Project, University of Dar es Salaam*

IAN J JACKSON *Lecturer in Geography, University of Dar es Salaam*

SÖREN JENSEN *Formerly of Planning Division, Ministry of Health and Housing, Dar es Salaam*

ADOLFO MASCARENHAS *Lecturer in Geography, University of Dar es Salaam*

JOHN McKAY *Research Fellow, Bureau of Resource Assessment and Land Use Planning, University of Dar es Salaam*

JOHN E MOORE *Lecturer in Geography, University of Dar es Salaam*

JOSEPHINE KADUMA *Tutorial Assistant, Department of Geography, University of Dar es Salaam*

HILARY PAGE *Research Student, Princeton University, formerly of University of Dar es Salaam*

ABDUL M H SHERIFF *Assistant Lecturer in History, University of Dar es Salaam*

BOB SIMKO *Associate Professor in Geography, Middlebury College, Vermont. Formerly Lecturer in Geography, University of Dar es Salaam*

JOHN SUTTON *Lecturer in History (Archaeology), University of Dar es Salaam*

PAUL TEMPLE *Reader in Geography, University of Dar es Salaam*

IAN THOMAS *formerly Lecturer in Geography, University of Dar es Salaam*

JOHN WHITE *Senior Education Officer, Ministry of Education, Tanzania*

GLORIA YOUNG-SING *Formerly Lecturer in Geography, University of Dar es Salaam*

ACKNOWLEDGEMENTS

The four maps showing atmospheric pressure and winds on p. 35 have been taken from *The Climate of Africa* by B W Thompson published by Oxford University Press, East Africa.

Maps were drawn by Mr M M Mwanjoka, Mr M K Ulaya and Mr F A Msuya, Cartographers in the Department of Geography, University of Dar es Salaam.

INTRODUCTION

This book is addressed primarily to people in Tanzania, both in formal education and outside it, who wish to know more of the spatial aspects of their country. At a time when the nation is concerned not only with overall national development but also with the need to achieve as wide a regional spread of development as possible, it is opportune to survey some aspects of the great diversity of the country and to attempt a preliminary analysis of some of the components of this diversity. For readers outside Tanzania we have tried to present a general picture of a fascinating country and to review the main elements of the economy.

Tanzania in Maps generally follows the format and presentation of its fore-runner, *Sierra Leone in Maps* by J I Clarke.

There are 65 block of maps and diagrams in this book, most of them dealing with the distribution of a particular element of national resources, production or of national culture. The accompanying text attempts to supplement the map or series of maps with added description and some explanation. We have not attempted to cover all facets of the economy: many indeed are not readily amenable to this sort of treatment, and the choice of topics has to some extent been dictated by the availability of data. However, in some cases, though information was rather limited, we have felt it worthwhile to provide whatever was available. Major gaps which could perhaps be filled in a later edition include trading and marketing flows, communication flows and land-use patterns. Although in the maps of population and of rural economy we have tried to provide an analysis at district or sub-district level, the data is not available to attempt this for most subjects and indeed the scale of our presentation is such that this would in any case be difficult. This book is not therefore a detailed regional analysis of Tanzania—a task which needs much more research, though Jensen (*Regional Economic Atlas of Tanzania*) has made a preliminary attempt which may in some ways be regarded as complementary to the present publication. Within the constraints of the format the contributors have been given a fairly free hand to develop their own approach to the topic. Some articles are the preliminary results of detailed research work and investigation; others are compilations from existing material, but we have attempted throughout to keep technical jargon to the minimum. For those wishing to read further on the topics discussed there is a bibliography for each part of the text, though in addition we have provided a general bibliography for Tanzania which should be of use for rather less specific follow-up reading. Neither is exhaustive; we have rather attempted to give an indication of the most important material available up to mid 1969. The *East African Geographical Journal*, *The Journal of the Geographical Association of Tanzania* and the publications of the Bureau of Resource Assessment and Land Use Planning at the University of Dar es Salaam provide a continuing source of reference.

The list of contributors clearly indicates that this is the work of many hands: the core of the material has come from members of the Department of Geography of the University, with assistance from other geographers in the University and outside it, but a range of other subjects and Departments have been involved and these contributions are particularly welcomed. A number of authors have been able to base their work on topographic and other maps published by the Survey Department, Ministry of Lands and Settlement, Dar es Salaam, or by the Directorate of Overseas Survey, UK and a list of Tanzanian published maps with a short commentary on them is found in Appendix 1. The first edition of the *Tanzania National Atlas* was published while this book was in preparation and we thank the director of the Survey Department for early access to this important basic document and for considerable other assistance in the progress of this work.

Most maps reproduced here were drawn at a scale of 1 : 3 000 000 and reduced for publication to a scale of approximately 1 : 7 700 000 so that there cannot be a high degree of accuracy in location and measurements based on them. The cartographic work has been entirely in the hands of the small team of Tanzanian cartographers in the Department of Geography and the finished volume owes much to their perseverence and ability in a demanding task. The University has in this and other ways provided very considerable support for this book and we are very pleased to acknowledge this help.

Some indication of sources and origins of basic data is given both in the text and in the bibliography, but the authors wish particularly to express their thanks for the assistance provided by the Ministry of Agriculture, Food and Co-operatives, the Ministry of National Education, the Ministry of Lands and Settlement, the Ministry of Commerce and Industries, and the Ministry of Health and Housing together with a host of individuals and organizations who have been helpful in the original research. I would also like to thank John B Mndolwa and Philbert K Rwejuna for much of the typing of the manuscript and Mrs J Carthew for assistance in the final stages of editing.

LEN BERRY

1 TANZANIA IN AFRICA

Tanzania is a large country located on the eastern side of the African continent. It lies just south of the equator between the great lakes of Central Africa (Victoria, Tanganyika and Nyasa) and the Indian Ocean. With an area of 931 082 square kilometres (363 708 square miles) and a population of twelve million, three hundred thousand (1967 census) it is the largest and most populous of the East African countries and one of the larger African nations. Officially known as The United Republic of Tanzania, the country consists of mainland Tanzania (formerly Tanganyika) and the islands of Zanzibar (1638 sq. km.) and Pemba (973 sq. km.), both lying about 32 km. from the mainland.

There are few written records which tell us of the history of inland Tanzania, but archaeological studies linked with the work of oral historians reveal a long and complex history of people in the area beginning in the Pleistocene and evolving up to the present day. Written records are available for the coastal area which has been known to Persian, Arabic, Chinese, Indian and Portuguese traders for many hundreds of years. The colonial period can be said to have formally begun in 1885 when at the Berlin Conference Germany gained control of Tanganyika. After the First World War this area was administered by Britain, first as a League of Nations Mandated Territory, and then as a United Nations Trusteeship. Independence was achieved on 9 December 1961 under the leadership of Julius K Nyerere, who became President of the Republic when it was declared a year later. Zanzibar experienced many years of Arab and Portuguese rule before becoming an independent Arab Sultanate in 1856. In 1890 a British Protectorate was established and the country obtained independence under minority Arab control in December 1963. The revolution that swept over Zanzibar the following month deposed the Sultan and in April 1964 Zanzibar merged with Tanganyika to form Tanzania. The Republic is a member of the United Nations, of the British Commonwealth, of the Organization for African Unity and of many other international commissions and organizations.

Tanzania is a part of the underdeveloped or 'developing' world. Per capita income is about 570 shillings ($81) and the economy is dominated by the agricultural sector with most smallholders obtaining an important part of their income from subsistence production. In comparison with other African nations Tanzania occupies a middle position with regard to economic progress. Comparative figures are somewhat out of date but in the early 1960s Tanzania had, for example, more miles of railway track than all African countries excepting Algeria, the UAR, the Sudan, Nigeria, the Congo and South Africa but in terms of surfaced roads she had a very low standing. For per capita income Tanzania appears to be in the middle of the list of African countries; similarly for indices of industrial output and services. Tanzania is fortunate in comparison with many African countries in that she avoids the risks inherent in a heavy reliance on one or two products as four items account for the bulk of the country's export trade: sisal, coffee, cotton and diamonds. In addition there are a number of other significant exports with future potential, though they are all in the agricultural sector. Tanzania, however, shares with many African countries the international marketing and price structure problems for her agricultural products. An important and growing industry in Tanzania is the tourist industry.

Tanzania has, since her independence, played a significant political role in Africa. President Nyerere has maintained a well defined foreign policy and has been a staunch supporter of the OAU. The country has attempted to follow an independent international position, developing relations with both east and west. In recent years difficulties have arisen with Britain over UDI in Rhodesia and with the USA and West Germany, but relations are now normal with all these countries. Because of its proximity to the white-controlled portions of southern Africa, Tanzania has become a centre for the various African liberation movements. Groups with headquarters in Dar es Salaam include FRELIMO (Mozambique), SWAPO (South-West Africa), ZANU and ZAPU (Rhodesia), and ANC (South Africa).

In the past few years Tanzania and the other East African countries have made a particular effort to expand African links and contacts. Air routes now provide closer contact with the Congo and with West Africa, and road links are planned with Burundi. Tanzania has also been influential in the 'Good Neighbours conference', a periodic meeting of Heads of State of East and Central Africa which is a little noticed, but consistently successful meeting, cutting across the division between French- and English-speaking Africa. As a longer term attempt to bridge the language barrier the study of French is being encouraged in Tanzanian schools and at the University of Dar es Salaam.

An internal development that may have considerable significance in Africa is Tanzania's policy of Socialism and Self-Reliance, as laid down in the Arusha Declaration of February 1967. Future development is to follow the guide-lines of the Declaration which strongly commits the country to socialism in the African tradition of communal labour and land ownership, to rural development and to a policy of self-reliance with less emphasis on foreign assistance and more on the land and people of Tanzania. Many African countries are watching with interest and hope Tanzania's progress in this policy.

BOB SIMKO

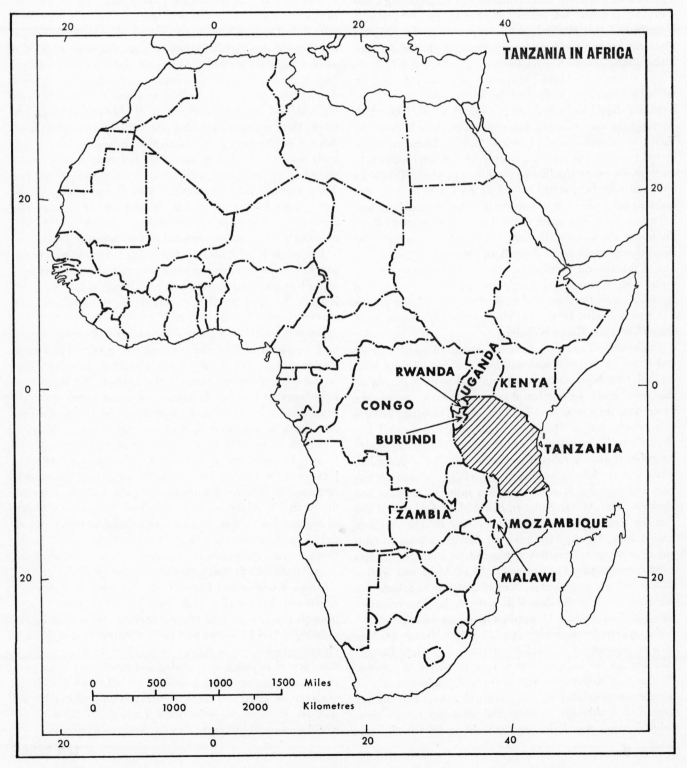

TANZANIA IN AFRICA

RWANDA

CONGO

UGANDA

KENYA

BURUNDI

TANZANIA

ZAMBIA

MOZAMBIQUE

MALAWI

| 0 | 500 | 1000 | 1500 | Miles |
| 0 | 1000 | 2000 | | Kilometres |

2 TANZANIA AND HER NEIGHBOURS

Tanzania has common frontiers with eight other states, more than any other African country except Congo (Kinshasa). Inside Tanzania the distribution of population is such that nodes of dense population tend to occur on the outer fringes of the country, promoting links across the frontiers. Many of the peoples of Tanzania have tribal or other affiliations in neighbouring countries: for example, the Masai with Kenya, the Bahaya with Uganda and the Makonde with Mozambique. Despite this Tanzania has had few boundary problems, the major one with Malawi being, however, as yet unsolved.

The dispute with Malawi is over the position of the frontier on Lake Nyasa. Logically and by international practice the boundary should be located near the middle of the lake which separates the two countries, but some maps show it along the Tanzanian shoreline of the lake and Malawi claims this as the correct frontier. The southern frontier of Tanzania follows for much of its course the line of the Ruvuma River. This is an awkward boundary, particularly if the river is to be developed and utilized at some future date, but it is clearly demarcated and has given rise to no dispute so far. The western frontier follows the line of the western rift valley which is partly occupied by lakes, though in the north Rwanda and Burundi fall within the line of this natural frontier. In contrast the boundaries to the north with Kenya and Uganda are arbitrary straight lines agreed upon by Germany and Great Britain as colonial powers and later modified by the birthday gift of Kilimanjaro from Queen Victoria to Kaiser Wilhelm.

Traditionally Tanzania has shown closest links with Uganda and Kenya, as between 1918 and Independence all three were controlled by the same colonial power and towards the end of this period evolved a number of common facilities and services between the three countries. The East African Common Services Organization was set up in 1948 (at this time it was called The High Commission) together with the East African Legislative Assembly (formerly called the Central Legislative Assembly) which was the international body controlling the common services and related matters. The services included Railways and Harbours, East African Airways, East African Agricultural and Forestry Research Organization, a number of other research bodies, East African Meteorological Service, a joint customs union, an integrated taxation system and for a number of years a common currency. The University of East Africa with its constituent colleges at Makerere, Nairobi and Dar es Salaam was another example of the close links between the three countries, although three separate Universities have now evolved.

Tanzania under the leadership of President Nyerere has long been an advocate of regional co-operation, and when Tanganyika was due for Independence in 1961, he offered to postpone the date until Kenya also could become independent in order to increase the possibility of closer political union. This did not happen, and although economic and other ties remain close, political union now looks very unlikely, at least in the near future.

Although many aspects of the Common Services Organization worked well, problems arose particularly over the tendency for most of the bodies to be centred in Kenya, and in 1966 a commission was set up under Professor Phillip of Denmark to 'review existing arrangements and propose means of increasing their effectiveness and equalizing the distribution of regional gains among the partners'. Out of this commission's report grew the East African Community Treaty which came into force on 1 December 1967. The treaty with its ninety-eight articles sets out to preserve and reform economic co-operation. Most of the common services are retained, though some headquarters have been relocated. The new community centre is Arusha, in Tanzania, but it is the geographical centre of East Africa. In addition a whole range of new economic proposals was put forward. These include the introduction of a transfer tax, which serves to aid the development of industry in Tanzania and to some extent in Uganda, and an agreed programme of industrial development in the three countries. One important mechanism for such industrial development is the creation of an East African (industrial) Bank which will give preference to industries which serve the whole of the region rather than any one national market. These measures are important to Tanzania which has a persistent trading deficit with her East African partners. In 1966 this amounted to over 230 million shillings, though in 1967, the unfavourable balance was reduced to 120 million shillings.

The attractiveness of the community arrangements is apparent from the number of outside countries which have already applied to join, and negotiations are already under way with Zambia, Somalia, Burundi and Ethiopia for membership or association with the community.

Following UDI in Rhodesia Tanzania's links with Zambia have expanded rapidly and movement of goods from Dar es Salaam and Mtwara to Zambia is already an important part of that country's re-orientation to the north. Politically the two neighbours are very closely linked, and contacts at all levels are expected to continue to grow. It may well be that in the long run Tanzania may serve in a similar way as one of Malawi's outlets to the sea, but at present the frontier dispute and difference in international policies have handicapped relations between them. In a similar way, in the long term, Tanzania is interested in close and harmonious relations with the people to the south, but at present the frontier with Mozambique is part of the 'hot line' across Africa where colonial or minority controlled governments meet independent African states. As the struggle for independence continues inside Mozambique, normal links with the south must necessarily wait.

Congo, Rwanda and Burundi, the last three of Tanzania's neighbours, have until recently remained rather remote, partly through the lack of inter-communications engendered by the differing colonial histories and partly through the considerable distances from Dar es Salaam to the western frontier. Now there is a clear policy of renewing and developing links, road communications are being improved, air links with the Congo are being increased and closer political and economic exchanges planned. In these and other ways Tanzania's links with her neighbours are all part of the slow decolonization process.

LEN BERRY

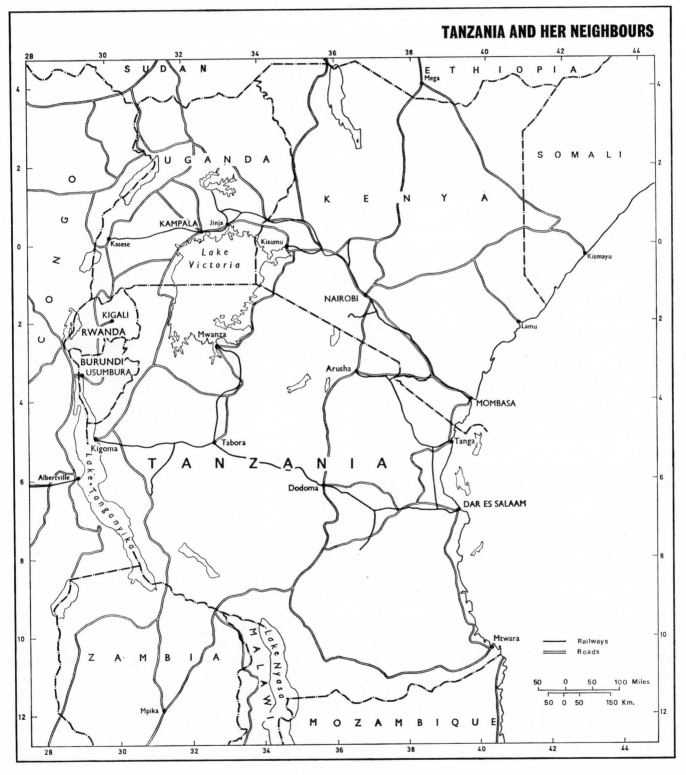

TANZANIA AND HER NEIGHBOURS

3 ADMINISTRATIVE AREAS, 1967

The division of a country into administrative areas seeks to achieve varying aims. The central government needs to manage the affairs of the nation, and to this end requires a system for disseminating its aims, objectives and proposals, and an organization for controlling the activities and providing for the needs of the populace. In turn it must be able to receive the views and aspirations of the people and devise a mechanism of tax collection. The physical size of Tanzania (886 177 sq. km.) and the nature of the population distribution mean that it is not possible to administer the whole effectively from a single centre—especially one as peripheral to the national area as is the capital city. The variety of the country's environments, peoples and problems means that there must be local as well as central government and locally-based executive and advisory services. Yet the limited skilled manpower—administrative and technical—necessitates some hierarchical structure of areal organization.

Tanzania has a well-defined administrative structure with eighteen Regions and sixty-two Districts.[1] There are seventeen Regions on the mainland. Zanzibar, united with Tanganyika since April 1964, has its own administrative structure. Zanzibar Island and Pemba Island may be added to the fifty-nine Districts of the mainland and the island of Mafia to constitute the full complement for the United Republic. The more important urban areas have a separate administrative hierarchy. Dar es Salaam (pop. 272 821 in 1967), the capital, has at different periods been given separate recognition as a district, a municipal area and, since the time of independent government, as a City. Zanzibar Town (68 490) is the main town of the offshore islands, while on the mainland Tanga (61 058) is the only municipality. Thirteen other urban areas have separate town councils and, although they are subordinate to the regional administration, they are administratively independent of the district in which they are located. However, functionally they are interdependent and all of these towns—with the exception of Lindi—are the site of the regional headquarters, and all are district headquarters. There are another forty-six urban areas which do not have their own town councils but which serve as district headquarters. This framework is set out in Table 1, p. 157. In the list of district headquarters those with town councils are italicized.

The German administration (1891–1917) created the first territorial administrative structure (see Map 44). German East Africa included Rwanda and Burundi (former Ruanda-Urundi) which, however, became the responsibility of Belgium in 1920. Zanzibar (which included Mafia Island until 1922) remained a separate entity until 1964 and has had its own administrative system of Districts Mudirias, and Shehias. The German system of districts was inherited by the British and elaborated between 1920 and 1961 (see Map 45). During this period the number of Districts was increased from twenty-two to fifty-seven as a result of changes in the concept of local government, the improvement of communications, changing economic and social conditions in

[1] There have been sixty-three districts since 1 May 1969 when Hanang was separated from Mbulu.

different parts of the country, and the increase in the population. From 1925 the Districts were grouped for administrative convenience into Provinces (eventually renamed Regions). There were initially eleven (1925–1931), but this was subsequently reduced to eight (1932–1958), and then increased to nine which remained the number until 1961. Since Independence, while the basic framework of Districts and Regions has been maintained, there has been considerable reorganization in detail as the emphasis on local development has been increased. At present the political officer in charge of a Region is the Regional Commissioner and his administrative counterpart is the Administrative Secretary. At the District level there is an Area Commissioner and his Area Secretary. It has been usual to have police, prison and medical staff at District headquarters, but the Districts have throughout been too numerous to have a full complement of technical staff for agriculture, survey, lands and mines, water development, etc. These have tended to concentrate at the regional headquarters and to organize their activities at this level. The increase from 9 to 15 regions in 1963 in part reflects the attempt to increase the distribution of technical expertise.

For the purposes of local government and the administration of justice, the Districts are too large. The establishment of law and order, the collection of revenue and, in recent years, the stimulation of economic and social development, are community level activities which require organization at the village or parish level. Between 1925 and 1963 each District was the charge of a District Commissioner and his District Officers, but these areas were sub-divided into chiefdoms and sub-chiefdoms. The subordinate councils of the chiefdoms and the informal parish councils provided a link with the district council, the provincial administration and thereby with the central government. The chiefs, sub-chiefs and *jumbes* (village headman) carried out the executive work at these sub-district levels and were responsible for tax collection, customary law, and undertook to organize the maintenance of roads and buildings. They provided the link with the local community. In 1963 the African Chiefs Ordinance (Repeal) Act dismantled this structure. The chiefdoms and sub-chiefdoms of the earlier period were replaced by Divisions and Sub-divisions which currently constitute the first breakdown of the total district area. In 1948 there were approximately 420 chiefdoms. In 1967 there were 360 Divisions and almost 1300 Sub-divisions on the mainland. These post-Independence Divisions and Sub-divisons were first defined as the areas of operation of, respectively, the Divisional Executive Officer and the Assistant Divisional or Village Executive Officer. Initially the delimitation of the geographic area was rather loose, but certainly in the case of the Divisons their areal location and extent is now more firmly established. They are shown on the map. Parallel with this development of the local administrative areas has been the strengthening of the political party structure and the creation of village development committees. The operation of the ten-house cell system takes this local involvement and mobilization down to the household level. However, this system is still evolving and at the sub-district scale a uniform areal organization is only just beginning to emerge. The dimensions of these units are summarized in Table 2, p. 157.

IAN THOMAS

ADMINISTRATIVE AREAS 1967

40   0   30   160   Miles
Kilometres   40   0   80   160   240

KARAGWE
Bugene
• Bukoba
L. Victoria
N. MARA
Ngara
NGARA
BIHARAMULO
Biharamulo
UKEREWE
Nansio
Mwanza
MWANZA
Geita
Ngudu
KWIMBA
Nyalikungu
MUSOMA
Musoma
Tarime
MASWA
MASAI
Monduli
ARUSHA
Arusha
KILIMANJARO
Moshi
PARE
Same
Kibondo
KIBONDO
KASULU
Kasulu
Kigoma
KIGOMA
Lake
Tanganyika
KAHAMA
Kahama
Shinyanga
SHINYANGA
Nzega
NZEGA
Mbulu
MBULU
Kiomboi
IRAMBA
Singida
SINGIDA
Kondoa
KONDOA
KOROGWE
LUSHOTO
Lushoto
Korogwe
Handeni
HANDENI
Tanga
TANGA
Pangani
PANGANI
PEMBA
Chakechake
TABORA
Tabora
Manyoni
MANYONI
DODOMA
Dodoma
Mpwapwa
MPWAPWA
ZANZIBAR
Zanzibar
MPANDA
Mpanda
Kilosa
KILOSA
Morogoro
MOROGORO
BAGAMOYO
Bagamoyo
Dar es Salaam
MZIZIMA
Kisarawe
KISARAWE
RUFIJI
Utete
MAFIA
Kilindoni
SUMBAWANGA
Sumbawanga
CHUNYA
Chunya
MBEYA
IRINGA
Iringa
MUFINDI
Kibau
Mahenge
ULANGA
KILWA
Kilwa
MBOZI
Mbeya
Vwawa
Tukuyu
RUNGWE
NJOMBE
Njombe
NACHINGWEA
Lindi
LINDI
Mtwara
MTWARA
Lake
Nyasa
MBINGA
Mbinga
SONGEA
Songea
TUNDURU
Tunduru
Nachingwea
Masasi
MASASI
NEWALA
Newala

REGIONS
WEST LAKE
MARA
MWANZA
KIGOMA
SHINYANGA
TABORA
SINGIDA
ARUSHA
DODOMA
TANGA
ZANZIBAR
KILIMANJARO
MBEYA
IRINGA
MOROGORO
COAST
MTWARA
RUVUMA

—·—·—   International boundary   ● Regional headquarters
—··—··— Regional boundary   • District headquarters
—···—···— District boundary
— — — — Divisional boundary

15

4 POLITICAL GEOGRAPHY

The District

The District is the basic political and administrative unit in Tanzania. From colonial times, the apparatus through which Dar es Salaam administers the country has had a two-tier structure. At the higher level, the colonial 'Provinces' were renamed 'Regions' after Independence, while in 1963 the nine Regions on the mainland were sub-divided into seventeen. But the units at the lower level—the Districts—were left the same. In fact the only change in boundaries of districts in the last generation or so has been the sub-division of some of the bigger ones, so that from fifty-four mainland Districts in 1957 there are now (1969) sixty-one, excluding Dar es Salaam.

As well as being the basis for the administration of the country, the District is also the area on which local government, the organization of the single national movement—the Tanganyika African National Union (TANU), and the Parliamentary constituencies are all based. Something of the working of these will be discussed in the following paragraphs. However, it is first necessary to describe the nature of the Districts themselves as social and political entities.

The District boundaries tend to enclose an area which has an ethnic of cultural homogeneity. Just over half of the Districts have a single predominant tribe, from which the majority of the population is drawn. Sometimes the Districts represent distinct ecological zones, but given the varied nature of the Tanzanian landscape, and the great number of differing ethnic groups, some of them were originally somewhat arbitrary units. Administrative difficulties have been increased by the fact that even when the population of a District had a common language and culture, it seldom owed allegiance to a single political authority. Only the present-day Districts of Ufipa, Lushoto, Karagwe and Iringa-Mufindi correspond to traditional 'states' in this way.

While the social coherence and the geographical compactness of some of the highland, densely populated Districts minimizes administrative problems, the difficulties in many other Districts are very great. The largest Districts in area—Tabora and Masai—are almost 64,000 square kilometres (25,000 square miles), and the largest in population, Kilimanjaro and Maswa, are approaching half a million, which means they are as big as some small independent states such as Sierra Leone, or the Gambia. Often, too, the population is fairly sparse, and for the most part scattered in separate family homesteads rather than residential centres. When, in addition, communications are but little developed, the administration of a District with only limited numbers of personnel becomes a very challenging task.

Administration

The seventeen mainland Regions are ruled as a unitary state, while the islands of Zanzibar and Pemba have a government of their own which has certain powers reserved to it. The main arm of central government in reaching out into the country is the Regional Administration, which is under the President's Office. In each Region and District it is embodied in the persons of Regional and Area Commissioners. These officers with the assistance of their staff are responsible for general administration and for the co-ordination of all government services as well as the overall development of their areas. They are also automatically the TANU Secretaries for the Region or District. The Regional Commissioners are key figures as they are also ex-officio Members of Parliament and of the TANU National Executive Committee (NEC). During 1969, for the first time, the administration extended below the District level with the appointment of Divisional Secretaries who, like the Commissioners, combine administrative and party functions.

Most other central government departments have an official presence at regional, and often district level. The main extension agencies concerned with development in the countryside, like Agriculture or Veterinary, Health and Rural Development, have field staff posted in the divisions or even below.

The Party

Elected and appointed officials of TANU extend down to the village level and even below, in the person of the *balozi* (leaders of cells based on ten houses). One of their main responsibilities is to assist governmental agencies in promoting development efforts and in organizing the people. The party also aims to channel the 'grass roots' demands and responses up to the central authorities. In particular, it is the medium through which competitive elections are held for various representative bodies from the Village Development Committees, through the District Councils, up to Parliament itself.

Parliament

The main body of parliamentarians consists of 107 Members, each elected for a single constituency (indicated in the map) under a unique, single party, electoral system introduced in 1965. Under this system, any party member (that is anyone who subscribes to TANU's basic socialist principles and has no financial interest in any private business) can put his name forward. Then branch representatives, meeting as the District Conference of TANU, vote for those candidates in each constituency of the District whom they prefer. Usually the top two in each constituency are then approved by the NEC to stand as the candidates. Finally, a campaign to present the pair of TANU candidates culminates in one being elected by popular vote. The largest District, Kilimanjaro, has as many as four constituencies; the smaller Districts form a single parliamentary seat. The constituency of the United Republic has recently been changed so that some of the Districts were divided or further sub-divided before the last elections (held in November 1970) so as to provide 120 constituencies.

In addition, Parliament contains some nominated and indirectly elected Members, as well as a number of representatives from Zanzibar. The unhappy history of pre-Independence elections, coupled with the revolution, make it difficult to extend the electoral system there—except for the election of President, which is done on the basis of a simple Yes/No for a single candidate.

Local government

Local authorities in Tanzania consist of District Councils, which in almost every case are responsible for education and other social and economic services within the confines of a single administrative District. There are in addition eleven urban areas which have Independent Town Councils, as well as the City of Dar es Salaam, and the Municipality of Tanga. These urban areas also have a separate TANU district organization. As with the parliamentary representatives, the party selects a short list of two competitors who contest for each Ward into which the District or Town Council area is divided.

LIONEL CLIFFE

5 POPULATION, 1967

Many of the maps of this book depict the activities of the inhabitants of Tanzania and the resources with which they work. The general characteristics of any population are its size, distribution, composition and quality, and the rate at which it is growing. Two outstanding and important features of the population of Tanzania are its uneven distribution and rapid rate of growth.

At the time of the population census of August 1967 the United Republic of Tanzania had a population of 12 313 469, of which 11 958 654 were on the mainland (but including Mafia) and 354 815 in Zanzibar. This total compares with the 1967 estimates for Kenya of 9 948 000 and 7 934 000 for Uganda. Thus of the three East African countries Tanzania has the largest population. However, it also has the largest land area (886 177 sq. km.), and the average population density at 13.9 per square kilometre is only moderate even for an African country (Table 3, p. 158). A number of near neighbours in East and Central Africa are small countries with high population densities. Zambia is only slightly smaller in area than Tanzania but has even fewer people. Morocco, Algeria and Congo (Kinshasa) have similar population totals, while Nigeria has a comparable area.

The distribution of the total population among the various Regions of the country is shown in Table 4, p. 158, which also gives the area of each administrative unit, the proportion of the total national area and total national population in each, and the regional population density. The distribution of population among the Regions is relatively even, the proportion on the mainland ranging only from 3.2 per cent in Ruvuma to 7.9 per cent in Mbeya Region. The areas of the Regions differ markedly and range from Tabora which has 13.8 per cent of the national area, to Kilimanjaro which covers only 1.5 per cent of Tanzania. The population densities are correspondingly variable. The islands of Zanzibar and Pemba have a very high density (134 psk) which is more than twice as great as that of Mwanza (54 psk) the most densely populated mainland Region. Tabora, Ruvuma, Arusha, Singida, and Morogoro Regions all have low overall population densities (less than 10 psk).

At the District level further features of the population distribution may be illustrated by grouping the Districts according to their level of population density and examining the proportion of the total national population and national area in each category (see Table 5, p. 158). Almost two-thirds of the area of the country (63.4 per cent) carries less than one quarter (23.8 per cent) of the population at average densities of under 15 per square kilometre, while 26 per cent of the people occupy 4.5 per cent of the area at densities of more than 50 per square kilometre. Within District areas there are also very considerable variations in the pattern of distribution (see Map 48: Population density, 1967) but contrary to the experience of many countries of the world these local patterns are not markedly affected by the process of urbanization, and the vast majority of the inhabitants of Tanzania live in rural settlements and, furthermore, remain in agricultural occupations.

The population of Tanzania is predominantly rural. There are only 830 678 in the sixty-two 'urban' centres which constitute the district headquarters and this is only 6.7 per cent of the total population. Of this total, 272 821 are accounted for by Dar es Salaam alone, while normally only thirty-four of the other centres are classed as fully urban. Tanzania ranks very low in the world by degrees of urbanization of the population. This is illustrated in Table 6, p. 158, which presents figures only for African countries.

More Tanzanians are living in urban areas than ever before, but the proportion is not increasing very quickly. Though comparisons over time are not easy, it has been estimated that whereas 3.2 per cent of the population were urban in 1948, this had risen to 4.8 per cent by 1957, and only reached 6.2 per cent by 1967. The average annual percentage growth-rate was 6.0 per cent over the two decades. The map shows the location and population size of those sixteen urban areas which have separate town councils, and indicates the extent to which they grew from 1957 to 1967.

A large proportion of those living in towns is non-African, and another characteristic of the country's population is the different ethnic and racial groups which inhabit the area. In 1957/58 the population composition in Tanganyika and Zanzibar was as indicated in Table 7, p. 159.

This diversity has had an impact on the culture of the country, has provided a lingua-franca derived from Bantu and Arabic sources, and finds expression in the morphological variety of the towns as well as in the contrasted land-use patterns of the agricultural areas.

IAN THOMAS

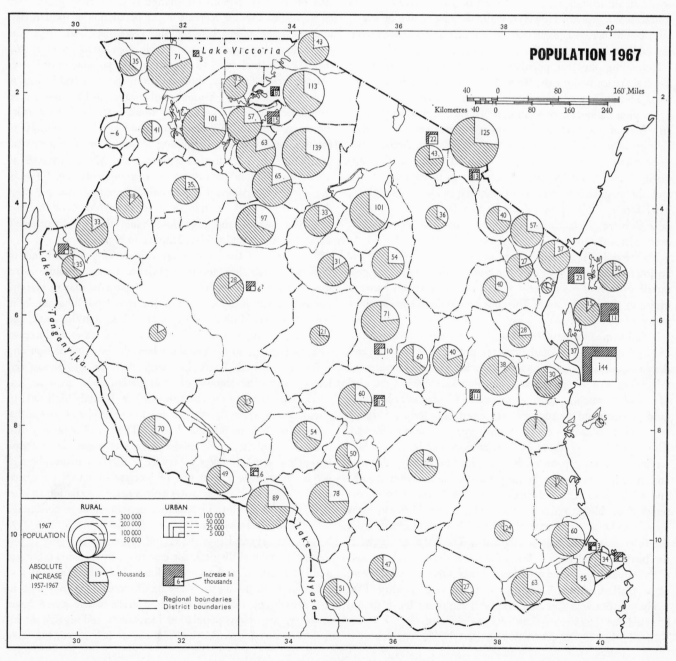

POPULATION 1967

RURAL

1967 POPULATION

ABSOLUTE INCREASE 1957-1967

Increase in thousands

Regional boundaries
District boundaries

6 POPULATION CHANGE, 1957-67

The first full enumeration of the population of Tanganyika and Zanzibar took place in 1948. The number of inhabitants was not known with any certainty until that time and the trend in the population size was a matter of some debate. The political, economic and social conditions in East Africa until at least 1925 were not seen as conducive to an increase in the number of people. Internecine warfare exacerbated by the activities of the slave traders was reinforced by the military operations of the Germans, in creating instability and causing loss of life. Epidemics for the human and the livestock population—influenza and rinderpest respectively—only served to make the situation worse. The upheavals of the First World War and attendant economic difficulties were only the last of a succession of events inimicable to growth. However, while the rate cannot be stated with confidence, it is clear that the population has grown considerably in the past thirty-five to forty years.

Estimating the real population growth in any country of tropical Africa is not easy. There are many difficulties encountered in trying to make a complete count of the people of a developing nation. As one can never be sure of the comparative efficiency of any two enumerations it is never certain whether changes in population are real or merely apparent. Account has to be taken of changes in boundaries and it is possible that successive censuses are increasingly efficient as the administrators and the populace become more familiar with enumerations. Therefore a certain proportion of apparent growth is attributable to more efficient coverage. The estimates of population at census dates are given in Table 8, p. 159.

The recorded increment of 3.22 million from 1957 to 1967 is an intercensal increase of 35.5 per cent. With a continued geometric growth of 3.0 per cent per annum such as this increase indicates, the population of Tanzania would double in the short period of 23.5 years.

This increase in the national total is the result of changes in the vital rates for the population—the proportions of births and deaths—and, to a lesser extent, variations in the amount of migration. The principal change has been a decrease in the level of mortality which, in 1967, was estimated to stand at 22 per thousand (the estimate for 1957 was 24/25 per thousand). It is likely to have been above 30 per thousand three or four decades ago. The expectation of life at birth is now greater because health services are more capable of dealing with the common diseases, and more infants survive the early years of life to become youths and adults who in turn raise families. On the other hand, the number of births remains high. The crude birth-rate was thought to be 46 per thousand in 1957, and the first estimate from the 1967 census data is 47 per thousand. The difference between the birth-rate and the death-rate indicates the natural increase of the population. In most African countries the natural increase of population is high. Table 9 presents the vital rates for Tanzania together with those for other African countries. It should be noted that the rates are no more than estimates.

In addition to the population change for the country as a whole, there are significant differences in the amount of growth which the various parts of the country have experienced. Again this results from differences in the rate of national increase, for the numbers of births and deaths in different parts of the country vary according to customary practices, standards of living, and the sex and age composition of the population. But within a country an equally important, or in some areas more important, determinant of population change is the amount of in- and out-migration. Some areas—such as the towns, and areas of economic development where agricultural expansion is taking place or where non-agricultural employment is available—attract migrants, while other areas are common sources of out-migration.

Tanzania is fortunate among tropical African countries in having had three relatively reliable and equally spaced full population enumerations in the past twenty years so that the information on internal population change is moderately good. Map 6a shows the absolute increase of the population of the Districts and the main towns between the years 1957 and 1967. The towns have experienced considerable population increase, and this would be mainly by in-migration. The population of Dar es Salaam increased by 144 thousand from 129 thousand in 1957 to 273 thousand in 1967. A number of rural areas have also added considerably to their population total: notably Maswa from 292 to 431 thousand, Kilimanjaro (excluding Moshi) from 351 to 476 thousand, Musoma (excluding Musoma Town) from 227 to 340 thousand, Geita from 270 to 371, and Mbulu from 188 to 289 thousand. Of all the districts of Tanzania only one, Ngara in the north-west, recorded a population decrease (from 102 to 96 thousand). All of these changes come about from a combination of natural increase and migration, though the latter is probably especially important in Geita, Mbulu and Ngara.

Some areas of the country are experiencing a rapid rate of increase though they do not experience a large absolute increment to their numbers. This is illustrated by the map of percentage population increase (p. 23). Karagwe and Biharamulo in the north-west; Mufindi, Mbinga, and Newala in the south; and Mbulu, Mpwapwa and Mzizima have high rates of increase. With the exception of Newala, where the base population and actual increment is large, these high rates are also almost certainly due to the amount of in-migration these areas are experiencing. Many of the areas showing moderately high rates of population increase (40–50 per cent) are peripheral to the districts with high population density. These well-populated districts show only relatively moderate rates of population increase (30–40 per cent). It takes a very large increase in numbers of people to produce a high rate of increase in a well populated district, whereas if the area has only a small population to start with, a small absolute increment represents a large percentage increase of population, see Table 10, p. 159.

Between 1957 and 1967 the rate of increase was higher in less densely populated districts, for example Mbeya, Iringa, Songea and Nachingwea in the south; Mbulu, Maswa, Shinyanga and Biharamulo in the north. The rate of increase was not high in the densely populated mountain districts where there have, however, been large population increments and significant increases in population density. The coastal belt remains an area

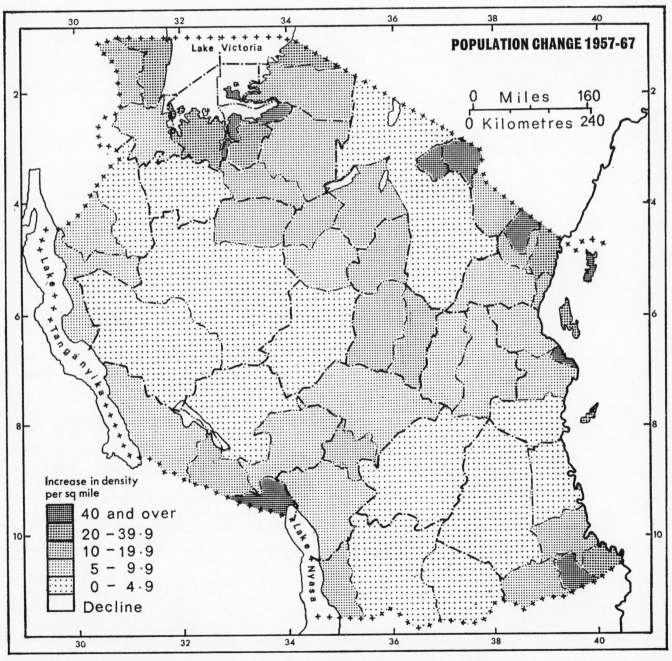

POPULATION CHANGE 1957-67

Lake Victoria

0 Miles 160
0 Kilometres 240

Lake Tanganyika

Lake Nyasa

Increase in density
per sq mile

40 and over
20 - 39·9
10 - 19·9
5 - 9·9
0 - 4·9
Decline

of low growth-rates, while large areas in the north and centre of the country have lower rates of change. There is, however, no direct relation between population density and rate of population growth in the districts.

It is useful in a predominantly agricultural country, therefore, to consider the increase in population not as a percentage but as an average increment per unit area (see Map 6b). This makes allowance for variations in the size of the area. A number of areas with large population clusters are found to have a large intercensal increase in density of population as well: e.g. around Lake Victoria—Bukoba, Geita, Mwanza, Kwimba, Ukerewe and North Mara; in the north-east—Kilimanjaro, Arusha, Lushoto, and Tanga; in the south—Rungwe; and in the south-east—Newala and Mtwara; finally, Dar es Salaam/ Mzizima, Mafia, Zanzibar and Pemba. These areas have to find sustenance for large numbers of additional people per unit area. This no great problem if paid employment is increasing, but if the people are agriculturalists who also grow much of the food they eat, it means there must be considerable increase in agricultural output which must be achieved by increasing acreage or yields per acre. Often neither of these is easy. The distribution of areas with a moderate increase per unit area bears a striking similarity to the general distribution of population in the country which serves again to illustrate the importance of natural increase in population change within the country as well as for the country as a whole, and points out the need for widespread technological and social development. The large, sparsely populated districts of the south-east and western plateaux, and of the Masai district have experienced little increase in density. These are areas of environmental difficulty where it is not easy to support more people without considerable technical innovation, change in customary attitudes and capital outlay of a high order.

IAN THOMAS

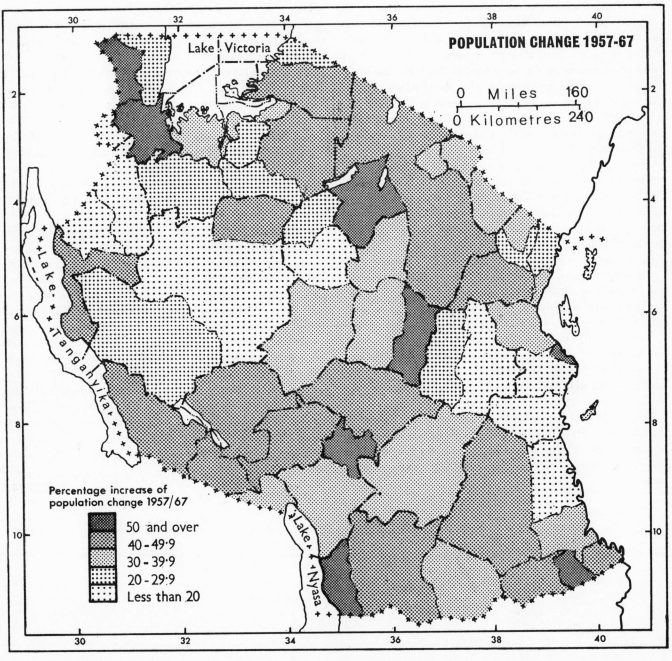

POPULATION CHANGE 1957-67

Lake Victoria

0 Miles 160

0 Kilometres 240

Lake Tanganyika

Lake Nyasa

Percentage increase of
population change 1957/67

50 and over
40 - 49·9
30 - 39·9
20 - 29·9
Less than 20

This section of the text provides an explanatory description of the next two maps: the one opposite—Relief—and the map of physiographic regions on page 27.

Tanzania is a land of attractive and varied landscape. Although most of the country is made up of plains and plateaux, significant areas of diversified relief occur, some on the grandest scale. Tanzania includes both the highest and the lowest parts of the African continent (Mount Kilimanjaro 5950m and the floor of Lake Tanganyika 358m below sea-level). Kilimanjaro is rightly famous as a landscape feature with its range of scenery and vegetation. Elsewhere inland there are many striking contrasts between swampy river valleys and arid plateaux, rocky granite hills and smooth volcanic cones, steep mountain slopes and gently rolling plains, though parts of the central plateau are noteworthy mainly for the monotony of the interminable undulating terrain. Such a variety of conditions is difficult to represent adequately on the scales used in this book, but some of the more useful 1:50 000 topographic sheets which may be used to gain a more specific picture are listed in the references. Other information is contained in the descriptions of relief and geomorphology included in the geological survey map notes and memoirs.

Only a small proportion of the country lies below the 200m contour but this includes the important islands of Pemba and Zanzibar and the sites of Tanga, Dar es Salaam and Mtwara. Excluding the Rufiji and Ruvu flood plains, the lowland area is made up of two physiographic regions (1 and 2), the Coast and the Coastal Hill Region.

The Coast typically includes a number of zones. Offshore and below low-water level there is often a line of coral reefs sometimes marked by small sandy islands. This is followed inland by a deeper channel with a shelving fringing reef or an erosional platform leading to the beach. The beach is either sandy or consists of low cliffs cut in coralline rock. Inland low terraces of coralline material mark former relatively high stands of the sea. However, in inlets and river estuaries mangrove grows quite luxuriantly (though in much smaller stands than those of the West African coast) and access to the coast is difficult.

The *Coastal Hill Region* begins typically some few kilometres inland and consists of dissected hills and plateaux rising to 300m in a few places. The area is underlain by rocks ranging from Pliocene to Jurassic in age giving rise to a variety of local scenery.

Inland there is a general rise of country to the west. The plateaux begin at about 300m above sea-level, rising steadily to about 800m and over in the south, and to over 1000m in the north. The so-called 'high plateau' of west central Tanzania varies in height between 900m in the Malagarasi basin to over 1500m in the Serengeti Plains. These plateau areas are divided into three physiographic regions, 10, 7 and 14 on the map.

Zone 10 *The South-east Plateau*: The whole plateau area shows a dome-like slope outwards from a point east of Songea and streams have a radial pattern from this node. The landscape varies considerably throughout the area. In the east (10a) predominantly crystalline rocks have produced a varied inselberg type topography. In the central zone (10b) Karroo rocks predominate and the plateau surfaces are very gently sloping, though deeply dissected by the major streams. In the west a subdued undulating topography occurs.

Zone 7 *The Masai and Handeni Plateau*: In the east the plateau surface is comparatively featureless and rises slowly westward to the higher Masai plateau over 1000m above sea-level. This is mainly rolling countryside but with many scattered small ridges and hill ranges—mostly bare rock inselberg-type hills.

Zone 14 *The Eastern Plateau*: Although this vast area, over one-third of the country, possesses a basic unity, there is considerable variation in the landscape from place to place. The area outlined in 14a is a gently undulating plateau covered with miombo woodland and with very little variation in landscape apart from occasional low hills and shallow drainage courses. 14b is mainly an alluvial basin which is an extension of the Lake Eyasi lowland and which includes most of the area formerly covered by the now vanished Wembere Lake. 14c is the high grassland plateau of the Serengeti with very flat undissected surfaces underlain for the most part by volcanic ash and lava resting on rocks of the Basement Complex. 14d is quite similar to 14a but with more pronounced drainage lines and generally lower ground as the plateau merges into the Malagarasi basin. 14e contains large areas of swampland and alluvial flats in the lower basin of the Moloyosi River and local relief is often only one or two metres. The Lake Victoria basin (14f) is an area of varied though generally low relief. The typical landscape south of the lake is one of low granite hills, rising perhaps 100m above gently sloping foothills which lead down to rather narrow flat valley bottoms. On the lake margins long narrow flooded inlets and the lake shore diversify the scenery. The remaining sub-division (14h) is an area in which the plateau surface is broken up by long narrow hill ranges which rise above rather flat lowlands.

LEN BERRY

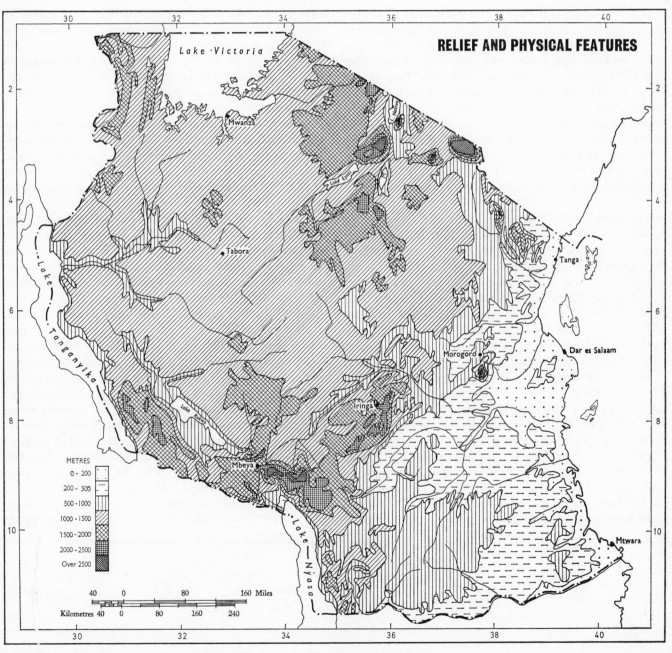

RELIEF AND PHYSICAL FEATURES

Lake Victoria

Mwanza

Lake Eyasi

Tabora

Tanga

Lake Tanganyika

Morogoro

Dar es Salaam

Lake Rukwa

Iringa

Mbeya

METRES

0 - 200	
200 - 500	
500 - 1000	
1000 - 1500	
1500 - 2000	
2000 - 2500	
Over 2500	

Lake Nyasa

Mtwara

40   0   80   160 Miles

Kilometres 40 0   80   160   240

There are four main upland zones in Tanzania: a line of mountains extending inland from Tanga to near Lake Manyara (the North-east Zone; 8 and 6 on the map); a line of high country extending from near Lake Natron to north of Dodoma (the Central Zone, 5 and 16); a line extending from north of Lake Nyasa to the north of Morogoro (the Southern Zone, 12 and 9); and a line associated with the western rift valley (the Western Zone, 13.)

The North-east Zone: This zone consists of two distinct types of upland, the fault block mountains of the Usambara and Pare ranges and the line of volcanic mountains which runs almost east-west and includes Kilimanjaro (5950m) and Meru 4600m).

The Usambaras which reach to over 2300m are a typical uplifted plateau with steep-sided slopes dropping about 1000m to the Pangani valley on the south-west. The upland is characterized by undulating country with some areas of spectacular mountain landscape. The north and south Pare Mountains are similar in origin but narrower and lower than the Usambaras. The same type of earth movements that resulted in the block mountains were also responsible for the rift-like trough of the Pangani valley which lies at their feet (8b). Much of the floor of this depression was a lake at some period in the Late Pleistocene or Recent, and soils are locally saline. The line of volcanoes terminating in Kilimanjaro may also be related to a line of weakness in the earth's crust, though the age of the vulcanism ranges considerably from one end of the line to the other. Kilimanjaro and Meru are cones of still active or very recently dormant volcanoes. Kilimanjaro has three main peaks: Kibo the highest, Shira and Mawenzi, and of these only Kibo still maintains its crater form, with periodic emmission of gases from the crater. The slopes of this mountain, which sweep down to Moshi at 1000m in one continuous line, must be one of the highest continuous slopes, and one of the most impressive sights in the world. Meru, rising 3400m above the town of Arusha, could only be dwarfed by such a gigantic neighbour. The crater of Meru is broken on the eastern side, where in a huge fall and flow of material the crater wall broke away and is now represented by a pile of debris stretching some 15 kilometres towards Kilimanjaro. The other volcanoes in this line have been strongly denuded and no traces of the craters are left.

The Central Zone: This is a complex area of high ground associated with the eastern rift valley but the rift faulting gives way southward to a whole series of fault lines. In the north the highland zone borders the faulted area of Lake Natron and Lake Manyara. Part of the altitude is due to relative upward movements of the blocks, but this has been increased by the addition of much volcanic material. Oldonyo Lengai is still active and many extinct cones occur including Hanang Mountain over (3300m). The second largest caldera in the world, Ngorongoro, is also found here. In the south the upland decreases in altitude breaking up into parallel ridges, and little trace of Pleistocene vulcanism is found.

The Southern Highland Zone: This is a north-east trending block of high ground generally rising above 1500m and with summits reaching 2000m in many areas. Upland relief is fairly subdued but the margins of the block are characterized by steep slopes. As the block has been uplifted streams have incised into it and the Great Ruaha gorge which cuts across the upland is an impressive landscape feature. North of about the latitude of Morogoro the upland breaks up into a number of hill areas though the fault line boundary on the west of the Wami valley is still very clearly defined. The Uluguru Mountains are an isolated block which may be considered part of the southern zone. Although these hills are well dissected, high plateau areas occur at over 2800m above sea-level.

The Western Zone: The western rift is a very clearly defined topographic feature in Tanzania with a well demarcated fault scarp (or fault line scarp) making up much of the eastern wall. In the south (13a) the land rises steadily towards the crest of the scarp and the Livingstone Mountains show greatly contrasting landscape on their east and west sides. To the north, volcanic activity has occurred and, around Mbeya town, heights reach over 3000m and there are many small craters and cones. The Lake Rukwa depression appears to be a subsidiary downfaulted area and between it and the Lake Tanganyika depression there is a range of high ground which rises to over 2200m (13d). Farther north the wall is less clearly defined except in two areas north of Kibwessa and Kigoma (13e). The remaining physiographic division in this area (15) is the extreme north-west corner of Tanzania; a hilly country with long north-south trending ridges rising to 1600m above sea level.

Alluvial Lowlands: Small alluvial valley floors are a feature of many parts of Tanzania, but there are four more extensive alluvial areas large enough to be considered separately. The Rufiji lower flood plain (3a) is an area of abandoned meander channels and low river terraces which is still subject to periodic flooding. The Ruvu flood plain is much narrower but forms a well defined area also susceptible to flooding. These are normal flood plains common in the lower courses of many rivers, but the interior alluvial lowlands of the Wami River (4a) the Great Ruaha (4b) and to a lesser extent the Kilombero (4c) have been caused by earth movements reducing the gradient of the rivers and resulting in deposition.

LEN BERRY

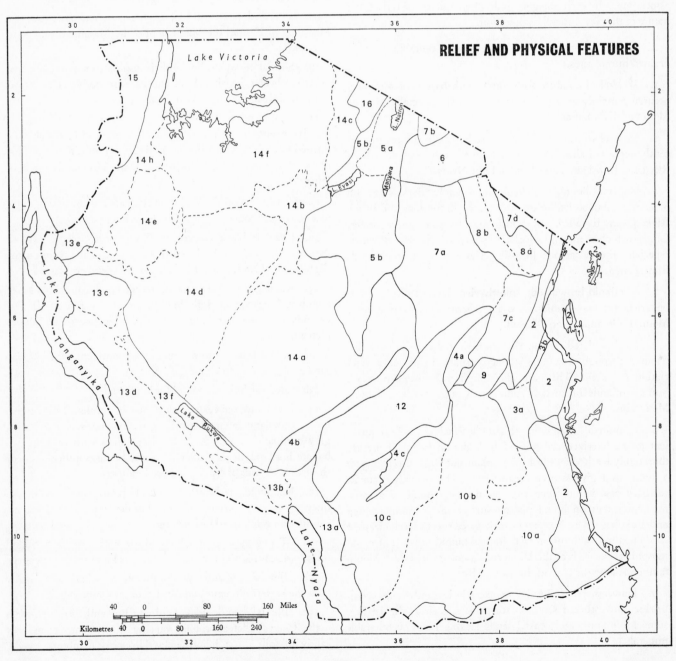

RELIEF AND PHYSICAL FEATURES

Lake Victoria

Lake Tanganyika

Lake Rukwa

Lake Nyasa

15

14 h

14 f

14 e

13 e

13 c

14 d

14 b

14 c

16

5 b

5 a

7 b

6

L. Eyasi

L. Natron

Manyara

5 b

7 a

7 d

8 b

8 a

7 c

2

3 b

2

2

1

2

13 d

13 f

14 a

4 a

9

12

3 a

2

4 b

4 c

13 b

13 a

10 c

10 b

10 a

11

2

Miles

40   0   80   160   Miles

Kilometres 40   0   80   160   240

27

9 SOILS

The major problem in presenting a map of Tanzanian soils is the choice of classification. That used here was developed by W Calton (1954) and used in the 1957 *Atlas of Tanganyika*. More recent classifications are used in the map by G H Gethin Jones and R M Scott in E W Russell (1962) and in the new *Atlas of Tanzania* (1969). Calton's classification has, however, the advantage of relative simplicity and is suitable for a small scale map. It is based, essentially, on genetic characteristics. Thus it combines the age of the soil, in terms of clay-mineral formation in tropical soil processes, with the nature of leaching. Three major categories are recognized, comprising eluvial and illuvial types, of regional or quasi-regional extent, and catenary associations. In each category individual soil types reflect the nature of the clay-mineral composition.

A. Eluvial (Quasi-regional leached soils occurring on well drained humid sites.)

1. Skeletal—immature soils, often with bare rock outcrops, occurring mainly on recent volcanic uplands especially Mounts Meru and Kilimanjaro.

2. Skeletal to montmorillonoid—soils mostly comprising recently deposited alluvium, especially in the valleys of the Rivers Ruvu and Rufiji and at the head of Lake Nyasa.

3. Montmorillonoid to kaolinoid—mainly dark clays on older alluvial deposits, for example on the Rufiji delta and in the River Grumeti valley, and which may be saline in character. Other such clays may be associated with particular parent rocks, especially the calcareous Jurassic series extending southwards from Tanga.

4. Kaolinoid brown soils—mostly rich clays weathered from base-rich, recent volcanic rocks. They occur extensively around Mount Kilimanjaro and Oldeani.

5. Kaolinoid red-earths—characteristic red clays widely distributed through Tanzania, though usually in catenary association (type 15). They are also found more extensively on humid uplands of metamorphic rocks such as the Uluguru Mountains.

6. Sesquioxidic-kaolinoid—highly leached old soils equivalent to the laterized red soils of B Anderson (1963). They are thoroughly leached and lacking in plant nutrients, except where a forest cover gives a deep organic layer. They usually occur in catenary association (type 16), but may be found to a more regional extent on broad plateau surfaces as in Sumbawanga and Bukoba, where the parent rock gives rise to freely-drained sandy-textured soils, or on well drained humid uplands of metamorphic rocks such as the Uluguru, Usambara and Pare Mountains and along the edge of the Eastern Rift.

7. Unweathered residuum or excessively sandy soils—comprising unweathered scree on scarp faces, such as the Livingstone Mountains, and coastal sands lacking easily weatherable minerals.

B. Illuvial (Quasi-regional soils in which transported leached minerals or the direct products of rock decomposition in situ accumulate.)

8. Skeletal soils—all soils of types 1 to 4 in which there is an accumulation of soluble salts. They occur especially in semi-arid river valleys, particularly that of the Pangani, where there is a problem of salinity through the evaporation of salt-rich flood waters.

9. Skeletal montmorillonoid soils—all soils of types 1 to 4 in which there is an accumulation of calcium carbonate either deposited by groundwater or accumulated by the capillary rise of groundwater from a carbonate-rich parent rock. These soils include the mbuga, or black cotton, soils occurring in poorly drained valley bottoms where rainfall is markedly one-seasonal. Characteristic extensive sites are the Lake Rukwa trough, the upper Great Ruaha valley and the Igombe-Moyowosi valleys.

9a. The arid phase of type 9—the principal areas are the Mkomazi plains and the Masai steppe (the Masailand rain-pond catena).

10. Similar to type 9 but with ironstone concretions formed as groundwater laterite above the calcium carbonate. This is found mainly in the upper Wami valley.

11. Similar to type 6 but with a depositional horizon of massive ironstone (or murram). This appears to be a palaeosol formed under previous climatic conditions or an earlier erosional phase. The major area is in the Southern Highlands south of Iringa.

C. Catenas (Associations of soils, both eluvial and illuvial, in a repetitive sequence determined by relief and drainage.)

12. Grey or black calcareous clays—these occupy level or depressed land in semi-arid areas. Grey clay-loams form on the slightly raised land. The typical area is the Wembere steppe.

13. Kaolinoid red-earth catena with a black calcareous lower member, intermediate soils have murram concretions—largely extends from the dry scrub thicket of Ugogo to the Mbulu plateau.

13a. Calcareous bottom member dominant—the Ugogo catena.

13b. Red-earth dominant—Mbulu plateau.

14. Kaolinoid red-earth, calcareous bottomland sequence—the Sukumaland catena comprising red or grey sandy hill soils, grey hardpan lower slopes and mbuga clays with calcium carbonate horizons in the valley bottoms. In the southern half of the area dark soils of types 2 to 4 predominate.

15. Kaolinoid red-earth, non-calcareous bottomland sequence—generally occurs in more humid areas where lime accumulation is inhibited by leaching.

15a. Topography generally subdued with grey bottomland soils dominant. Most of the coastal plain belongs to this category.

15b. Illuvial sesquioxides dominant—associated principally with the karoo sediments and consists of grey silty soils.

15c. Illuvial sesquioxides dominant but with little red-earth—the Central Plateau catena varying in sequence from grey sandy hill soils, through hardpan and ironcrust to mbuga.

15d. Red-earths dominant—this usually occurs in humid areas on coarse-grained Basement rocks or on quartzites, for example in Nachingwea, Masasi and Tunduru Districts, on the Nguru and Rubeho Mountains, and along the uplands of the Western Rift.

16. Sesquioxide catena—brownish-red sesquioxide soils with a non-calcareous lower member and a murram horizon. This is found largely on the ancient peneplain surface extending northwards from the Livingstone Mountains.

D. Complex associations in which the soil development has been interrupted by geological or geomorphological phenomena.

17. Pumice layered soils of varying maturity largely found around Mbeya.

18. Sesquioxide catena (type 16) partly overlain by volcanic ash which has weathered to a mature soil. The type areas are Njombe and Mbozi Districts.

19. Unweathered sandy residium or excessively sandy soils (type 7) with massive ironstone concretion in a catenary association similar to type 16 or partly overlain by recent alluvium. This is limited to the Kilombero valley.

The fertility of these soils is related primarily to age. Thus, of the eluvial soils, types 1 to 4 normally have moderate to high fertility, except where saline. Types 5 and 6, however, have lost much of their nutrient status and the clay complex has broken down to less useful forms. The illuvial soils are generally fertile though often subject to drainage problems. Where excessive soluble salts are present they cannot be cropped. At the stage when the illuvial soils have developed a massive ironstone horizon, as in types 10 and 11, the upper horizons have been depleted of plant nutrients, while the murram itself is devoid of any cropping value.

JOHN E MOORE

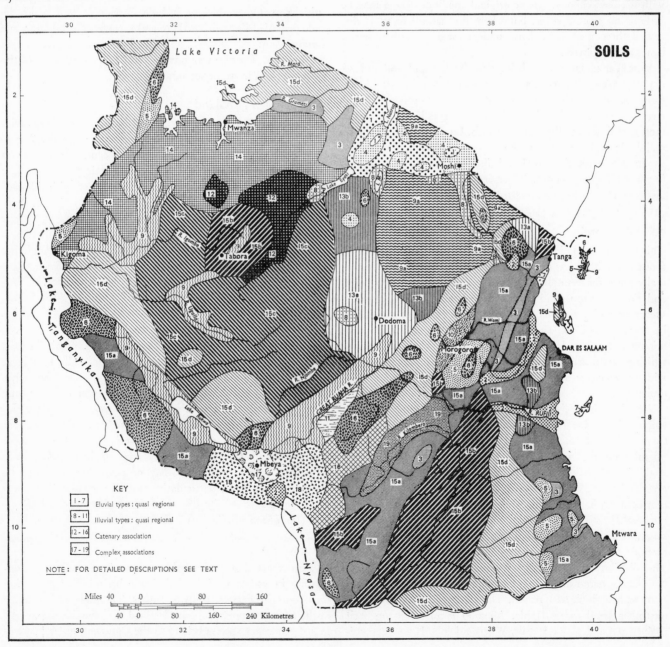

SOILS

KEY

1 - 7	Eluvial types : quasi regional
8 - 11	Illuvial types : quasi regional
12 - 16	Catenary association
17 - 19	Complex associations

NOTE : FOR DETAILED DESCRIPTIONS SEE TEXT

Miles 40   0   80   160
40   0   80   160·   240 Kilometres

The map opposite is based on that of C Gillman (1949) accompanying his classic essay on vegetation types in what was then Tanganyika. The vegetation is classified physiognomically (P J Greenway, 1943), that is according to the dominant life forms of those plant associations which actually occur. Seven principal categories are recognized: forest; woodland; bushland and thicket; wooded grassland; grassland; swamp; desert and semi-desert. These may be sub-divided according to variations in habitat and to the dominant plant species.

1. Forest

Forest comprises a dense stand of tall trees up to 60m in height with a closed canopy. Under original conditions there may be little or no ground cover, but where the natural forest is disturbed there may be a dense undergrowth of bushes, herbs, lianes and epiphytes.

Most Tanzanian forests belong to the lowland and upland dry evergreen type, though areas of rain forest and deciduous forest occur as well as a range of groundwater (swamp and riverine) types. The total forested area is small and is for the most part limited to the major uplands. Lowland forest is found mainly in Bukoba and on the Makonde plateau. Forest tree species are extremely varied and discussion of them is beyond the scope of this account. Major economic trees are, however, discussed in the section on forestry (pp. 68–9).

2. Woodland

This type of vegetation comprises trees of lesser height than in forest and with a less closed canopy. The ground cover is normally grass, for example *Andropogon* spp., *Panicum maximum* and *Eragrostis* spp., and herbs. There is a distinction between evergreen and deciduous types, but the most useful division is by dominant species. The most extensive form of woodland is miombo, dominated by *Brachystegia* and *Isoberlinia* species, which covers nearly one half of the country. It is often associated with *Pterocarpus angolensis*, Tanzania's major commercial timber.

Woodland is rarely simple in distribution. Miombo, for example, almost invariably occurs in catenary association. The Central Plateau catena, which is most significant, comprises miombo on the well drained hill slopes, *Combretum* spp. wooded grassland on the less well drained lower slopes, and grassland on the mbuga. *Acacia* and *commiphora* species thicket may occur on hardpan soils, while where the water-table is high, pure stands of *Borassus* palm may occur. Along permanent streams there may be a fringing strip of riverine forest, as for example the *Syzygium guineense-Ficus* spp. forests of Tabora. The distribution of miombo is essentially climatic, it being dominant where rainfall is between 800 and 1200 mm. per annum with a single wet season. The catenary relationships, on the other hand, are edaphic. Miombo occurs only on well drained red and grey hill soils. Where miombo is not predomi-

nant *Combretum* spp. woodland often occurs as in parts of the lake region, in Shinyanga and on the Bereku ridge.

3. Bushland and thicket

This dense shrub and low tree form of vegetation is often found on hardpan soils in the miombo woodland, but there are also areas of more regional extent which are dominated by thicket. The primeval Itigi thicket in central Tanzania is an edaphic phenomenon related to duricrust soils. It is dominated by *Bussea massaiensis* and *Baphia massaiensis*, though there are many associated, and locally dominant, species. They form a dense cover of coppicing shrubs in contrast with the open nature of the surrounding miombo or *Combretum* woodlands. The Msua thicket west of the River Ruvu is a variegated dense mass of bushes and low trees verging on low forest. Along the coast an evergreen thicket comprising many shrub and low tree species is often found. It appears to be the result of earlier periods of cultivation. Other thickets include *Euphorbia* spp. which invade degraded slopes in the Pare and Usambara Mountains, and *Commiphora* spp. thickets on rocky hilltops in Usukuma, and on murram. Termite mounds are also often thicketed, distinguishing them from the surrounding land.

4. Wooded grassland

This type of vegetation is dominated by grass and herbs with low trees or bushes either grouped or scattered according to type. Canopy cover is less than fifty per cent. It may form a natural community, but it seems likely that in most areas it is a fire climax. The most common trees associated with this type are *Combretum* and *Acacia* species, usually fire-resistant. Associated grasses vary from tall *Hyparrhenia* species to shorter *Panicum, Setaria* and *Themeda* species. It generally occurs in catenary relationship on the lower hillslopes of undulating country. Some high-level wooded grasslands occur, for example in the Southern Highlands, as a result of forest clearance.

5. Grassland

In this type of vegetation grasses are dominant and tree cover, if any, is less than ten per cent. Most examples of this type are the result of edaphic factors. They occur principally in valleys, especially where subject to seasonal flooding, hence the rather linear pattern on the map. Grass species vary according to the poverty of drainage. On mbugas *Setaria holstii* is most significant with *Digitaria regularis* and *Themeda triandra*. Occasionally dwarf grasses such as *Microchloa indica* and *Sporobolus* spp. may occur. On less flooded sites *Hyparrhenia rufa* is common but there is a wide variety of possible species. In the Southern Highlands, particularly, montane grasslands of *Londetia simplex* show the effects of forest destruction. Bracken fern (*Pteridium aquilinum*) is also common on such sites.

6. Swamp

Swamp vegetation grows where there is permanent waterlogging in valleys or inland drainage basins. The vegetation may comprise grasses, reeds or rushes. The mangrove swamps of the coast are more properly classified as swamp forests. Common fresh water species belong to the *Cyperus* (reeds), *Echino-*

chloa and *Phragmites* (grasses) families. Rushes include *Typha* spp. while locally, ferns such as *Dryopteris* spp. and *Acrostichum* spp. are important.

7. Desert and semi-desert

In Tanzania this type includes the rock and ice of upper Kilimanjaro and the salt flats of Lakes Eyasi and Natron. Few climatically induced semi-desert areas occur. A notable example is the Mkomazi plains between the Pare and the western Usambara Mountains. The vegetation normally consists of stunted shrubs, especially *Acacia* and *Commiphora* species or saltbush (*Suaeda monoica*), and scattered tussocks of grass, for example *Sporobolus robusta*.

This brief account serves only to illustrate the wide range of variation in Tanzanian vegetation types. It does not, for example, include the altitudinal zonations on Kilimanjaro with their characteristic giant *Lobelia* and *Senecio* and tree heathers, but such examples are extremely localized.

JOHN E MOORE

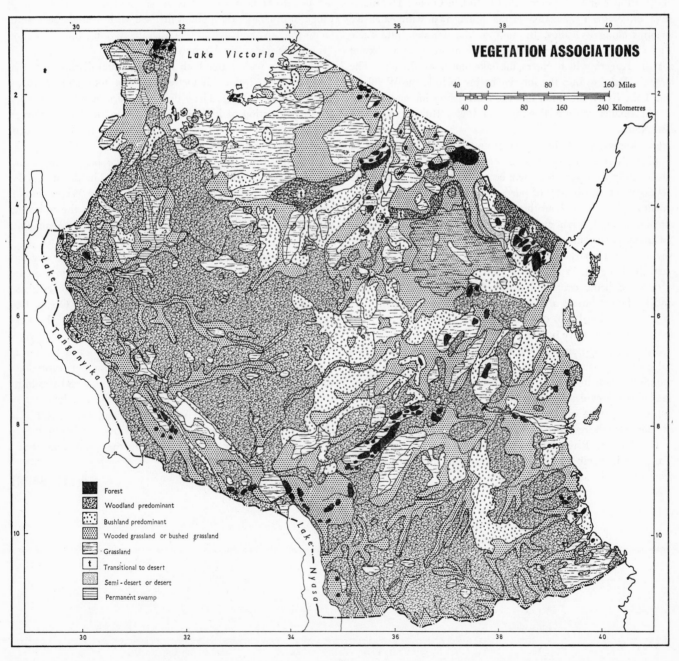

VEGETATION ASSOCIATIONS

40   0   80   160 Miles
40   0   80   160   240 Kilometres

Lake Victoria

Lake Tanganyika

Lake Nyasa

■ Forest
▨ Woodland predominant
⁙ Bushland predominant
▤ Wooded grassland or bushed grassland
▭ Grassland
t Transitional to desert
⬚ Semi-desert or desert
≡ Permanent swamp

11 HYDROLOGY OF MAJOR RIVERS

The rivers of Tanzania drain into four major drainage basins, the Indian Ocean, the Nile and the Mediterranean, the Congo and the Atlantic, and the interior basins. Five major rivers and many minor ones drain directly to the Indian Ocean. The Pangani in the north drains the Kilimanjaro–Usambara upland area, the Wami, the northern Uguru hills and part of the Central Plateau, while the Rufiji, the largest of Tanzania's rivers, drains a large part of the Southern Highland zone. The Ruvu is a small basin but drains the high rainfall area of the Uluguru Mountains, and the Ruvuma draining the southern part of the country also forms the southern boundary of Tanzania. A small part of the country around Lake Nyasa discharges into the lake and via the Zambezi system into the Indian Ocean. The major river of Western Tanzania is the Malagarasi with extensive swamps along its valley. In contrast, the drainage into Lake Victoria is mainly through short, rather minor streams, except for the Kagera which enters the lake north of Bukoba. The streams draining into the interior basins include the Wembere into Lake Eyasi, the Bubu into the Bahi depression and a number of smaller streams flowing into Lakes Rukwa, Manyara and Natron.

Our knowledge of the discharge and other characteristics of Tanzania's rivers is based on a comparatively short period of study. Only since 1950 has there been a real appreciation of the development possibilities of our water resources and the consequent need for facts about them. Stream gauging of many small streams around Meru and Kilimanjaro has been in progress for many years, but until quite recently the major national survey of river discharge concentrated on the main rivers draining east, the Pangani, Wami, Ruvu, and Rufiji. Now the gauging network is being expanded in the Ruvuma and Bubu basins and in the catchment around Lake Victoria—the latter as part of an international project for investigating lake hydrology. For the rest of the country little is yet known of surface flow.

The graphs opposite provide a summary picture of our knowledge of some river régimes. The shaded bars represent the mean monthly runoff in cusecs for the recorded period while the unshaded bar provides an index of comparison of flow from one part of the year to another. The index 1.0 is the average monthly discharge for the recorded period.

The Mngoro River north of the Usambaras is unusual for Tanzania in having a December maximum, the result of rain from the north-easterly winds, and a secondary peak in May. A May peak is typical of most Tanzanian rivers. The Karanga record shows the discharge characteristics around Mt Kilimanjaro characterized by high variability and maximum discharge in May. Farther east at Mauri on the Pangani, flow is much more uniform with the May peak almost sustained through June and July. The Pangani has the most uniform flow of Tanzanian rivers and perhaps partly because of this has been developed for hydro-electric power.

The records for Turiani and Kilosa, both on the Wami River, are probably typical of the east-central part of Tanzania. Discharge is quite uniform with peak flow in April and May. Kilosa, farther to the south, shows increased discharge in February and March and there is a suggestion of the appearance of a double peak. The Kidunda and Utari gauges are both on the Ruvu River and show the pronounced April–May peak characteristic of this river. Although details of the Rufiji régime are not given in graphs, it is to be noted that there is a high range in discharge throughout the year with a single peak similar to that on the Ruvu at downstream stations, though station 1Ka5 on the Great Ruaha shows two peaks.

There is a wide range both in total annual discharge and in discharge per square kilometre from the four gauged basins (see Table 11, p. 159). These differences are mainly a reflection of the proportion of high rainfall areas in the basins, though the Ruvu with only 10 per cent of its area in the Ulugurus shows relatively high rates of discharge.

Although records are short, there have been considerable fluctuations in discharge from year to year. The driest year for many stations was 1960 when discharge in the Wami, for example, was less than 25 per cent of the flow in the following year, which was the wettest on record. Even the Pangani flow in 1960 was only 30 per cent of that in 1961.

The river basins of Tanzania offer huge potential for development both for hydro-electric power and for irrigation. So far hydrology and development possibilities have been investigated mainly for the four rivers draining to the Indian Ocean. Our knowledge of these basins has now reached a stage where development projects can be properly assessed. Already the hydro-electric potential of the Pangani has been harnessed for use in the coastal and Arusha–Moshi area. Plans for agricultural development in the Ruvu basin are well under way and feasibility studies are likely in the near future for the development of hydro-electric power and irrigation on the lower Rufiji at Steiglers Gorge. In the meantime Tanzania is beginning to assess the potentiality of other basins in the south, central and western parts of the country.

LEN BERRY

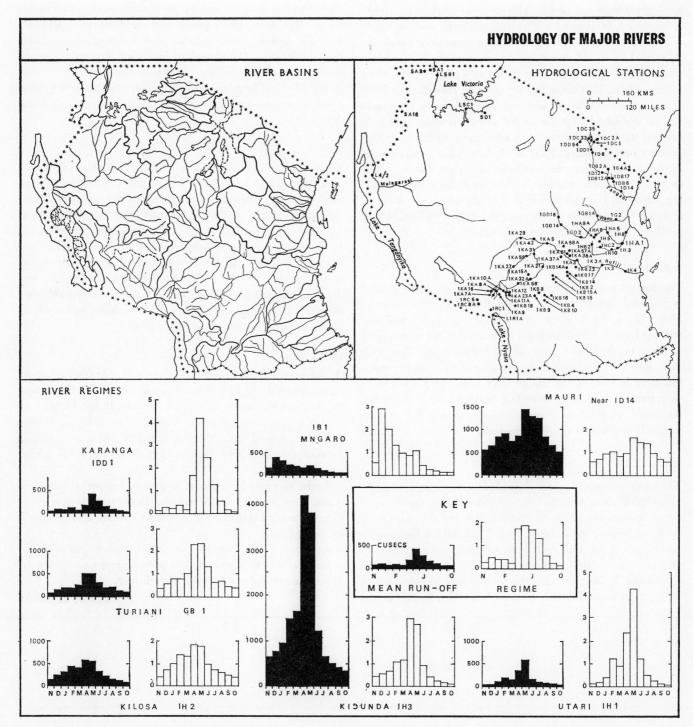

HYDROLOGY OF MAJOR RIVERS

RIVER BASINS

HYDROLOGICAL STATIONS

RIVER REGIMES

KARANGA IDD 1

IB 1 MNGARO

MAURI Near ID 14

TURIANI GB 1

KEY

500 CUSECS

MEAN RUN-OFF

REGIME

KILOSA IH 2

KIDUNDA IH 3

UTARI IH 1

Mean charts at the 850 mb. level for the months January, April, July and October (see p. 35) are used to illustrate the pattern at various times of the year, although it must be emphasized that daily synoptic features often differ considerably from average conditions.

The country is seasonally under the influence of two major airstreams: a south-easterly one during the northern hemisphere summer, and a north-easterly one during the southern hemisphere high sun period. The character of these airstreams is important in determining rainfall over the country, particularly its comparatively low total over most areas. Both are influenced by the effects of subsidence under the high pressure ridges extending from the two strong anticyclones from which they originate. This has a limiting effect on rainfall. The lower layers of the south-easterly airstream are fairly moist after crossing the southern Indian Ocean, but aloft, conditions tend to be dry and stable. The north-east monsoon, originating from high pressure over Arabia and the north Sahara has a much more meridional track than the south-east airstream, moving either over a land surface, or at best, a short sea distance before reaching Tanzania. It is therefore drier than the south-east monsoon, and this, together with the fact that the airflow will tend to run parallel to the coast, greatly limits the rainfall.

January

The surface equatorial trough over the Indian Ocean at 10°S is displaced farther south to 15°–20°S over the lower areas of Mozambique due to surface heating. The north-east monsoon moving from the Arabian high, after crossing the equator, becomes a northerly and eventually a north-westerly flow as it turns into the circulation of the trough. At 850 mb. (see map), the mean latitude of the trough is 15°S and at 700 mb. 13°S over the continent and extending eastward over the ocean. Again the airstream at these levels, on crossing the equator, gradually acquires a westerly component.

April

The surface trough, poorly defined, is now located over the coast and offshore waters of Kenya and Somalia, appearing as a duct between the collapsing Arabian high and the intensifying southern Indian Ocean anticyclone. The Arabian high moves southwards at this time and eventually disappears by late May or early June. The surface trough near the equator also diminishes during the following months and, simultaneously, falling pressure over Arabia creates a low which by July is very marked. There is no suggestion therefore that the southern hemisphere surface trough remains as a finite entity moving gradually north. It dies at the equator at the same time as a new continental low forms over Arabia. The 850 mb. chart (Map 12B) repeats much of the sea-level pattern, the Arabian high weakening and the southern high intensifying with a duct on the equator between the two. The troughs at 700 mb. and 500 mb. are near the equator and have almost reached their most northerly mean position in April.

April may therefore be regarded as a transitional period when the predominant low tropospheric airflow across the equator into the southern hemisphere trough is changing to a predominant movement of south-easterly air from the south Indian Ocean high across the equator into the northern hemisphere low. The airflow is from due east more frequently than at other times of the year. The pattern on individual days varies greatly, however, as the controlling sub-tropical highs fluctuate rapidly in intensity and location with the progression of extra tropical pressure systems over Europe, the Mediterranean and South Africa.

July

The surface trough over North Africa and Arabia, part of the vast, deep Asiatic low is near 20°N. There is therefore a meridional pressure gradient extending from the southern hemisphere anticyclone to these deep lows over North Africa and Asia. At 850 mb. (see map), the trough axis is 15°N, but at 700 and 500 mb. only between 0°–5°N. At the surface and 850 mb., ridges from the strong southern anticyclone extend across the equator, the resultant subsidence limiting any tendency for rainfall to develop. This is therefore the period when the south-east monsoon-flow from the southern Indian Ocean high dominates conditions over Tanzania.

October

At the same time as rising pressure over the Arabian peninsula creates a surface high, a new surface low begins to form across the Arabian Sea and Somalia. The southern Indian Ocean anticyclone begins to weaken. The 850 mb. chart (Map 12D) illustrates the general situation, the new low pressure area lying between the developing Arabian high and the weakening high over Madagascar.

Again, this may be regarded as a transition period but, as in April, there is a great daily variation in the pattern in response to extra tropical systems. By November, the low-level trough is on the equator.

A feature evident on all the charts to some extent is the presence of a semi-permanent low pressure area over north-west Tanzania, particularly the Lake Victoria area.

IAN J. JACKSON

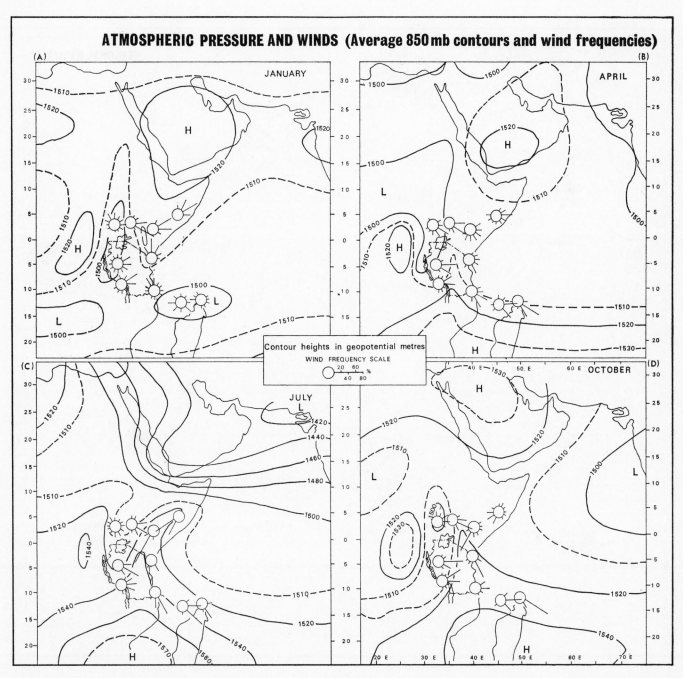

ATMOSPHERIC PRESSURE AND WINDS (Average 850 mb contours and wind frequencies)

Contour heights in geopotential metres

WIND FREQUENCY SCALE

13 RAINFALL

Water is a key factor in the development of Tanzania and clearly, therefore, rainfall, together with evaporation, are the most important climatic elements. The seasonal rainfall distribution in particular greatly influences agricultural practices. Much is not understood about rainfall over East Africa, and lack of data, particularly in the upper air, precludes the making of a complete physical interpretation.

Examination of mean monthly rainfall maps suggests in general terms that a rain belt shows a north–south seasonal movement which can be linked to the average pressure and wind conditions. In January, the belt of heaviest rain lies between 10°S and 15°S when the surface low pressure trough is at its southerly limit. In April, the main rainbelt appears to be moving north in conjunction with the shift of the pressure systems so that by July it is mainly north of Tanzania. October sees the rainbelt again moving south so that in November, when the low-level trough is on the equator, northern Tanzania has its second rainy season, although the rainfall is erratic and failure is not uncommon. The major cause of rainfall in the tropics is convergence of air leading to an upward movement, and resultant cooling. The seasonal pattern of rainfall would seem therefore to be simply explained by convergence of air in

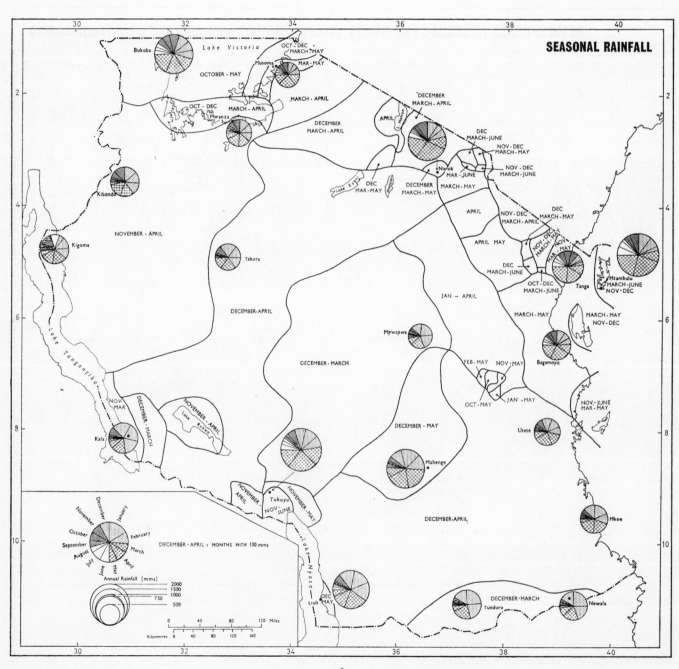

36

the low-pressure trough and, in particular, at the meeting of the north-east and south-east airstreams (a feature often called the Inter-Tropical Convergence Zone or ITCZ). There is, however, no simple association of rainfall with this feature. The great daily variation in pressure and wind conditions during the transitional periods (see April, October section 12) has been pointed out and it is incorrect to picture the ITCZ as a finite entity moving north–south. Often it is not possible to trace it and even when it can be located, rainfall is far from being always associated with it but often occurs elsewhere. Particularly during the transitional periods illustrated by April and October, when pressure and wind conditions are changing rapidly, daily rainfall areas show sudden jumps and irregular short term fluctuations often run against seasonal rainfall trends, being due to a variety of synoptic processes. Rain areas are often not zonal (as would be expected if they were associated with the ITCZ) but meridional and daily falls are often patchy, some stations within a general rain area having none. With the exception of coastal areas, where moving belts of rain are observed, rainfall areas tend to develop in situ, persist for a time and then die out without moving. Associated with the semi-permanent low-pressure trough in the lake area (see Map A, p. 35, for example) is a local convergence region, resulting in increased rainfall.

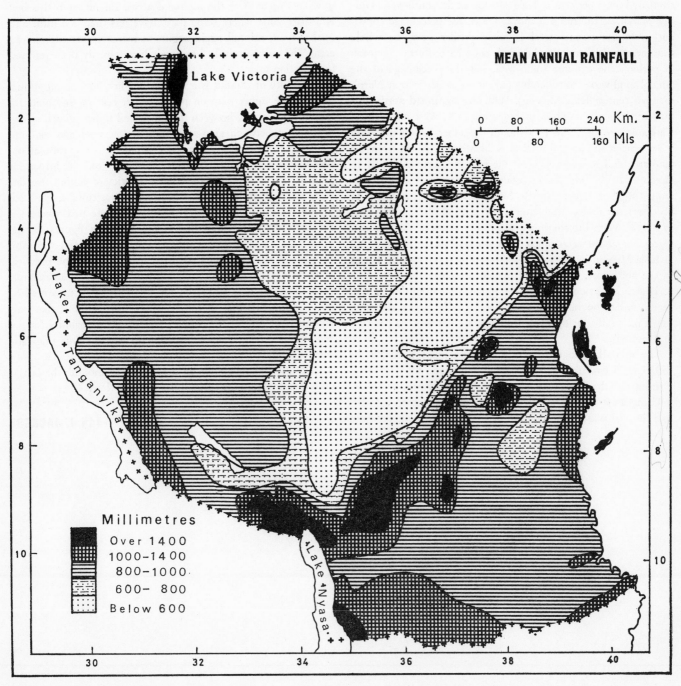

Apart from the far from simple meteorological factors influencing rainfall, relief provides a further complication. Under the general easterly airstream, north–south aligned highland areas create striking rainfall gradients. Other highland areas such as the Usambaras in the north-east, which have a more east-west alignment, can radically alter the seasonal rainfall régime. Over the Usambaras, the rainfall maximum may be received during the north-east monsoon on north-facing slopes, and in the south-east season on south-facing ones.

Ignoring the effects of highland areas, the seasonal pattern is as follows (Maps on pp. 36 and 41): During January and February the area south of an irregular line Dar es Salaam to Lake Victoria can be considered 'rainy'. At Tanga in the north-east, these two months produce only 5 per cent of the annual total compared to 42 per cent at Kala Mission in the south-west. During March, as the rainbelt moves north, the percentage contribution to the annual total is fairly similar over the whole country. April is wet over the whole country, with the exception of perhaps the extreme south-west, but the percentage of the annual total varies considerably (e.g. from 28 per cent at Narok to 7 per cent at Kala Mission). With the continued northward movement of the rainbelt in May and June, west and central Tanzania are dry, the two months together producing only 1 per cent of the annual total at Kala Mission. Apart from the lake area and to a lesser extent the extreme north-east, July to October is dry, this period producing only 1 per cent of the annual total at Mpwapwa. By November, rain has returned to north-eastern areas, producing 9 per cent of the annual total at Narok. With the continued movement south of the rainbelt, December produces as much as 21 per cent of the annual total at Kala Mission in the south-west but only 6 per cent at Tanga in the north-east. The semi-permanent low over the Lake Victoria area has associated with it a much more even distribution of rainfall throughout the year than in other areas, although much of it falls during the period March–May (e.g. 52 per cent at Musoma).

The rainfall histograms of the map on p. 41 illustrate the difference between the double rainfall maxima in the north (e.g. Arusha) and the single season in the south (e.g. Mtwara).

Using a fairly arbitrary figure of 100 mm. per month to define the wet season, the map on p. 36 shows the complexity of the seasonal rainfall distribution, with 43 regions altogether. Over much of the country except the north and north-east, the 'wet' season is from November or December to March or April. In the north and north-east, some or all of the months March to May are wet, together with another wet period in November/December in certain areas. The complex patterns and longer seasons of the highland areas such as the Usambaras and Kilimanjaro in the north-east, the Uluguru Mountains west of Dar es Salaam and the Southern Highlands stand out noticeably as do the longer seasons of the Lake Victoria area.

The annual rainfall distribution (the map on p. 37) shows a simple pattern in general terms. The wedge-shaped coastal belt, most of which has more than 800 mm. is narrow in the north, highland areas having the largest totals. Very striking rainfall gradients occur over the highland areas. Inland from this belt is a drier zone where some parts have less than 400 mm. and farther west, rainfall again begins to increase over the plateau area. The comparatively low totals have already been referred to in Section 12.

Variability of rainfall is a key factor illustrated on an annual basis by the upper map on p. 39. 50 per cent of the totals for individual years lie between the lower and upper quartiles (e.g. at station 5, between 1400–2000 mm., and between 590–760 mm. at station 10). Extreme values range from 1202–3957 mm. at station 5 and from 459–1083 mm. at station 10. An important point is that many areas experience a series of consecutive dry years which may have a drastic effect on agriculture. Data for Mvumi Mission in central Tanzania illustrate this where the average over a 30 year period is 544 mm., but figures for the years 1948–54 were 360, 374, 391, 576, 377, 459 and 340 mm. In view of the variability, there is a need, from the practical point of view, to assess the reliability of rainfall and an example of the kind of map produced for this purpose is presented on p. 39. From this map it can be found, for example, that only about 20 per cent of the country has a high probability (90 per cent) of receiving at least 750 mm. in a year. This map also further emphasizes the dry conditions of central Tanzania. Variability and reliability on a seasonal or monthly basis is a critical factor from the agricultural point of view.

IAN J. JACKSON

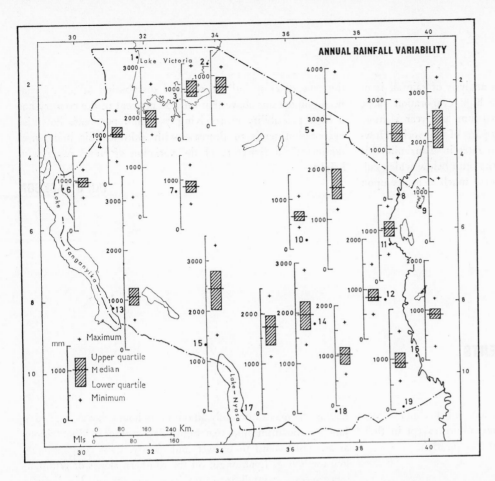

ANNUAL RAINFALL VARIABILITY

mm

Maximum

Upper quartile

Median

Lower quartile

Minimum

0   80   160   240 Km.

Mls   0   80   160

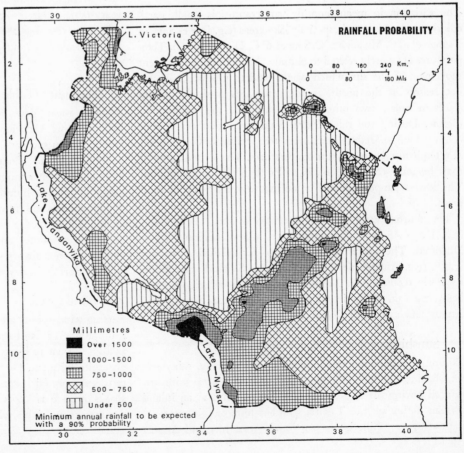

RAINFALL PROBABILITY

0   80   160   240 Km.

0   80   160 Mls

Millimetres

Over 1500

1000-1500

750-1000

500 - 750

Under 500

Minimum annual rainfall to be expected
with a 90% probability

14 EVAPORATION

From the practical point of view, an analysis of rainfall is of limited use without reference to the high evaporation rates, Table 12 on p. 160. A rainfall of 750 mm. per year is more than adequate for agriculture in many parts of the world. However, because of the high evaporation rates in Tanzania, this figure is taken by some people to be the limit below which cultivation is marginal, although of course much depends upon the type of crop and the seasonal distribution of rain. It has been pointed out above that only 20 per cent of the country has a high probability of receiving 750 mm. per year. Potential evaporation tends to decrease with altitude, this being predominantly a reflection of the variation of cloud cover with height.

IAN J JACKSON

15 OTHER CLIMATIC ELEMENTS

Compared with rainfall and evaporation, other climatic elements are of limited importance to agriculture except in that they influence rates of evaporation and transpiration.

1. Temperature (map p. 41)

The variation in mean monthly temperatures is small, particularly on the coast and especially lake areas (e.g. Dar es Salaam a range of 4°C, Mwanza 2°C, Songea 6°C, Dodoma 5°C). Temperatures are closely related to altitude. Apart from the apparent movement of the sun which would tend to produce a double hot season in the north, trending towards a single one in southern areas, two other factors influence the temperature régime. During the rains, extra cloud cover and evaporative cooling tend to reduce maximum temperatures. Cloud cover also tends to raise minimum temperatures. The second factor is that the south-east monsoon is cooler than the north-east one. The lowest temperatures occur during June and July in most areas.

The diurnal variation in temperature is least on the coast (e.g. Dar es Salaam compared to an inland location such as Dodoma). The maximum daily range occurs during the dry season (e.g. August, September at Dar es Salaam). Few places regularly report screen frosts, and ground frosts seldom occur below 2500 m. except in the Southern Highlands in July and August and occasionally in cold air drainage hollows.

2. Sunshine

The number of hours of sunshine varies seasonally, rainy seasons having the lowest figures, and also areally, areas with low rainfall having the highest sunshine hours. Thus at an inland plateau station such as Tabora, with 892 mm. of rain per year, the average sunshine hours per year is 3142, July and August having the maximum daily amounts (10 hours/day average) and January the minimum (6.9 hours/day average). Mountainous areas, which tend to be wet and cloudy, have comparatively low totals (e.g. Lyamungu, on the southern slopes of Kilimanjaro, average rainfall 1679 mm./year, average sunshine hours/ year 1571). Dar es Salaam, with an average rainfall of 1080 mm./year, has 2800 hours of sunshine per year, April having the least (5.3 hours/day) and October the most (9.1 hours/ day).

3. Humidity (Table 13, p. 160)

Monthly mean dew point temperatures show comparatively little seasonal variation, the range being about 4–5°C at a coastal station such as Dar es Salaam or a lakeside station such as Mwanza, and about 6–7°C at an inland station such as Iringa. The wetter months have the highest values. The diurnal range in relative humidity is approximately indicated by the values at 0300 and 1200 GMT. Since relative humidity is determined both by the water vapour in the air (indicated in the table by dew points) and temperatures, the pattern of seasonal variation is not always simple, although the lowest values tend to occur during the dry season.

4. Wind speed

Surface wind speeds are generally fairly low with a night-time minimum. At inland stations during the night, speeds are normally less than 10 knots but during the day, 11–16 knot winds are quite frequent. On the coast and lake areas, speeds of up to 16 knots are fairly common at night and during the day wind speeds of up to 21 knots are not infrequent. Marked relief variation may create higher winds locally.

IAN J JACKSON

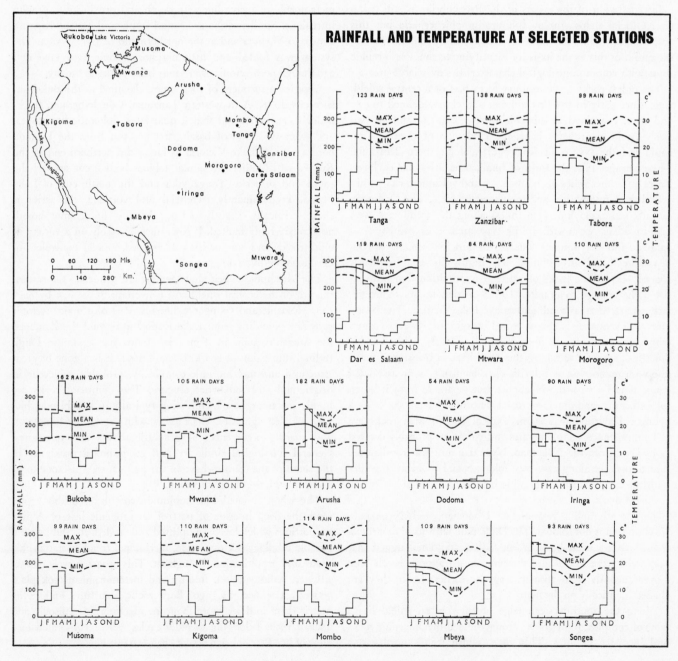

RAINFALL AND TEMPERATURE AT SELECTED STATIONS

Tanga — 123 RAIN DAYS

Zanzibar — 138 RAIN DAYS

Tabora — 99 RAIN DAYS

Dar es Salaam — 119 RAIN DAYS

Mtwara — 84 RAIN DAYS

Morogoro — 110 RAIN DAYS

Bukoba — 162 RAIN DAYS

Mwanza — 105 RAIN DAYS

Arusha — 182 RAIN DAYS

Dodoma — 54 RAIN DAYS

Iringa — 90 RAIN DAYS

Musoma — 99 RAIN DAYS

Kigoma — 110 RAIN DAYS

Mombo — 114 RAIN DAYS

Mbeya — 109 RAIN DAYS

Songea — 93 RAIN DAYS

Tanzania is underlaid by some of the world's oldest rocks. Some were originally formed more than 3000 million years (my.) ago. Precambrian, sedimentary and metamorphic rocks (older than 500 my.) cover over 40 per cent of the land area. Associated plutonic rocks of comparable age cover a further 25 per cent. Karroo (270–160 my.) terrestrial sediments cover less than 2 per cent of the land area while marine rocks of Jurassic (160 my.), Cretaceous (135 my.), Tertiary (70 my.) and Quaternary (2 my.) age cover a belt of limited width adjacent to the present coastline. Contemporaneous accumulations of terrestrial sediments are found inland in local basins while volcanic eruptions (covering 4 per cent of the land area) became regionally important from the Neogene (20 my. ago).

Interpretation of the events of the Precambrian is still tentative. Official maps employ lithostratigraphic criteria but this account emphasizes a chronology established by radiometric dating and uses this as the basis for identifying tectonostratigraphic units with common geological characteristics over large areas.

The oldest rocks of the country form part of a central shield, rigid since early in the Precambrian and clearly defined to east and west. Ingrained in this shield are vestiges of at least two Early Archean orogenic belts, the Dodoman of Central Tanzania and the Nyanzian–Kavirondian of Northern Tanzania. These vestiges take the form of small, often irregular enclaves, lenses and other relics of sedimentary and volcanic rocks within a setting of migmatites and mobilized granites. The Dodoman extends some 480 km. (300 miles) along the trend east–west and broadens westward. In its type area, it is composed of banded and ferruginous quartzites, sericitic schists, aplites, pegmatites and ironstones, all highly-altered, frequently coarsely–crystalline rocks of extreme composition that have resisted the change to granite. The Nyanzian occurs in irregularly separated areas south and east of Lake Victoria. The Nyanzian type sequence is characterized by acid and basic volcanics (rhyolites, trachytes and corresponding tuffs with basalts, dolerites and basic tuffs) together with banded ironstone (quartzite with magnetitic or chloritic dark bands). Closely associated geographically with the Nyanzian, but separated from it by an unconformity and intense crustal deformation, are rocks of a younger Kavirondian system. Typical Kavirondian rocks are grits, mudstones, conglomerates and volcanics, probably derived as molasse from the Nyanzian. Nyanzian and Kavirondian are folded together along east–west fold-axes and probably, together with the large associated granitic intrusions and emplacements, represent one complex orogeny.

The stratigraphic relation of Dodoman and Nyanzian–Kavirondian is not known. The Dodoman, with its higher metamorphic grade, may be older but radiometric dates suggest that both belts were folded and metamorphosed approximately contemporaneously 2500–2600 my. ago or earlier; hence they are shaded identically on the map.

Along the south-western edge of this central shield lies a zone of complex, high-grade, strongly-folded metamorphic rocks and intrusive granites. This zone, which trends north-east—south-west parallel to Lakes Tanganyika and Rukwa and is known as the Ubendian belt, is structurally younger than the central shield. The rocks are mostly pelitic and volcanic in origin, and hornblendes, biotites, garnets and kyanite are common in the gneisses. The Ubendian is clearly overlain by equivalents of the Karagwe–Ankolean and Bukoban. Radiometric dates suggest that this belt was folded and largely metamorphosed around 2100–1950 my. ago, though post-tectonic events here may be considerably younger. It is thus of late Archaean age, though it may be polycyclic.

The early Proterozoic is represented by the Karagwe–Ankolean. K–A rocks, occuring principally over north-west Tanzania are largely argillaceous, mildly metamorphosed to phyllites, argillites and low-grade sericitic schists, while arenaceous formations have been changed to quartzites. Comparatively simple major folds are characteristic, deformation and metamorphism increasing with depth and proximity to granite intrusions. Similar rocks are found south and east of Kigoma almost to Mpanda and at the northern end of Lake Nyasa. The system was folded and metamorphosed some 1300–1100 my. ago though post-tectonic events may be as young as 850 my.

A varied assortment of rock types, classified as the Bukoban, succeeds the K–A in western Tanzania. Conglomerates, thick-bedded sandstones, red shales, quartzites, dolomitic limestones, and extensive flows of basalt stretch south from the Uganda border west of Lake Victoria as far as the northern end of the Rukwa rift. Outliers of similar tabular beds occur around the south end of Lake Tanganyika and the north end of Lake Nyasa. Predominantly terrestrial and volcanic, the series is characteristically slightly-folded, virtually unmetamorphosed, and considerably faulted. It rests uncomfortably on a variety of older rocks, and may be the undeformed, tabular equivalent of the Mozambiquain orogeny.

The Mozambique belt abuts against and truncates the eastern margin of the central shield and is overlain to the east by Karroo, Mesozoic and younger sediments. Part of a major tectonic province extending from Lake Rudolf to beyond the Zambezi, the Mozambiquain in Tanzania attains its maximum longitudinal dimension of 400 km. (250 miles). It is a zone of great structural and metamorphic complexity, probably polycyclic in origin and still somewhat obscure. The dominant rocks are highly metamorphosed, consisting typically of hornblende, biotite, pyroxene gneisses, charnokites with crystalline limestones and sparing occurrences of graphitic schists and quartzites. General lithological similarity and geographical proximity in the south of the country have in the past caused this zone to be grouped with the older Ubendian.

The whole foliated Mozambiquain complex probably represents the deep interior of part of an orogenic belt of Alpine proportions which has been uplifted and eroded. It exhibits comparable lithology, tectonic style, meridional trend, metamorphic grade and granitization throughout. This orogenic cycle of subsistence, sedimentation, folding and metamorphism took place between 1100–600 my. ago. Both rocks, structures and radiometric dates indicate more than one metamorphic episode, and ancient rocks belonging to older cycles were incorporated in a zone of late Precambrian activity 730–600 my. ago.

Following the Mozambiquain there was apparently a long erosional interval before the deposition of rocks of Karroo (Upper Carboniferous – Lower Jurassic) age. Principally terrestrial sediments, consisting of sandstones, conglomerates, tillites, shales, red and grey mudstones, coal measures and occasional limestones, they show limited marine facies in the east-central region. The rocks were principally laid down in downfaulted or downwarped areas and have been preserved, though easily eroded, because they occupy structural basins. The Karroo formations are the oldest containing undoubted plant and animal remains.

Marine rocks – chiefly marls, limestones, sandstone and shales of Jurassic, Cretaceous, Tertiary and Quaternary age – make up a belt of limited though variable width parallel to the present coast. The sequence is disconformable and indicates long in-

stability of the continental margin. No marine rocks of this age are found west of this belt. Contemporaneously with this marine deposition a variety of terrestrial deposits accumulated inland, mainly in rift troughs. Sands and sandstones, siltstones and limestones occupy a variety of warped and faulted depositional basins notable among which are the Cretaceous sandstones of the Nyasa rift and the Pleistocene playa sequence of the Olduvai and Natron basins.

Volcanic activity, commencing in late Cretaceous times with carbonatite centres, caused the local and regional accumulation of typically-alkaline volcanics in the Neogene, particularly north of Lake Nyasa in Rungwe; from Hanang to Kilimanjaro and north to Lake Natron. Typical of these rocks are olivine and alkali basalts, phonolites, trachytes, nephelinites and pyroclastics.

PAUL TEMPLE

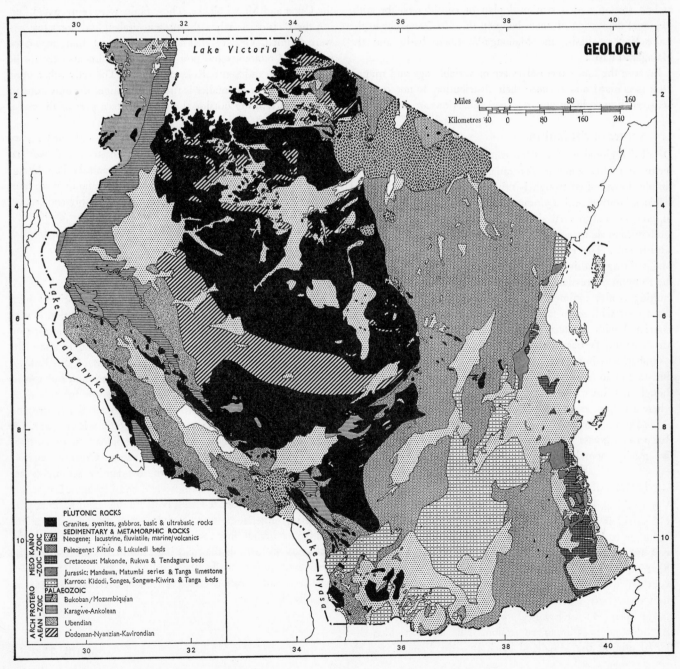

GEOLOGY

PLUTONIC ROCKS
Granites, syenites, gabbros, basic & ultrabasic rocks
SEDIMENTARY & METAMORPHIC ROCKS
Neogene: lacustrine, fluviatile, marine/volcanics
Paleogene: Kitulo & Lukuledi beds
Cretaceous: Makonde, Rukwa & Tendaguru beds
Jurassic: Mandawa, Matumbi series & Tanga limestone
Karroo: Kidodi, Songea, Songwe-Kiwira & Tanga beds
PALAEOZOIC
Bukoban/Mozambiquian
Karagwe-Ankolean
Ubendian
Dodoman-Nyanzian-Kavirondian

MESO KAINO -ZOIC -ZOIC
ARCH PROTERO -AEAN -ZOIC

Both the Western and Gregory rifts are represented in Tanzania. However, the map shows that the general plan of these fault systems and the zonal pattern of faults is more complex than is commonly supposed. In addition to the pattern of faults the map shows the distribution of volcanic areas and zones which have been downwarped or depressed as the result of faulting. These patterns are superimposed upon a background of Bouguer contours.

Much of the country not directly affected by faulting and volcanic activity has been indirectly affected by rift tectonics. Regional doming preceded faulting in the Gregory rift zone and is presently evidenced by elevated rift margins of semi-arched section and a semi-oval plan of considerable breadth. Regional depression of zones between the rifts is evident in the Lake Victoria basin, the Manonga-Wembere basin and the Malagarasi basin.

Because the faults themselves are of variable age and magnitude (see map) and because their distribution is not comprehensively known in certain areas, generalizations are difficult.

1. Nature of rift faulting

Detailed regional mapping has conclusively demonstrated that for many faulted zones in Tanzania, the concept of the rift as a simple downfaulted trough is misleading. Much more general is block-faulting and asymmetric structures, involving steeply-dipping normal to vertical faults, and consequent tilting of the land surface about a central axis of tilt, without large vertical adjustments. The result is a basin-range type of topography. Major tilting of this type in the Gregory rift is to the west; in the Ruhuhu depression it is consistently to the east. Such block-faulting is also common in the coastal zone where blocks are tilted west with scarp faces facing east. The coastal faulting is associated with spectacular flexures and downwarping of the Mesozoic and Tertiary rocks of that zone.

Graben and horst features tend to be produced fortuitously due to the interaction of opposed block faults, frequently – though not invariably – of different ages. Trough faulting, where a strip of crust is let down between simultaneous vertical or near-vertical faults, is less common. It is exhibited only in the Rukwa and Nyasa troughs associated in both with strong negative gravity anomalies.

2. Pattern of rift faulting

A general lack of block faulting and tilting in the central granitoid shield is noticeable. By contrast the Mozambiquain and Ubendian rocks are affected in wide curves. Particularly in the west and south-west, faulting shows a general parallelism with the trend of Precambrian structures. In northern Tanzania there is little such parallelism and in this southern terminal section of the Gregory rift, the rift system splits into three distinct units like an open fan: the Eyasi rift, the Manyara-Balangida rift and the Burko-Meru-Kilimanjaro section. This last section is deflected around the Masailand block into the Pangani trough where it is bounded on the east by the horsts of the Pare and Usambara Mountains.

3. Age of rift faulting

The age of fault movement varies. The oldest faulting is in the south-east, extending from the Ruhuhu depression north-eastwards into the Kilombero valley, around the Mahenge block and northward into the Kidodi-Mkata trough and around the Uluguru block. This faulting is of Karroo age, though some of the faults have experienced subsequent rejuvenation as, for example, along the western side of the Kilombero valley and along the eastern Uluguru boundary faults. Some Jurassic faulting of the coastal zone is evident but its extent and significance is not well known. A major period of faulting in the Cretaceous period led to the initiation of the Nyasa-Rukwa and Lake Tanganyika depressions and to the structural delimitation of the Ufipa and Mbozi blocks. These faults were rejuvenated during the Pleistocene when the present graben and horst features were defined. Gravity measurements suggest that 2000–2500 metres of Cretaceous and post-Cretaceous sediments exist in the north Nyasa and south Rukwa troughs. The only other zone with comparable anomalies is the Eyasi trough, the only zone of Cretaceous faulting outside the south-western part of the country.

Apart from Eyasi, the oldest faults associated with the Gregory rift are the Tertiary faults forming its eastern and western limits, Eyasi to Ol Doinyo Ogol on the west and the Pare-Usambara faults on the east. These major bounding faults were later rejuvenated by Plio-Pleistocene movement, probably contemporaneous with complex grid-faulting of the central part of the zone between Lake Natron and Lake Balangida. Some of these grid-faults are Pleistocene-Recent in age.

4. Associated features

Volcanic zones are clearly though irregularly associated with rift faults. In the Gregory rift zone, such an association is very prominent with a massive group of major volcanoes located on the zone of major fault intersections. In a similar location, the Rungwe volcanic zone marks the intersection of the Rukwa, Nyasa and Mbeya-Usango faults: volcanics are not, however, a feature of the Western rift in Tanzania except for this area. Except for the Cretaceous carbonatites of Mbozi, Kilombero and Speke gulf, all the volcanics are of upper Tertiary-Recent age.

Indications of structure at depth as opposed to the surface are provided by the Bouguer gravity values. Greatest negative values, indicating great depths of low-density sediments are associated with the Nyasa, Rukwa and Eyasi troughs. Large deficiencies are also associated with both Rungwe and Kilimanjaro, indicating either the lower density of these volcanic formations relative to surrounding rocks or some mass deficiency at depth. The gradient towards the coast indicates the wedging out of the continental crust while the positive gravity anomalies of localized coastal sections and particularly the islands are as yet unresolved.

PAUL TEMPLE

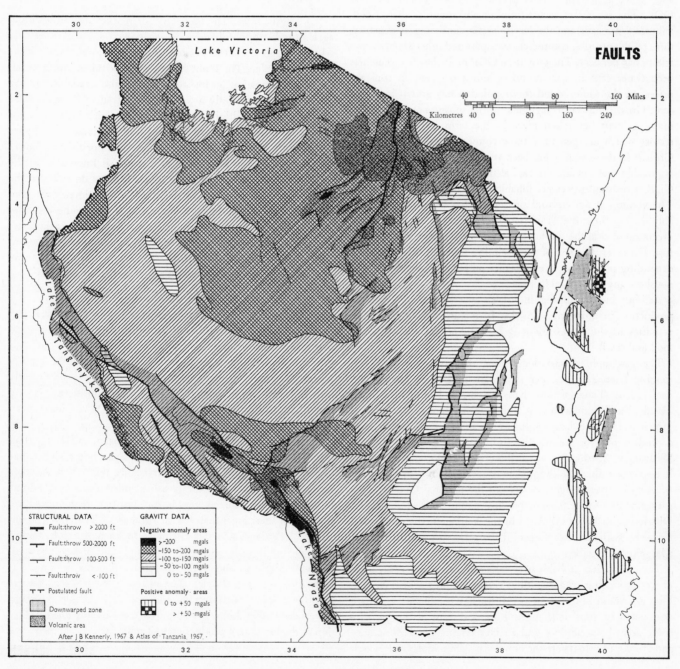

FAULTS

Lake Victoria

Lake Tanganyika

Lake Nyasa

STRUCTURAL DATA

Fault:throw > 2000 ft

Fault:throw 500-2000 ft

Fault:throw 100-500 ft

Fault:throw < 100 ft

Postulated fault

Downwarped zone

Volcanic area

After J B Kennerly, 1967 & Atlas of Tanzania, 1967.

GRAVITY DATA

Negative anomaly areas

> −200   mgals

−150 to−200 mgals

−100 to−150 mgals

−50 to−100   mgals

0 to − 50   mgals

Positive anomaly · areas

0 to + 50   mgals

> + 50 ·mgals

40   0   80   160 Miles

Kilometres 40 0   80   160   240

The usual yardstick for measuring a country's standard of living is by an estimate of (1) what is earned or (2) what is produced. In Tanzania a combination of these two is used. The national standard of living is expressed in terms of Gross Domestic Product (GDP), which means an approximation of the sum of incomes earned by all factors engaged in production-peasant, labour and capital (see Table 14, p. 160). In 1967 the GDP for Tanzania was 5690 million shs. which is 480 shs. per inhabitant. Slightly more than half (52 per cent) of the GDP is contributed by the agricultural sector (including fishery and forestry). The subsistence agricultural sector produces 28 per cent of the total GDP. The secondary sector (mining and manufacturing) contributes 8 per cent and the service sector consisting of construction, public utilities, commerce, transport and other services contributes 35 per cent. The growth in GDP in the last five years has been 6 per cent in current prices and 4 per cent in constant prices. In the same period the population has grown by 3 per cent. Growth has been negligible in the subsistence sector. The major growth has taken place in the secondary and tertiary sectors which are generally those connected with urban areas. Growth in these sectors has been very fast in Dar es Salaam. It is possible that outside the capital there has been no growth in GDP at constant prices per inhabitant during the last five years. The volume of agricultural production has increased considerably during these five years (see Table 15 on p. 161). With the exception of sisal the production of most crops is increasing very fast. However, in view of the declining trend in prices and the expanding population, the monetary output per inhabitant does not show any substantial increase.

Activity in the mining industries concentrates on diamond production in Shinyanga District. In manufacturing the major activities are the processing of agricultural products, particularly food and textiles.

The geographical variation among the districts is very big, ranging from 4200 shs. per inhabitant in Dar es Salaam and 1200 shs. in Tanga to less than 200 shs. in Kasulu, Kibondo, Handeni and Sumbawanga. Almost 20 per cent of the GDP is earned in Dar es Salaam. Kilimanjaro and Tanga Districts have a product of over 300 million shillings, while the product in Shinyanga, Arusha, Mwanza, Bukoba and Morogoro Districts is over 150 million shillings. These seven main provincial districts cover twenty-eight per cent of the national GDP and together with Dar es Salaam produce almost half of the GDP. Districts with lower GDP are in the south-east, the centre and the west, with the exception of Tabora District which includes a large service sector.

The calculation probably over-values urban employment. Most of the processing of agricultural products and the service facilities are found in urban areas. All the low production areas are dominated by subsistence agriculture and most of the high income areas by secondary and tertiary production. Kilimanjaro and Pangani Districts are the only areas with a high GDP which are dominated by monetary agriculture, followed at a lower level by Korogwe, Kilosa and Ulanga Districts.

Estimation methods

The Tanzanian GDP is an approximation of the total incomes earned by all those engaged in production and expressed net of any subsidies and indirect taxes: i.e. factor cost of production. GDP (for all sectors other than agriculture and mining)=wages and salaries plus income from property and entrepreneurship, taking into account depreciation of capital equipment.

The agricultural output is calculated by adding the farmer's output and deducting what is spent in the production process (input of goods and services). GDP (agriculture)=value of output at producer's price less cost of input, less indirect taxes and subsidies. At present only a part of the district product can be calculated directly:

(1.) Agriculture. The monetary (or marketed) production of agricultural crop husbandry is fairly well known in all districts, though even the present material in some cases seems rather unreliable. The input cannot easily be taken into account. District information on livestock sales is also available, but the registered sales are only a part of the output of livestock. District figures are multiplied by a coefficient which is the same for all districts – in such a way as to reach the national GDP figure for livestock. The same is done for forestry. For fishery, figures for the actual catch have been used. Little is known about the total output of subsistence agriculture. Figures do exist for the total production in each district, but these estimates are considered so unreliable that it is necessary to use another assumption: that the subsistence production per inhabitant is the same all over the country. Therefore the district figures only represent the population figure of the districts multiplied by 136 shs. – the national average for subsistence production per inhabitant.

(2.) Secondary and Tertiary Sectors

Annual figures for wages and salaries are known by district for each industrial sector (on punch prints in the Central Statistical Bureau). On the assumption that the ratio of wages to output is the same all over the country, the GDP by district in the remaining sectors can be estimated. Around Lake Victoria, particularly near Mwanza and Shinyanga, output is also considerable, and a belt of high production follows the Great North Road from Dar es Salaam through Morogoro to Mbeya. Capital equipment per worker is certainly greater in Dar es Salaam and Tanga than in the rest of the country. Output is correspondingly higher, but higher wages in these areas counterbalance this factor. Another factor which outbalances the possible undervaluation of output in the highly mechanized areas is that statistics are more comprehensive for these areas than for the rural areas. The GDP (Secondary and Tertiary factors) is calculated for each district by taking the wage bill in each industrial sector and multiplying it by a coefficient. Table 16 shows the major components in the GDP estimation for each district. The estimate of GDP per district involves a lot of assumptions and not very reliable statistical material. Despite this it seems to give a reasonably good indication of the location of production in Tanzania.

SÖREN JENSEN

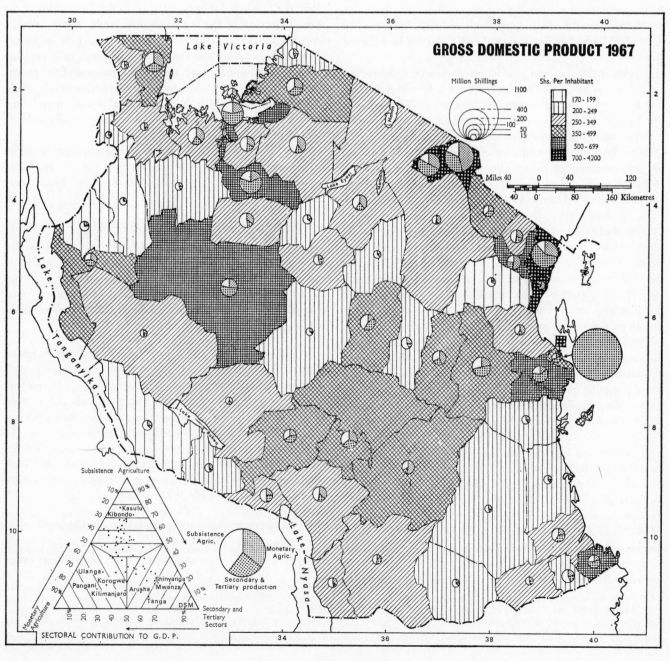

GROSS DOMESTIC PRODUCT 1967

Million Shillings

1100
400
200
100
50
15

Shs. Per Inhabitant

170 - 199
200 - 249
250 - 349
350 - 499
500 - 699
700 - 4200

Miles 40   0   40   120
40   0   80   160 Kilometres

Lake Victoria

Lake Natron

Lake Eyasi

Lake Manyara

Lake Tanganyika

Lake Rukwa

Lake Nyasa

Subsistence Agriculture

10%   90%
20   80
30   70
40   60
50   50
60   40
70   30
80   20
90%   10%

Kasulu
Kibondo

Subsistence
Agric.

Ulanga
Pangani
Korogwe
Kilimanjaro
Shinyanga
Mwanza
Arusha
Tanga
DSM

Monetary
Agric.

Secondary &
Tertiary production

Monetary Agriculture

10%   20   30   40   50   60   70   80   90%

Secondary and
Tertiary
Sectors

SECTORAL CONTRIBUTION TO G.D.P.

19 TYPES OF RURAL ECONOMY

In this attempt at differentiating between types of rural economy in Tanzania, 'rural economy' is taken to refer specifically to the major economic sectors of the rural areas, namely crop and livestock farming. Furthermore, only the marketed (export and domestic) products of these activities have entered into the analysis. There are many reasons for this, the most obvious being the lack of reliable statistics relating to the value of production in the subsistence sectors. In fact, availability of data of a reasonable degree of reliability has largely determined the criteria used in this classification. This means that it has not been possible either to pursue differentiation below the district level or to introduce into the study many of the factors relevant to an examination of farming systems, such as farm unit size, input measurements, farming methods and techniques etc., for none of which is there sufficiently detailed and reliable information.

In spite of this less-than-ideal approach, however, the present study has this value, albeit a limited one: it identifies the relative importance of the commercial or market element in the district agricultural economies and variations in agricultural incomes, and relates these to population distribution and densities to obtain more realistic income indices. The justification for thus emphasizing money values may be seen in this fact: in Tanzania's agrarian economy, subsistence farming still plays an important role, but one which will and must diminish with economic development. By accenting monetary indices it is possible to distinguish those districts which are making positive contributions to national economic development from those which are not. Moreover, by correlating this map with others showing environmental conditions, especially rainfall distribution; transportation routes; distribution of towns; livestock densities and so on, further inferences may be drawn about variations in development potential from district to district.

The key in the bottom left-hand corner of the map isolates the four components of the classification scheme. The two most important are (1) agricultural income *per capita* (vertical lines) and (2) population density per square mile (horizontal lines). Each of these has been divided into three orders or levels (high, medium and low) and then both have been combined to produce nine basic classes or types of economy, eg. high income/high population; high income/medium population; high income/low population, and so on. Thus from type 1 through to 9 there is a descending scale with respect to degree of commercialization, of wealth, and of contribution to the national economy. Superimposed on the resultant pattern and creating sub-divisions of the major classes are symbols denoting (a) the district agricultural wage labour force expressed as a percentage of the national total, and (b) livestock sales as a percentage of the national total, and (c) livestock sales as a percentage of dis-

trict agricultural income. The former gives a rough indication of the spatial distribution of large estates and medium size holdings, which are the chief employers of wage labour – the fifteen districts designated on the map together accounting for 84 per cent of the national agricultural wage labour force. The latter identifies those districts in which livestock sales contribute over 20 per cent of the district agricultural income. The crop/livestock income ratio of the ten districts involved, deviate in varying degrees from the national norm – for Tanzania as a whole, crops accounted for 89 per cent of the agricultural income and livestock for only 11 per cent.[2]

The composite key at the top of the map illustrates the main classes and the sub-divisions which emerge from the combination of the four criteria used. Especially worthy of notice is the way in which the wage labour factor coincides with the upper half of the scale, i.e. with districts of high and medium incomes, while the livestock factor is restricted to the lower third of the side or districts of the lowest income levels. Among the inferences which may be drawn from this are (1) the important contribution of large-and medium-size holdings to Tanzania's monetary agricultural sector, and (2) that in some of the poorest districts of the country, the obstacles to economic development, besides those of a physical environmental nature, may be aggravated by the more conservative attitudes generally ascribed to pastoralism.

In the interests of clarity and ease of interpretation, no attempt has been made to show on the map the distribution of major crops. This is done in the brief descriptive summary which follows.

1. High income/high population density

a. *Korogwe, Tanga*: Large sisal estates are responsible for the dominant position of these two districts. Both are markedly export orientated, with export crops (tea taking a very poor second place to sisal) accounting for about 95 per cent of total crop sales. The remaining 5 per cent is made up largely of maize in Korogwe and bananas and citrus fruits in Tanga.

b. *Kilimanjaro, Arusha–Meru*: Parts of the rich Northern Highland zone of Tanzania, in which coffee, grown on small- and medium-size units, is the leading export crop. In quantity as well as value Kilimanjaro's crop is three times greater than Arusha's. Sugar is also an important product of the former but less so of the latter. Both districts show certain similarities in the variety of minor export crops and in those earmarked for the domestic market. Included among the former are sisal, pyrethrum and seed beans, and among the latter maize, bananas, wheat, millet and vegetables.

2. High income/medium population density

a. *Kilosa* b. *Pangani*: Predominantly sisal-producing areas, which differ from each other in the wage labour factor

[1] The statistics on which this study is based are taken from *District Data, 1967*, by S B Jensen and J Mkama, Land Survey and Development Planning, Dar es Salaam, 1968, in which, in the absence of reliable figures, the compilers assumed a *per capita* subsistence production of 136 shs. all over the country.

[2] In 17 of the 60 districts there were no livestock sales at all, i.e. the districts of Coast Region with the exception of Bagamoyo; all the districts of Mtwara and Ruvuma Regions; and Ukerewe, Pangani and Tanga. However, it should be noted that in the remaining 43 districts relatively small percentages of animals reared are sold on the market, and also that generally livestock are not integrated into the crop farming systems.

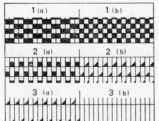

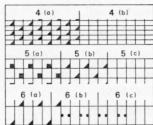

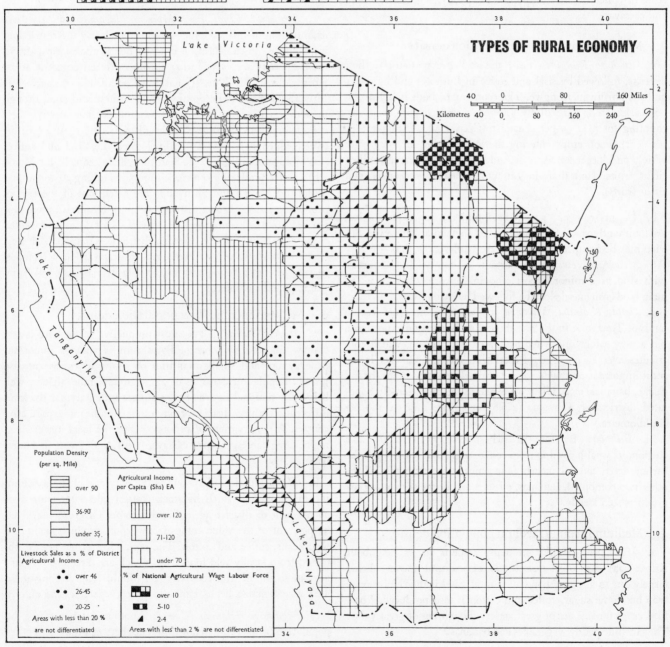

TYPES OF RURAL ECONOMY

L`ake Victoria

Lake Tanganyika

Lake Nyasa

40   0   80   160 Miles
Kilometres 40 0   80   160   240

Population Density
(per sq. Mile)

over 90

36-90

under 35

Agricultural Income
per Capita (Shs) EA

over 120

71-120

under 70

Livestock Sales as a % of District
Agricultural Income

over 46

26-45

20-25

Areas with less than 20 %
are not differentiated

% of National Agricultural Wage Labour Force

over 10

5-10

2-4

Areas with less than 2 % are not differentiated

and from (I a) in this as well as in population density. Sisal alone accounts for 64 per cent of total agricultural income in Kilosa and 72 per cent in Pangani. In Kilosa, cotton is a minor export crop while millet and oil seeds are the chief crops marketed locally. In Pangani some copra is produced for export, while maize, bananas and cassava are for domestic sale.

3. High income/low population density

a. *Ulanga*: Sugar is the leading estate crop contributing 83 per cent of the income from crop farming. Cotton and sisal are minor export crops, while the local market is largely restricted to beans and paddy.

b. *Tabora*: This differs from (a) not only in the insignificance of the wage-labour factor but also in the type of crops grown. Over 80 per cent of crop income is derived from tobacco. The remaining 20 per cent is made up of a wide range of food crops of which the most important are paddy, vegetables, onions and cassava.

4. Medium income/high population density

a. *Lushoto, Rungwe*: Tea is the leading export crop in these districts, followed by sisal and coffee in Lushoto, and by coffee and pyrethrum in Rungwe. The economy of both is highly export orientated, particularly Lushoto's with export crops accounting for over 90 per cent of total crop sales (Rungwe: 80 per cent). Food crops entering the local market are of greater variety and larger amounts in Rungwe (paddy, bananas, millet, citrus fruits, etc.) than in Lushoto (bananas, vegetables and citrus fruits).

b. In this category are to be found the more productive, predominantly small farming areas of Tanzania. The seven districts may be grouped according to crop differences, thus –

i. *Mtwara, Newala*: Important cashew-producing areas, with sisal as a minor export crop in Mtwara. Cassava is the main food crop on sale locally, followed by citrus fruits.

ii. *Geita, Kwimba, Mwanza, Ukerewe*: The chief cotton lands of Tanzania. In the first three, sisal is a second export crop but a very minor one when compared with cotton, which contributes over 80 per cent of total crop income. Cassava is the most important of a wide variety of marketed food crops (beans, maize, bananas, etc.). Ukerewe is one of the most densely populated districts of Tanzania (436.8 per square mile or 169 per sq. kilometre.)

iii. *Bukoba*: By far the richest district in West Lake Region, its wealth coming from coffee, sugar and tea, though the income from coffee is nearly four times larger than that of the other two combined. Bananas, oil seed and beans are among the products sold locally.

5. Medium income/medium population density

a. *Morogoro*: Similar in many respects to its neighbour Kilosa (2a), its lower *per capita* agricultural income being largely due to a higher population total. Sisal is the chief money crop but some sugar, coffee and cotton is also produced. Local food crops for sale are of great variety though not of great value. They include paddy, vegetables and bananas.

b. *Mbulu, Njombe, Mbozi*: Productive highland districts, though considerably less wealthy than those of (1b). The crop patterns of these three districts show certain similarities but also some marked differences. Coffee and pyrethrum are grown in all three but the former is the main export crop in Mbulu and Mbozi, while in Njombe it is of minor importance. Here pyrethrum is in the dominant position, in fact, Njombe is the most important pyrethrum-producing district in Tanzania, with 45 per cent of the national total. Seed beans and sisal in Mbulu and tea in Njombe are other export crops. Mbulu differs markedly from the other two in the predominance of wheat in domestic crop production, the value of this product being only slightly less than that of coffee. This helps to explain why domestic crop sales are as high as 50 per cent of Mbulu's total crop income, in great contrast to Mbozi and Njombe (9 and 3 per cent respectively), made up of small quantitites of millet, bananas and beans in the former, and paddy, oil seed, wheat, etc. in the latter).

c. *Kisarawe, Lindi, Pare, Mbinga, Maswa, Shinyanga*: An examination of this sub-type shows quite clearly the restrictions imposed by the classification criteria. For in their crop patterns these districts are very similar to others (often adjacent areas) already discussed. Thus (i) Kisarawe and Lindi are similar to Mtwara (4bi) in the predominance of cashew and sisal, though in addition both produce small amounts of copra; (ii) Pare's export crops are also those of the districts of (1a) and (1b) between which it is geographically located, i.e. sisal and coffee; (iii) Mbinga, marginal to the South Highland zone is like Mbozi (5b) a coffee-producing centre, with tobacco taking a poor second place; (iv) Maswa and Shinyanga are extensions of the cotton-producing Lake Victoria districts of (4bii). Similarities will also emerge from a comparison of their lists of locally marketed crops with those of the relevant districts. Kisarawe: cassava, citrus, oil seed; Lindi: Oil seed, millet, cassava; Pare: bananas, maize; Mbinga: beans and wheat; Maswa: beans; and Shinyanga: paddy, onions and beans.

6. Medium income/low population density

a. *Iringa/Mufindi*: The most productive factor here is tea, closely followed by tobacco. Pyrethrum is another important export crop, and small quantities of sisal and coffee are also grown. Population densities of 23 per square mile, that is, well below the national figure (35 per square mile/13.7 per sq. km.) differentiate these districts from other significant export crop centres. A wide variety of produce enters the local market, e.g. maize, vegetables, beans, cassava, Irish and sweet potatoes, bananas, etc.

b. *Masai* District stands out as the only one of the medium-income group in which livestock (cattle) sales contribute over 20 per cent of district agricultural income. Of crops marketed 55 per cent of the value comes from export products including seed beans, coffee and cotton. The remaining 45 per cent is obtained from locally sold food crops which are therefore very important to the district economy (cf. Mbulu (5b). Among these are: wheat, maize, beans, bananas, millet, vegetables and onions.

c. *Bagamoyo, Kigoma, Mbeya*: Another instance where the population factor is the major difference between these and other districts occuring higher up the scale. Bagamoyo's cashew-sisal-copra complex is akin to that of other coastal districts described in (4bi) and (5ci); Kigoma may be considered an outlier of both the lake cotton and coffee (Bukoba) lands, though production is at a rather low level (small amounts of tobacco are also grown); and finally Mbeya, like Njombe (5b), is a pyrethrum–coffee area. Crops marketed locally are as follows: Bagamoyo: paddy, oil seed, bananas, cassava; Kigoma: cassava, bananas, palm kernels and beans among others, the total value of which is seven times higher than its export crops; Mbeya: paddy, sweet and Irish potatoes, vegetables and bananas.

7. Low income/high population density

a. *North Mara*: Livestock (cattle) sales make up about 28 per cent of district agricultural income. Three-quarters of all crop sales are food crops (maize, millet, cassava, bananas, paddy, vegetables) and the remaining quarter consists of coffee and sisal for export.

b. *Mzizima*: Typical coastal district crop pattern of cashew and sisal for export. Local sales are restricted to paddy, oil seeds and vegetables. The very high population density (279 per sq. mile/109 per sq. km.) is largely due to its proximity to Dar es Salaam.

8. Low income/medium population density

a. *Nzega*, b. *Mpwapwa*, c. *Kondoa, Dodoma, Iramba, Singida*: In all of these, livestock sales make sizeable contributions to district agricultural income – least (20 per cent) in Nzega and most in Dodoma (75 per cent i.e. the largest in the country). In Mpwapwa, Kondoa and Dodoma no export crops are grown at all. Iramba and Singida produce very small amounts of cotton and are marginal cotton areas when compared with Nzega, which participates more fully in the lake cotton complex. The chief crops on sale locally in each district are as follows: Nzega: paddy, groundnuts, millet, maize; Mpwapwa: maize, oil seed, groundnuts; Kondoa: maize and oil seed; Dodoma: groundnuts and oil seed; Iramba: onions; Singida: millet and sweet potatoes.

d. *Musoma, Kasulu, Masasi, Karagwe, Ngara*:

i. Musoma is another lake cotton-producing area. Sisal, the only other export crop is by value only 3 per cent of the cotton crop (the value of which is about 60 per cent of the cotton crop of neighbouring and richer Mwanza). Large quantities of cassava, millet, sweet potatoes and maize enter the local market. Livestock sales, slightly less than 20 per cent of district agricultural income are, however, important to the district economy.

ii. Kasulu, Karagwe, Ngara – crops dominate the list of marketed agricultural products (livestock sales contribute 4, 13 and 5 per cent respectively of agricultural income) but this is crop farming at very low production levels. Kasulu grows very small amounts of cotton and sisal for export; Karagwe and Ngara small amounts of coffee. Three show marked similarities in types of crops sold locally – bananas, beans, oil seed.

iii. Masasi, like its neighbour Newala (4bi) is a cashew-producing area. Groundnuts, cassava and citrus fruits are among the chief products for the domestic market.

9. Low income/low population density

a. *Handeni*: Cattle sales make up 20 per cent of a very low district agricultural income. Crop sales, small in quantity as well as in value, include cotton, sisal and cashew (export), and maize, beans and oil seed (domestic).

b. *Manyoni*: A predominantly livestock district, animal products contributing 62 per cent to agricultural income. No export crops are grown. Heading a rather short list of crops marketed locally are millet and sweet potatoes.

c. *Rufiji, Kilwa, Nachingwea, Songea, Tunduru, Mpanda, Chunya, Sumbawanga, Biharamulo, Kahama, Kirbondo*. In all of these, crop farming predominates but at very low productivity. Rufiji and Kilwa display the typical coastal crop pattern but very small quantities are involved. In the former are grown sisal, cashew and copra (small amounts of cotton as well) and in the latter cashew and copra. Food crops sold are as follows: Rufiji: paddy, oil seed, citrus; Kilwa: groundnuts, paddy. Nachingwea is another cashew-growing area, and to a lesser extent Tunduru and Songea as well. Tobacco is, however, a more important export crop in Songea. In these three districts oil seed is a common crop on sale locally; others are groundnuts and maize. In Tunduru citrus fruits bring in a sizeable income. Chunya grows small quantities of cotton and tobacco for export and even smaller quantities of maize, millet and groundnuts for the local market. In Mpanda tobacco, maize and groundnuts are the leading crops sold, while Sumbawanga, though it produces no export crops, markets a wide range of food crops, e.g. millet, beans, wheat, onions, Irish potatoes, etc. In Biharmulo cotton and coffee predominate (92 per cent of total crop sales) and bananas, cassava and beans in small quantitites are sold locally. Kahama produces some cotton for export, livestock sales contribute 12 per cent of agricultural: income and domestic crop sales include paddy, cassava and millet. Kibondo markets minute quantities of cotton and coffee (export) and millet, beans and bananas (domestic).

GLORIA YOUNG-SING

Since the 1930s Tanzania has been the world's leading producer of sisal. In 1892 an agronomist of the German East Africa company, Dr Richard Hindorf, became 'concerned to find a plant suitable to the conditions in the plains from Usambara to Tanga where there is neither too little nor too much rain'. He came across a reference to sisal plants in Mexico and he ordered material for planting, but found that its export was prohibited. Eventually a plant dealer in Florida dispatched 1000 bulbils to East Africa via Hamburg. Only sixty-two survived the trip to Tanga, but their progeny have provided planting material for most of the many sisal plantations in East Africa.

Compared with the low rainfall of 500–750 mm. (20–30 in.) and shallow calcareous soils of Yucatan, the Tanzanian environment is generally more favourable to the cultivation of sisal than that of Mexico. Rainfall in growing areas varies between 650 and 1250 mm. The xerophitic characteristics of the plant are important but its distribution in Tanzania is very much influenced by transportation factors.

The bulky nature even of the processed plant restricted early sisal enterprises to the vicinity of the tidal creeks in the Tanga region and later in the Mtwara region. With the building of the railway line sisal penetrated in the Tanga area to the drier area beyond Korogwe and eventually to the Kikuletwa plains near Arusha. The 'Tanga Line estates' produce nearly two-thirds of Tanzania's sisal. With the construction of the Central railway line westward from Dar es Salaam important nodes developed at Dar es Salaam, Ngerengere, Morogoro and Kimamba/Kilosa.

Until recently the cultivation of sisal was based on the plantation system. Estates were essentially capitalistic enterprises whose ownership was almost entirely in foreign hands. Greeks commanded about a third of the production, British and Asians a quarter each, while the Swiss and Dutch controlled about six per cent each. About five million shillings would be required to start an average estate today and the total capital investment of the sisal industry in Tanzania is probably well over £20 000 000 (400 000 000 Tanzania shillings).

The sisal plant or *Agave sisalana* perrine can be propagated either from suckers or from bulbils which are found on the pole of a mature plant. Bulbils are generally grown in a nursery for a period of one year before being transplanted. Sisal is then cultivated in blocks which can be planted in single or in double rows in densities varying from 2500 to over 9000 plants per hectare. The first cut of the leaves can take place two years after transplanting and the life-cycle of the plant varies from five years to ten years. Systematic and careful land-use planning is essential to ensure that the factory operates to its full capacity. In Tanzania fixed automatic decorticators are used in contrast to the small mobile raspadors frequently found in Mexico

and Brazil. An average decorticator can produce about 1500 tons of sisal per annum. Because of variations in soil, rainfall and age of the sisal plants, the area required to operate a factory at capacity and therefore most economically, is between 1200–2000 hectares. Nearly forty per cent of all sisal in the country orginates in estates producing over 2000 tons of sisal per annum, while less than two per cent originates from factories with a capacity of 250 tons or less.

Only two-and-a-half to five per cent of the leaf consists of fibre, so that about 40 000 tons of leaves per annum have to be cut and transported to the decorticator. To overcome this problem, an estate operates its own internal light railway or road services. An average estate requires a minimum of 4000 gallons of water per hour to carry away the waste leaf pulp and to wash the fibre.

Cultivation of the fields is carried out mechanically; however, the planting and transplanting and the subsequent upkeep of the fields such as hoeing, weeding and desuckering still rely on manual labour. The cutting of large quantities of leaves also requires an impressive labour force. At its zenith in 1952 over 142 000 labourers were employed, nearly forty per cent of those engaged as wage-earners in the country. An average estate employed about 1500 labourers. The source areas of the labour have varied, but most are outside the sisal-producing areas even including extra-territorial labour from Mozambique, Rwanda and Burundi. The labour required to produce a ton of fibre dropped from 1.04 in 1948 to 0.63 in 1958 to 0.23 in 1966.

By the middle of the 1920s sisal had become the most important export of the country and it was not until 1967 that sisal relinquished this position. At its peak in 1951, when prices were over £200 (4000 shillings) per ton, sisal accounted for over fifty-eight per cent of the value of all exports. To this must be added the indirect benefits from taxation, levies, employment, use of power, etc. With so much wealth derived from sisal it became important to maximize the national interest in the industry. Thus attempts have been made since Independence to increase African participation in sisal-growing through smallholder production. In 1967, through nationalization of several estates, the Government finally attained majority control in the industry.

In the past the contribution of individuals, the work of the Sisal Research Centre at Mlingano, the rationalization of effort through the Tanganyika Sisal Growers' Association and the host of improvements to machines and cultivation practices have been responsible for making Tanzania the foremost sisal-producing country both in quality and quantity of sisal. Now that sisal is under strong competition from synthetic products, the future prosperity of the industry will be dependent on a new flexibility in the industry. New alternative end-uses of sisal are being explored, and the production of paper pulp from sisal is a possibility. Costs will have to be maintained at par with, or lower than synthetics, and international agreements towards rationalizing output and stabilizing prices have been formulated.

ADOLFO MASCARENHAS

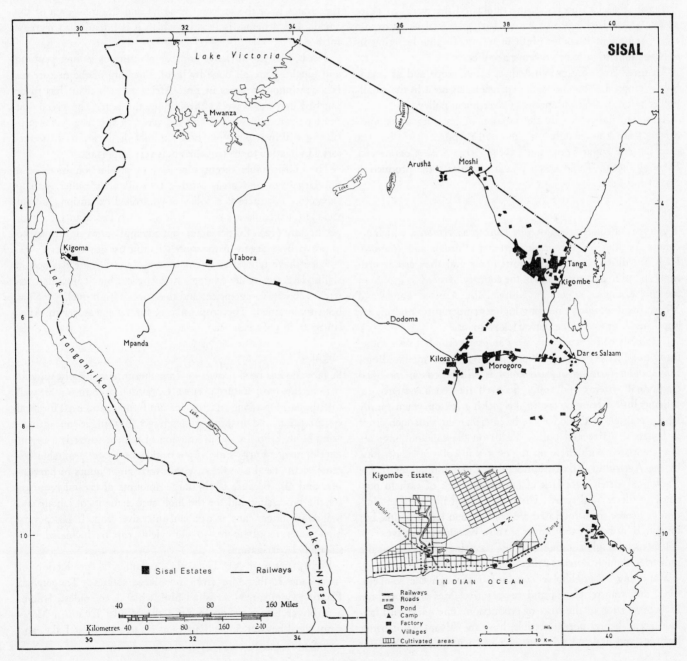

SISAL

Lake Victoria

Mwanza

Lake Natron

Arusha   Moshi

Lake Eyasi

Manyara

Tanga

Kigoma   Kigombe

Lake Tanganyika

Tabora

Dodoma

Mpanda

Lake Rukwa

Kilosa

Morogoro   Dar es Salaam

INDIAN OCEAN

Lake Nyasa

◼ Sisal Estates   —— Railways

40   0   80   160 Miles

Kilometres 40   0   80   160   2·10

Kigombe Estate.

Bushiri

Tanga

N

Railways
Roads
Pond
Camp
Factory
Villages
Cultivated areas

0   5   Mls
0   5   10 Km.

These are three major crops for Tanzania of which sugar is the most recently established and the only non-export crop, although it is hoped that when home demands are fully met continued expansion will provide a surplus for export. In 1967 production just about equalled mainland demand.

Coffee has for a long time been one of the three major exports of the country, currently holding second place, and first in terms of gross output value. Coffee also accounts for the largest area but production is likely to be contained by government policy as under the International Coffee Association agreement only about fifty per cent of the present production can be exported. Profits are lower from non-quota sales.

Tea is subject to no restricting quotas on the world markets as yet, and it is thought to have a high potential as an export crop. At present it comes ninth in terms of value bringing in only about a fifth as much revenue as coffee.

All three crops are grown both as estate crops and as smallholder crops, and much recent expansion has been in the smallholder sector, in line with present Government policy.

The map indicates only the location of growing areas since acreages are known only for the estates (coffee 19 874 ha, tea 9302 ha, and sugar 14 402 ha. *Census Large Scale Commercial Farming*, 1964). Table 17 on p. 162 provides some production and export data.

Coffee

Two types of coffee are grown in Tanzania: *Arabica*, which accounts for most of the production (two-thirds), and *Robusta*. Each has different physical requirements and they are accordingly found in different parts of the country. *Arabica* is grown in the cooler, higher regions of Kilimanjaro, Arusha, Tanga and Mbeya, while *Robusta*, needing higher temperatures and higher humidity, is grown in the central lake regions.

Originally coffee was exclusively an estate crop but now something like fifty per cent of the production is from smallholdings. Smallholder farming of cash crops is still based on modified traditional systems and coffee fits well into such systems, requiring little labour except in the picking season when family labour is often used. Coffee can be interplanted with such crops as bananas, maize and pulses. Yields on the smallholdings are low compared with those on the estates in spite of work done by the Agricultural Extension Service. Chief limitations in the traditional systems are lack of labour and lack of cash to purchase fertilizers and sprays. Up to the present increased production has come from increased area rather than larger yields, but improved husbandry techniques are now becoming effective.

It is increasingly common for the processing to be done at the pulperies, though *Robusta* coffee is often sun-dried.

Marketing of smallholder produce is through the co-operatives, and transport costs and co-operative dues account for a high proportion of the costs of production. The northern highland areas, being more accessible, have the advantage of better facilities and higher level commercial activity and are the most important producers. Annual production varies between 650 000 and 800 000 bags, of which 700 000 are now sold on quota. It is estimated that production could rise to one million bags in 1970 leading to marketing problems and need for diversification.

Tea

Tea is a crop which requires at least 1250 mm. (50 in.) of well distributed rainfall a year and *cool* temperatures so that it is confined to the higher regions of Tanzania (1500–2000 m.) The two main growing areas are the Usumbara Mountains, near Tanga, and the Southern Highlands, regions of Iringa, Mufindi and Mbeya. Tea has a high value/weight ratio and can stand fairly high transport costs.

It is still largely an estate crop, since it requires considerable initial investment, but recent expansion has been the result of Government-financed smallholder schemes. The total extent of the estates is of the order of 9000 ha and the total area of the smallholder schemes is 1200 ha which it is intended to increase further.

Tea is a labour-intensive crop, as planting, weeding, pruning and plucking are all done by hand. Plucking of the mature tea is a continuous process in East Africa as each plant has to be plucked every two weeks throughout the year. The green leaf must be carefully packed and delivered to the factory for processing within twenty-four hours so that the location of the factories in relation to the tea schemes is very important.

The considerable recent increases in production have been due largely to new areas coming into maturity rather than to expansion, but there is a policy of controlled expansion. Present yields in Tanzania are relatively low: often less than 1400 kilos per hectare (1200 lb. per acre), but attempts are being made to improve these largely by the more scientific use of fertilizers.

Prices have tended to fluctuate recently and there has been a slight decrease in the average world price, but Tanzanian tea fetches above average prices and the price of high quality tea has been maintained. The crop forecast for 1968 was 7·4 m. kilos (16·25 m. lb.) of made tea.

Sugar

Sugar-cane has been grown in Tanzania in climatically suitable regions (i.e. temperature over 21°C, rainfall over 1000 mm. well distributed) for a long time by peasant farmers and used for local consumption and making of jaggery *, but sugar-cane grown as an estate crop for the production of refined sugar is a recent development. Large-scale organization is more profitable because of the need to process within forty-eight hours of harvesting, and also because of the large amounts of capital required for the processing and for the high cost elements of labour and irrigation. Sugar-cane is a labour-intensive crop. It has a very high water requirement, so that yields can be increased considerably by irrigation.

Eighty per cent of Tanzania's commercial production of sugar-cane is therefore from five large estates: Tanganyika Planting Company at Arusha Chini, which is the oldest; Kilombero Sugar Estate set up in 1962; the Mtibiri Estate in Morogoro; the Bhagwat Sugar Estates at Kagera in West Lake; and

* Crudely refined brown sugar.

54

the Karangi Estate in Arusha. The first two produce about five-sixths of the total. The limiting factor in expansion is the availability of processing facilities. The factories at Kilombero are unable to process all the cane which is now being produced.

Smallholder schemes for sugar-cane growing are therefore of necessity, at present, outgrower schemes for the large estates, depending on the provision of refinery facilities. They produce ten per cent of the crop. The cane from the Sonjo Settlement Scheme is processed by the Kilombero Estate, and the cane from

the smallholder communal farm in West Lake is sold to the Bhagwat Sugar Factory. Although yields on smallholdings are lower than on the large estates, which have yields of 200 tons per hectare and a conversion rate to refined sugar of 10–1, higher than world average, the cash yield to the smallholder compares very favourably with other peasant cash crops.

FAO is giving assistance for the setting up of refineries on Pemba Island and it is hoped that a smallholder scheme will prove successful there.

EILEEN BERRY

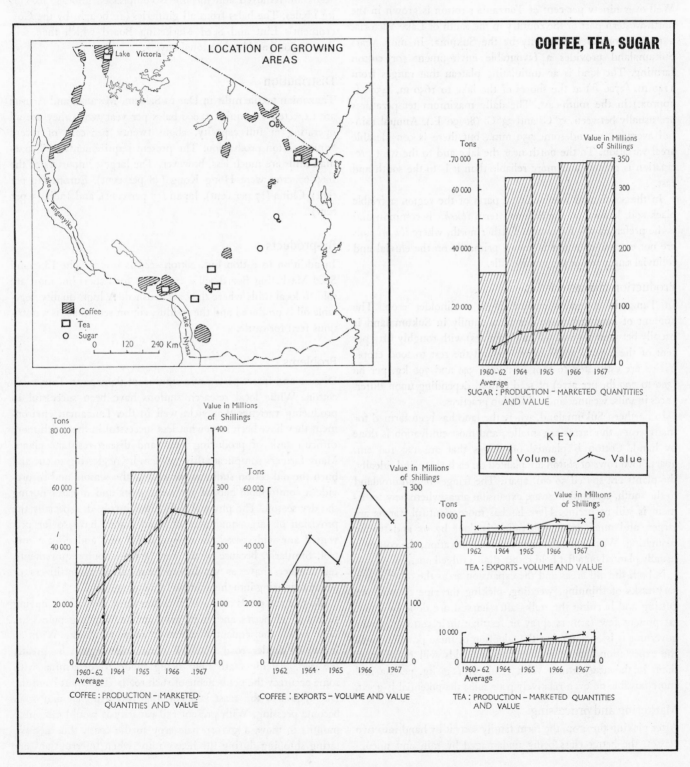

LOCATION OF GROWING AREAS

Lake Victoria

Lake Tanganyika

Lake Nyasa

▨ Coffee
☐ Tea
○ Sugar

0   120   240 Km

COFFEE, TEA, SUGAR

Tons / Value in Millions of Shillings

1960–62 Average   1964   1965   1966   1967
SUGAR : PRODUCTION – MARKETED QUANTITIES AND VALUE

KEY
▨ Volume   ✕ Value

Tons / Value in Millions of Shillings

1962   1964   1965   1966   1967
TEA : EXPORTS – VOLUME AND VALUE

Tons / Value in Millions of Shillings

1960–62 Average   1964   1965   1966   1967
TEA : PRODUCTION – MARKETED QUANTITIES AND VALUE

Tons / Value in Millions of Shillings

1960–62 Average   1964   1965   1966   1967
COFFEE : PRODUCTION – MARKETED QUANTITIES AND VALUE

Tons / Value in Millions of Shillings

1962   1964   1965   1966   1967
COFFEE : EXPORTS – VOLUME AND VALUE

During recent years cotton has become Tanzania's most important cash crop and its leading export commodity. From 1965 to 1967 the value of cotton from Tanzania averaged 280 million shillings per year, twenty per cent of the country's total exports.

Production area

Well over ninety per cent of Tanzania's cotton is grown in the north-western part of the country to the south of Lake Victoria, a region populated primarily by the Sukuma. In most years Sukumaland provides a favourable environment for cotton farming. The land is an undulating plateau that ranges from 1140 m. (3700 ft) at the shores of the lake to 1650 m. (4500 ft approx.) in the south-east. The daily maximum temperatures are usually between 27°C. and 33°C. (80–90°F.). Annual rainfall averages around some 750 mm., but there is considerable areal variation. To the north near the lake and to the west precipitation is greater and more reliable than it is to the south and east.

In the south and south-eastern parts of the region a friable black soil, known by the Sukuma term *ibushi*, is common and is the preferred soil for cotton. Farther north, where *ibushi* soils are not extensive, cotton is grown primarily on the eluvial and colluvial sandy soil of the granite hills.

Production characteristics

In Tanzania cotton is exclusively a smallholder crop. The amount of land cultivated per farm family in Sukumaland is usually between 2·4 and 3·6 ha (6–9 acres) with roughly fifty per cent of the land devoted to cotton and the rest to food crops. Yields are estimated to range between 340 and 790 kg. per ha (300 to 700 lb. per acre) of seed cotton, depending upon differences in soils, weather and cultivation practices.

In northern Sukumaland, where the land has been farmed for many years, the farms are smaller, and most cultivation is done by hand. Cotton is planted on ridges that are 130–190 cm. apart. Two rows of cotton are planted on each ridge and, ideally, the plants are spaced 50 cm. apart. The fringes of Sukumaland to the south, east and west are expansion areas where new settlement is still occurring. Here land is more plentiful, farms are larger, and much more cultivation is done by ox and tractor ploughing. When ploughs are used for cultivation, the cotton is usually planted on a flat field rather than a ridged one.

In both the old areas and the expansion areas the other necessary tasks of thinning, weeding, picking the ripe cotton, and cutting and burning the stalks after harvest are done by hand. At present few farmers spray or fertilize their cotton, but the government is encouraging the adoption of these practices with the expectation that large increases in yields will result from them in the near future. With yields of 1350 kg. per ha and more possible on even relatively poor soils, the potential is great.

Marketing and processing

After picking the crop, the farm family sorts it by hand into two classes, the better class being undamaged by rain and uncontaminated with dirt, weeds, or other rubbish. The farmer then takes his cotton to the local primary society buying-post of the Co-operative Union which inspects and weighs the crop and pays him at a price fixed for all producers regardless of their location. In 1967 this price was 46 cents per lb. (101 cents per kg.) for the better grade cotton and 21 cents for the lower grade (46 cents per kg.), thus providing producers with average gross returns of Shs. 320–875 per hectare (Shs. 130–350 per acre). The society bags the cotton and transports it to the ginnery where seeds are removed and the lint is compressed into 400 lb. (182 kg.) bales. The bales from all ginneries are bought by the Government's Lint and Seed Marketing Board which then sells them to local and international buyers.

Distribution

Tanzanian textile mills in Dar es Salaam, Mwanza and Arusha are expected to require 73 000 bales per year when they are all operating at full capacity, about twenty per cent of recent annual cotton production. The present requirements of Tanzanian mills are much less, however. The largest importers of the 1966–67 crop were Hong Kong (38 per cent), Europe (19 per cent), China (17 per cent), Japan (17 per cent), and India (5 per cent).

By-products

In addition to cotton lint, cotton seed is useful. The Lint and Seed Marketing Board sell a few seeds for export but most are sold to local mills where they are crushed. A high quality vegetable oil is produced and the residue, cotton seed cake, is a nutritious feed for cattle.

Problems

Disease and insect pests cause significant damage to Tanzania's cotton. While local research stations have been successful in producing varieties that yield well in the Tanzanian environment they have been somewhat less successful in the much more difficult task of producing pest- and disease-resistant plants. Many farmers complicate this problem by neglecting to cut and burn the old cotton stalks at the end of the season, and so provide a comfortable habitat for some pests and diseases during the dry season. The physical difficulties involved, especially the provision of large quantities of clean water, have so far prevented any widespread use of sprays for pest and disease control. Similarly, because of the very great labour requirements, few farmers have as yet incorporated artificial fertilizers or heavy manuring into their cotton farming systems.

Most of the roads over which cotton must move from buying points to ginneries and from ginneries to shipping points are very poor. Consequently transport costs are high. With an improved feeder road network these costs would be greatly lowered. Attempts are now being made to determine with some accuracy the net benefits of such roads. Transport from the lake region to the coast is a potential problem that may soon become pressing. With present rail capacity it would take nine months to move a 500 000 bale crop to the coast, thus necessitating shipping during the heavy rains when interruptions are frequent. To avoid this, substantial increases in rail capacity will be necessary as production increases.

Additional problems complicate production in the coastal region. There cotton is more prone to insect attack than it is in Sukumaland. Moreover, in many of the coastal areas so little cotton is grown that transport costs are excessive and ginneries cannot operate economically.

TOM HANKINS

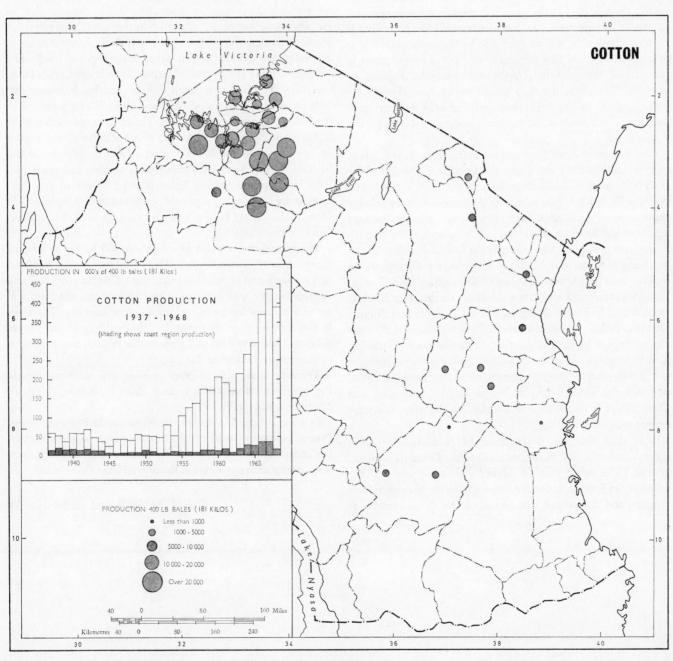

COTTON

PRODUCTION IN 000's of 400 lb bales (181 Kilos)

COTTON PRODUCTION

1937 - 1968

(shading shows coast region production)

PRODUCTION 400 LB BALES (181 KILOS)

- Less than 1000
- 1000 - 5000
- 5000 - 10 000
- 10 000 - 20 000
- Over 20 000

23 MAIZE, WHEAT AND OTHER GRAINS

It is extremely difficult to obtain an accurate and detailed picture of the pattern of grain production in Tanzania. Maize, the most important of the grain crops, is a staple food crop over much of the country, with millet being more important in the drier areas. However, our knowledge of the bulk of this crop, which is eaten by the producer and his family, is extremely sketchy, and the problems of getting a nationwide inventory of maize acreages and yields are immense. The figures used in this section refer only to that part of the grain output which is marketed. The map shows the amounts of grain crops marketed through the legal co-operative channels and then handled by the National Agricultural Products Marketing Board. These data are extremely inadequate. In most areas it is possible for a farmer who has maize surplus to his own food needs to sell this privately for a price far above the official price paid by the co-operatives. It is generally true to say that the maize sold to the co-operatives is that part of the marketed crop which cannot be disposed of privately. Therefore, the map should be interpreted with extreme caution. It has been estimated that only between one-seventh and one-tenth of the marketed maize passes through the co-operatives.

A second set of figures is presented in Table 19, p. 162. These are estimates made by the Regional Agricultural Officers of the grain crops marketed in their regions. Again, these data must be treated with caution. However, they do demonstrate the relative importance of each area, even though the absolute tonnage figures might be in question. In maize production, the importance of Iringa Region, and especially the Ismani Plains area, can be clearly seen, as can the areas of secondary importance in regions such as Arusha, Dodoma, Kilimanjaro and Tanga. Marketed maize and sorghum production, on the other hand, is concentrated in Mara, Morogoro, Mbeya, Dodoma and Singida Regions. Paddy production is even more concentrated, with Mbeya Region by far the most important producer. Such important irrigation schemes as Mbarali, make a very significant contribution here. Other important areas are Tabora Region, especially the western part of Nzega District, Morogoro and Coast. All of these have the well-watered valley areas necessary for rice production.

It is clear that the development of production of these major grain crops is an important key to Tanzania's overall growth. The wider use of higher yielding grain varieties would make it much easier for farmers to secure their own food supplies, and thus release land and labour for the production of market crops. It should also be remembered that grain crops can be in themselves remunerative cash crops. Much research work has been carried out on the development of improved strains of maize, millet and sorghum, and some farmers are already reaping the benefits of this. More will soon be encouraged to do so.

It is possible to be much more confident about the quality of data on wheat production, since this is concentrated in a few areas and output generally comes from a relatively small number of large farms. The overwhelming present importance of Arusha and Kilimanjaro Regions is clearly shown in Table 18, p. 162. Wheat is seen as a major growth crop over the next five years, with the immediate aim of making Tanzania self-sufficient in this crop. Recently a study was made by a team of Canadian experts, who picked out a number of areas for expansion. These are shown in the map.

The Arusha area, already important, has a high potential for expansion, especially in Mbulu District. In the area close to Arusha town most of the wheat production is on large estates of 400 hectares or more, but here there is little room for expansion. Similarly the Kitete-Oldeani area, made up of small- and medium-sized, hand-cultivated farms has little extra land. However, the Lolkirale area, south-west of Arusha, has some 800 hectares available for future use, and there is also potential in the Makuyuni and Lolindo areas. The major expansion will be at Basuto in Mbulu District. The wheat state farm was started in late 1967, and 140 hectares were seeded in 1968. Some 800 hectares will be seeded in 1969, and a further 2400–3200 hectares have good potential. There is another area of 6000 hectares to the north-east. At present, transportation is a problem in Mbulu District, but high priority is being given to the construction of access roads.

The second major point of expansion will be in the Sumbawanga area of Mbeya Region. The state farm at Milundukwa, 64 km. north-east of Sumbawanga, was started in 1967, and will expand to some 1200 hectares. It is envisaged that the farm will act as a nucleus for a series of smallholder satellites. Transport is also a problem in this area, but the building of the Dar es Salaam–Tunduma road will help in this respect, and may open up market possibilities in Zambia.

There are a number of other possible sites for expansion in the southern area, notably near Mbeya, Kitulo, Njombe, Mufindi and Sao Hill.

In all it is hoped to set up ten wheat-producing state farms. Present consumption of wheat in Tanzania is some 60 000 tons per annum, and it is expected that home production will reach this figure within the period of the Second Five Year Plan.

SALIM HAMEER and JOHN McKAY

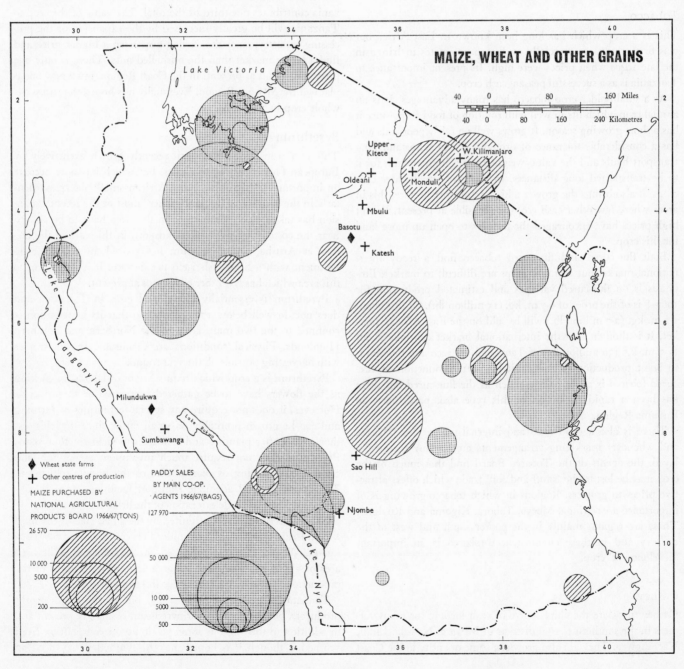

MAIZE, WHEAT AND OTHER GRAINS

Lake Victoria

Upper-
Kitete +

+ W. Kilimanjaro

Oldeani +
+ Monduli

+ Mbulu

Basotu ◆
+ Katesh

Lake Tanganyika

Milundukwa ◆

Sumbawanga +

Lake Rukwa

Sao Hill +

Njombe +

Lake Nyasa

◆ Wheat state farms
+ Other centres of production

MAIZE PURCHASED BY
NATIONAL AGRICULTURAL
PRODUCTS BOARD 1966/67 (TONS)

26 570
10 000
5000
200

PADDY SALES
BY MAIN CO-OP.
AGENTS 1966/67 (BAGS)

127 970
50 000
10 000
5000
500

40   0   80   160   Miles
40   0   80   160   240 Kilometres

These are all important crops to Tanzanian smallholders, who produce all of the cashew crop and at least half of the tobacco and pyrethrum. Their importance has increased in recent years through government promotion and help to smallholders, aimed at bringing more farmers into the cash economy and also to help diversify the export sector and lessen dependence on the three major export crops (coffee, cotton, sisal).

Map 25 indicates only the location of growing areas since no statistics of areas are available. Table 18, p. 162, provides some additional production and export information.

Tobacco

This is a crop which has long been known in East Africa but was first grown commercially on European estates in Iringa in the late 1940s when prices were high. Its present importance to Tanzania is as a successful peasant cash crop.

As a smallholder crop tobacco has many advantages. It is an annual crop which fits in well with rotation of food crops since it has a short growing season. It grows well on fairly poor soils and has a considerable tolerance of drought. It can withstand long transport hauls and the value/weight ratio is high enough for it to be transported long distances. In terms of smallholder cash crops, it also brings the grower a high return per hectare, this in areas where few other cash crops are feasible at present. Recent high prices have encouraged the farmers to open up more land for this crop.

Both flue-cured and fire-cured tobacco find a ready international market but aromatic crops are difficult to market. Emphasis is on flue-cured varieties and estimated production for 1967–8 is of the order of 6·7 m. kg. (15 million lb.). Of this about 1·2 m. kg. (2·7 million lb.) will be sold on the East African market. It is thought that the international market can take about 13·5 m. kg. (30 million lb.) of Tanzanian tobacco and the aim is to boost production to this limit by 1971. Production of fire-cured tobacco is about half as much as the flue-cured but there has been a rapid expansion of this type also, particularly in Ruvuma Region.

There is also a good local and internal market for tobacco, and whenever marketing arrangements are for any reason delayed, the agents of the Tobacco Board find that much of the crop may be lost to the 'snuff and coil' trade which offers attractive prices to growers. Regions in which tobacco-growing is of importance are: Iringa, Mbeya, Tabora, Kigoma and Ruvuma. These are regions mainly in the poorer south and west of the country and in these circumstances tobacco is an important 'development' crop.

Cashew

Cashew nuts are the chief source of cash income for many farmers in the southern coastal districts of Mtwara, Newala, Lindi, Nachingwea. They are also grown in some quantity in the Coast Region near Dar es Salaam, but here they are more often grown to supplement other sources of income.

The crop is a simple one in that it requires little attention once it is planted and the nuts are harvested from the ground after falling. Expenses are mainly incurred in clearing and planting, cleaning beneath the trees, harvesting nuts and transporting them to the co-operative society. Transport is often the highest cost element in production, since family labour is frequently used for the farm operations. The cashew trees are usually interplanted with food crops. Yields are not thought to be high, but it is a valuable cash crop in areas where there are few other sources of income. It is confined to the coastal areas by the requirement of high temperatures and also by the need for good transport facilities.

The annual crop is of the order of 80 000 tons, and most of this is still sold unshelled on the world market, to which Tanzania contributes one-third of the total. The value of the crop to Tanzania will be greatly increased by the expansion of the processing industry, since the shelled nuts fetch a higher price and find a larger market than the unshelled nuts. There is only one processing plant at present, in the Coast Region, but a new one is planned for Mtwara Region. Eventually it is hoped to process the whole crop in Tanzania.

Pyrethrum

This is a crop which was until recently grown exclusively by European farmers on large estates, but which has now become an important cash crop to many African smallholders, particularly in the Southern Highlands where most of the recent expansion has taken place. Cash crops in this area have to be able to bear the costs of long-distance transport, in this case to the factory at Arusha, and pyrethrum has proved an economic investment with a high cash yield per hectare. It is important to this area which has few other cash crops at present.

Pyrethrum is essentially a highland crop in Tanzania and does not do well below 1700 metres, so that its distribution is confined to the two main areas of the Northern and Southern Highlands. Physical conditions are favourable in the tropics with harvesting possible all the year round.

Pyrethrum is a crop which requires a lot of labour for picking as the flowers have to be gathered every two or three weeks. However, it does not require any special techniques of farming and can be grown profitably on small farms since it yields less than a year after planting and continues to yield for four years. Pyrethrum does not require much investment except for land clearing and buying of plants. One of the main problems in Tanzania is to find adequate transport facilities to the factory because delays lead to deterioration of the dried flowers.

Expansion of this crop is limited by the small size of the market and it is therefore grown under licence. A total of 6 631 400 kg. (14 589 000 lb.) was produced in 1967–8 from a licensed area of 31 600 ha. The southern area accounted for most of the production, 5 550 000 kg. (12 225 000 lb.) from 23 630 ha.

Tanzania, together with Kenya, is one of the major world producers, but the demand for pyrethrum is small at present and in addition to this there is some possibility of competition from synthetics, though it is hoped that the synthetics may need an addition of pyrethrum to perform effectively as insecticides. The government therefore attempts to limit the total quota of dried flowers to 5000 tons (5 m. kg.). The price for the extract, pyre-thrin, remains stable, in spite of recent production increases, and the product is of such small volume and weight that much is exported by air transport.

EILEEN BERRY

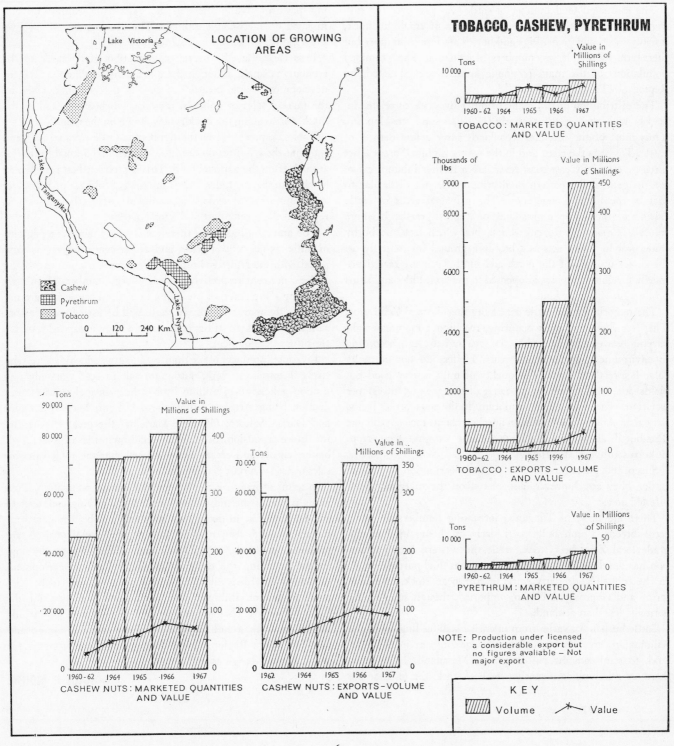

LOCATION OF GROWING AREAS

Lake Victoria

Lake Tanganyika

Lake Nyasa

Cashew
Pyrethrum
Tobacco

0   120   240 Km.

TOBACCO, CASHEW, PYRETHRUM

Tons
Value in Millions of Shillings
10 000
0
1960 - 62   1964   1965   1966   1967
TOBACCO : MARKETED QUANTITIES AND VALUE

Thousands of lbs
Value in Millions of Shillings
9000   450
8000   400
6000   300
4000   200
2000   100
0   0
1960-62   1964   1965   1996   1967
TOBACCO : EXPORTS – VOLUME AND VALUE

Tons
Value in Millions of Shillings
10 000   50
0   0
1960 - 62   1964   1965   1966   1967
PYRETHRUM : MARKETED QUANTITIES AND VALUE

NOTE: Production under licensed a considerable export but no figures avaliable – Not major export

Tons
90 000
Value in Millions of Shillings
80 000   400
60 000   300
40 000   200
20 000   100
0   0
1960 - 62   1964   1965   1966   1967
CASHEW NUTS : MARKETED QUANTITIES AND VALUE

Tons
70 000   350
60 000   300
40 000   200
20 000   100
0   0
1962   1964   1965   1966   1967
CASHEW NUTS : EXPORTS–VOLUME AND VALUE

KEY
Volume   Value

25 CATTLE

This map is based on figures obtained during the United Nations FAO census of livestock in 1965. In some districts there was an actual enumeration, whereas in others estimates only were derived. The Regions in which counts were made are Coast, Iringa, Kigoma, Mbeya, Morogoro, Mtwara, Ruvuma, Shinyanga (excepting Maswa District) and Tabora, and the district of Ukerewe.

The estimated total number of cattle was just over ten million. In addition there are large numbers of small livestock, notably sheep and goats. Pigs and horses are few in number but there are, locally, larger numbers of donkeys. The estimated populations of the main economic animals are tabulated, by Regions, in Table 20, p. 163.

The distribution of cattle and of other livestock correlates inversely with that of the tsetse-fly (*Glossina* spp., see Map 26). Thus most of the miombo woodlands carry a low density of cattle. Towards the coast and in the wetter highland areas other diseases, especially east coast fever, are a further inhibiting factor. In general the pattern of distribution is not dissimilar to that of the human population. The principal areas of cattle raising are the dry open grasslands or wooded grasslands whose rainfall is marginal for cultivation, but which lack the bushy undergrowth which acts as a breeding ground for tsetse-fly. In the cooler uplands of the north and south cattle are reared primarily for dairy purposes as opposed to the beef, hides and skins production of the dry lands.

The majority of the cattle are of the short-horned Zebu type. They are small and slow maturing, reaching a mature weight varying between 450 lb. and 800 lb. (204 and 363 kg.), according to environment, in about six years. Heifers do not normally calve before three years. The quality of milk is very good but yields are small, reaching 70–120 gallons (319–545 litres) per lactation. The only other significant indigenous breed is the Sanga or Ankole cattle which number about 100 000 and are distributed along the highlands in the extreme west from Bukoba southwards to Ufipa.

Sheep and goats have a very similar distribution to that of cattle. They are, however, also reared on the marginal tsetse infested areas.

There are now, in Tanzania, increasing numbers of exotic cattle breeds. Boron bulls particularly are being used to upgrade local Zebu beef stock, while the western breeding station has developed the Mpwapwa breed, as dual-purpose cattle. In the cool uplands dairy cattle of European stock, especially Jersey and Guernsey, are being imported, though supplies are normally less than demand.

Cattle husbandry varies from intensive stall-feeding, as in the Kilimanjaro area, through systematic grazing, as in Sukumaland, to semi-nomadic pastoralism in Masailand. In addition there are a few modern ranches for beef stock. Six of these are nationally owned by the National Development Corporation (see Table 21, p. 163). The majority of the cattle on these ranches are Boron × Boron or Boron × Zebu.

Several large prisons, for example Kingolwira in Morogoro Region, have herds and there are some private ranches.

Despite the large cattle population the industry is not as fully developed as it might be. In many parts of the country cattle are kept more as symbols of wealth and prestige, or are reared for payment of bride-price, rather than as an economic enterprise. Thus numbers tend to increase to the detriment of available pasture. Overgrazing leads to soil erosion and decreasing pastures, while there is no systematic culling of old, diseased or uneconomic animals. The development of the livestock industry is shown in Table 22 on p. 163.

It is clear that the overall contribution of livestock to the economy is small, although there is a considerable potential for development. Some measure of current production is given by the market sales of animals, most of which are moved to the market areas along the stock routes shown on the map.

Table 23, p. 163, gives the figures for cattle sales in 1961 and 1967 but these figures do not indicate the total annual offtake of animals from the national herd. This is probably best represented by the number of hides and skins sold. Table 24, p. 163, gives such numbers for exported production only, though exports represent the greater part of the total output.

The annual offtake was therefore, in 1967, about 10 per cent of cattle, 25 per cent of goats, and 23 per cent of sheep, as compared with the registered offtake (from market sales) of 2.9, 2.3 and 0.9 per cent respectively. Clearly large numbers of animals are being slaughtered or are dying by natural causes but are not entering the market. Many of these will be used for home consumption, but there still appears to be a large untapped resource for future development.

Livestock products other than meat, skins and hides are relatively insignificant. Milk output for sale in 1966 was only 1.45 million gallons (6.35 million litres), the principal areas of production being Arusha, Kilimanjaro, Tabora, Mara, Morogoro and Dar es Salaam. Of these Mara has the greatest potential for future expansion. In addition small quantities of ghee, fresh butter, cheese and cream are produced, but the total value of sales in 1966 was only 2.3 million shillings.

In terms of livestock per head of the human population, Tanzania is one of the most significant animal-rearing countries in Africa. There is no doubt that livestock will be a major focus for economic development in the future. Several projects are proposed in the 1969–74 Development Plan. Range developments, including the current Masailand Range Development Commission with a pilot ranch at Kolomonik, are to be allocated 20 million shillings with a further 5.9 million for the UNDP livestock scheme. State farm projects in the Plan include ranches at Uvinza and Singida and dairy farms at Oljoro and in North Mara Region. Other developments are proposed for goats, sheep and pigs, as well as cattle.

JOHN E MOORE

CATTLE

Lake Victoria

Bweri
Buhemba

Malya

Shinyanga

Bukene

Temi

Kelena

Korogwe

Manyoni

Dodoma

Lake Tanganyika

Mloa

Mbeya

Lake Nyasa

. One dot represents 5000 head of cattle
— Government stock routes
(H) Government holding grounds
(C) Check points

Songea

40   0   80   160 Miles

Kilometres 40 0   80   160   240

Development of the livestock industry in Tanzania faces many problems of which one of the most outstanding is the wastage of animals, by death or by emaciation, through diesease. The set of maps opposite summarizes the distribution and intensity of some of the major disease types.

1. Bovine trypanosomiasis

Commonly known as *nagana*, to distinguish it from human sleeping-sickness, this disease is carried by the tsetse-fly (*Glossina* spp.). It is caused by trypanosomae, microscopic protozoa, of which there are a number of species. Those mainly responsible for nagana are *T. brucei*, *T. vivax*, *T. cingolense* and *T. uniforme*. The seven species of tsetse-fly in Tanzania act as vectors of trypanosomes from host to uninfected animal. The infected host may be domestic stock or may be one of a wide variety of game animals. Of the tsetse-fly, those which act as important vectors of nagana are *Glossina morsitans*, *G. swynnertoni*, *G. pallidipes*, *G. brevipalpis* and *G. palpalis*. Each species has favoured types of breeding ground but in all cases a dense woody thicket or woodland is required.

The most widespread ecological type favoured by the fly is the miombo woodland, hence cattle-raising is excluded from a major proportion of the country (see Map 10). Elsewhere riverain forest and dry thorn scrub harbour other species of the fly.

The disease takes the form of fluctuating fever, loss of appetite, anaemia and swellings. Susceptible animals die in two to twelve weeks.

In 1967 the confirmed number of deaths from nagana was 4,597, but this certainly understates the true extent of wastage since in many parts of the country deaths and their causes are unrecorded, more particularly in those areas with most cattle. Curative drugs and prophylactic vaccines are available, but the task of immunizing twenty million stock is immense.

Most effort in Tanzania has, since 1920, been concentrated on control of the tsetse-fly by the use of insecticides and by clearing the trees and shrubs in which they breed. Large scale clearance is very costly and most current measures aim at the creation of tsetse-free bush-cleared cordons around zones in which insecticides may systematically be applied.

2. East coast fever

This disease is caused by the protozoa *Theileria parva*. The principal vector is the brown tick (*Rhipicephalus appendiculatus*). The parasites are passed on to livestock in the saliva of ticks attached to the skin especially around the ears. The infected animal develops fever, swollen lymph nodes, difficult breathing and becomes emaciated. Death usually follows in ten to twenty days, so the disease is essentially short and fatal.

The distribution of the brown tick is not related to any one ecological zone, although there is a very clearly defined enzootic area. The disease can, however, spread even when the density of ticks is very low, as little as one tick per three beasts. In general the tick is rare where rainfall is less than 500 mm. per year and

at heights above 2150 m. (7000 ft.). Elsewhere the density of ticks roughly corresponds to the density of cattle, but there is a marked concentration in the Lake Victoria basin in a belt 30–80 km. inland from the lake, and in a curving strip from Ufipa, through the Southern Highlands northwards to the Usambara and Pare Mountains thence through Kilimanjaro, Monduli and Mbulu to the Kondoa scarp and the north-west Kilosa Highlands. Areas where the tick is sparse are generally those where cattle are few due to tsetse infestation.

Deaths in 1967 numbered 5929, but this underestimates the dimensions of the disease.

The only form of disease control available at present is regular systematic dipping and the distribution of the 458 dips and spray races in Tanzania in 1968 is indicated on the map.

3. Blackquarter fever

Blackquarter fever is caused by the spore-bearing bacteria *Clostridium chauvoei*. It mainly affects cattle but does occur in sheep and goats.

The organisms live in the soil, and once an area is infected the disease will recur. Although in most parts of the world it is a disease of young animals, in Tanzania less than half of those infected may be described as immature.

The first symptoms are lameness followed by diffuse swelling in the region of the shoulder or of the rump, and accompanied by fever and depression. The affected animals normally die within two days. Few recover, but those that do are completely immunized against further attack. Since the disease does not rely on a vector it is widespread, but is particularly prevalent in Mara, Mwanza, Shinyanga and Tanga Regions.

Control of the disease can now be effected through a number of vaccines.

4a. Foot and mouth disease

This is an extremely contagious virus disease transmitted from animal to animal especially through the saliva. It affects all cloven hooved animals, and while it is not especially fatal it causes extreme wastage. Immunity gained by surviving infection is, unfortunately, only short-lived.

In some parts of the world, especially Europe and North America, control of foot and mouth epidemics is effected by slaughter of all infected stock. In Tanzania, where the disease is widespread, quarantine together with vaccination are applied. Movement along stock routes, particularly, is prohibited. No district is free from the disease and the map shows only those outbreaks occurring in 1967 when a total of 86 deaths was recorded and 36 000 animals were vaccinated.

b. Brucellosis

Of the various *Brucella* species of bacteria that which affects cattle is *Bacillus abortus* which causes infectious abortion in cows. It is transmitted by contact through the mucous membranes of the eye or through ingestion of infected discharges. It mainly infects the uterus causing abortion and consequently low calving rates. Treatment is by terramycin or penicillin.

c. Anthrax

This is also a bacterial disease caused by *Bacillus anthracis*. All herbivorous animals and man are susceptible. It can be transmitted in a number of ways: through infected pasture; through blood-sucking flies; through spores remaining in hides and skins. It is a short and fatal disease resulting in high fever and internal bleeding. Vaccination is available, but the carcases of those infected animals which die must be burned to destroy the spores. The number of confirmed deaths in Tanzania in 1967 was 1405.

d. Rinderpest

This highly contagious virus disease of cattle has now been con-trolled in Tanzania by the establishment of immunization centres throughout the country.

Other cattle diseases occur in Tanzania, most notably *Anaplasmosis* (1325 deaths in 1967), but are generally of less significance.

It is clear that the figures given do not reflect the actual extent of cattle disease through Tanzania and the concomitant losses of livestock productivity. Remedial measures, however, entail widespread reorganization of the cattle-raising industry, so that curative and prophylactic measures can be regularly and systematically applied.

JOHN E MOORE

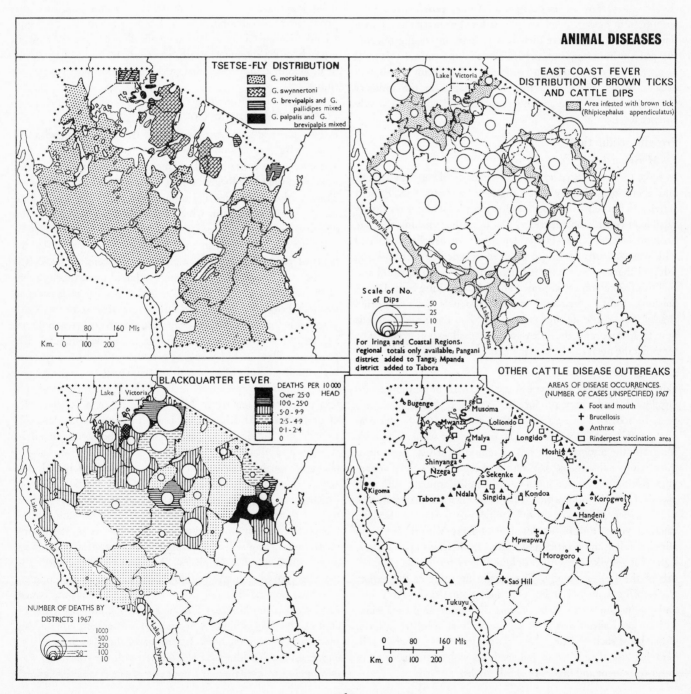

27 FISHERIES

Perhaps the most important aspects of the Tanzanian fishing industry are its great capacity for future development together with the problems which must be overcome in order to allow it to expand. In Table 25, p. 163, it can be seen that, whilst overall there has been an upward trend in production since 1962, progress has been irregular, particularly if individual fisheries are considered. It has been suggested that given training, modern equipment, techniques, processing facilities, improved communications and research, production could be increased tenfold. The operations of Japanese and Russian fishing fleets in the Indian Ocean are indications of future possibilities. Consumption, at 6·8 kg./head/annum, is low by international standards. In a country where diets lack protein, increasing the consumption is important but, particularly in remote areas, this must await improved transport and processing. It is estimated that, at present, about 38 000 fishermen are engaged in the industry although many of these are only part-time and operating at subsistence level.

Present production

1. *Marine fisheries*
In 1967, these produced 17 per cent of the total catch by weight and about one-third by value (figures are estimates). Present activity is limited to inshore production and while even this is capable of considerable increase, it is in offshore fishing that the greatest potential lies. Heavy landings are usually associated with seasonal runs of various kinds of pelagic fish such as kingfish and shark. There is some exploitation of octopus, squid and shellfish (e.g. commercial prawn and lobster fishing from Dar es Salaam). Other specialized marine products such as dried sharks' fins, *bêche de mer* (sent to the Far East) and seashells sent to Europe and the USA form a small export trade. The main fishing areas can be seen in the map.

2. *Fresh water fisheries*
Covering an area of over 51 000 sq. km. with more than 10 000 family fishponds, they produce an average of 112 kg./hectare/year. In 1967 (Table 25, p. 163), they accounted for 83 per cent of the total catch by weight and 66 per cent by value. The table illustrates the importance of Lake Victoria (nearly 40 per cent of the catch by value in 1967). With the exception of Lake Tanganyika, fishing for various species of tilapia is dominant, although even in Lake Victoria, which tends to be regarded primarily as a tilapia fishery, it makes up only some 35 per cent of the lake catch by value. Future development of Lake Victoria is especially dependent upon extending fishing farther into open waters. Lake Tanganyika supports a unique fishery for 'dagaa', a small fish of the sardine family. They make up most of the export trade, being sent to Zambia after being sun-dried on beaches, and production seems to be capable of considerable expansion. Fishing on Lake Nyasa is at present only at subsistence level. Other lakes such as Rukwa and Kitangiri present special problems because their shallowness leads to violent fluctuations in the environment and therefore of fish stocks.

The importance of water conservation projects in Tanzania makes the stocking and organizing of fishing on dams an important aspect of the work of the Fisheries Division. At very low cost, this provides fish resources important to the subsistence economy where communications or low income do not permit marketing of fish from the sea or lakes. In most areas, for a number of reasons, construction of ponds specifically for fish production is not a practical proposition, but in remote areas where there are abundant perennial streams, simple ponds make a useful contribution to diets, although these should be regarded as subsistence and not cash operations.

3. *Fishing and tourism*
Off the coast of Tanzania are found highly prized sport fish, including marlin, sailfish, tuna, barracuda and kingfish. This presents considerable potential as a tourist attraction, the Mafia Island Fishing Club of the Tanzania Tourist Board being an example of development. Fresh water fish, including game trout in highland streams, have led to the formation of a number of clubs.

Present and future developments
High priority at present is given to the training of staff who will then advise and pass on knowledge of fishing techniques, storage, etc., to the fishermen. Training centres exist at Mwanza on Lake Victoria and Mbegani on the coast north of Dar es Salaam. There is also a Fisheries Training Institute attached to the University of Dar es Salaam, which awards a Diploma in Fisheries (the first in Africa.)

Before the industry can expand, much development in the fields of processing, storage, marketing and communications is necessary. It is estimated, for example, that at present 20 per cent of the catch exported to Zambia is lost by inefficient processing methods before it reaches its destination and in some cases fish is rotten before it reaches the shore because the fishermen do not use ice. One important development is an experimental fish-processing plant at Mwanza, the products of which range from high quality tilapia fillets to fish protein concentrate for human consumption and fish meal for livestock. Plans for a food protein concentrate factory at Mwanza are at an advanced stage of preparation. At Kigoma on Lake Tanganyika, a plant will provide hot air drying of dagaa and will be accompanied by storage and distribution facilities. In coastal areas, a slow change towards consumption of fresh fish is anticipated, and with a cheap supply of ice it should be only fractionally more expensive to keep fish fresh than smoked or dried. Ice generators are therefore planned for Tanga and Dar es Salaam. In lake areas, the bulk of production will continue to be dried. Improved marketing will result from the concentration of landings at a limited number of places where buyers can gather, and from improved communications. Extension and development of fishing port facilities are proposed for Dar es Salaam, Tanga, Mikindani (near Mtwara), Mwanza, Bukoba and Musoma, including landing quays, wholesale fish markets, ice-making plants and storage facilities. Expansion of the Mwanza and Dar es Salaam boat-building yards, together with the construction of new ones at Mikindani and Itungi port (Lake Nyasa) is planned.

With these developments at major ports will arise a need for improved fishing techniques and equipment to meet increasing demand. New techniques, boats and equipment are being experimented with by Fisheries staff who will then recommend more efficient methods to fishermen. In the Second Five Year Plan, a number of marine and lake village fishing units will be established with modern boats, equipment, storage and marketing facilities. Initially, they will be supervised by Fisheries staff and then turned over to producers' co-operatives. Mobile fishing units are planned for Mbeya Region, to exploit the shallow lake areas.

Research projects to evaluate the resources of Lake Victoria and Lake Tanganyika involving all the lake countries are planned. The East African Marine Fisheries Research Organization (EAMFRO) is also examining resources, migration, feeding and breeding habits of fish in the Indian Ocean as well as new fishing techniques, concentrating particularly on deeper waters. Until the local industry undergoes expansion and modernization, however, it is felt that the work of EAMFRO is of more benefit to the major fishing countries such as Japan than to those which actually pay for the research.

IAN J JACKSON

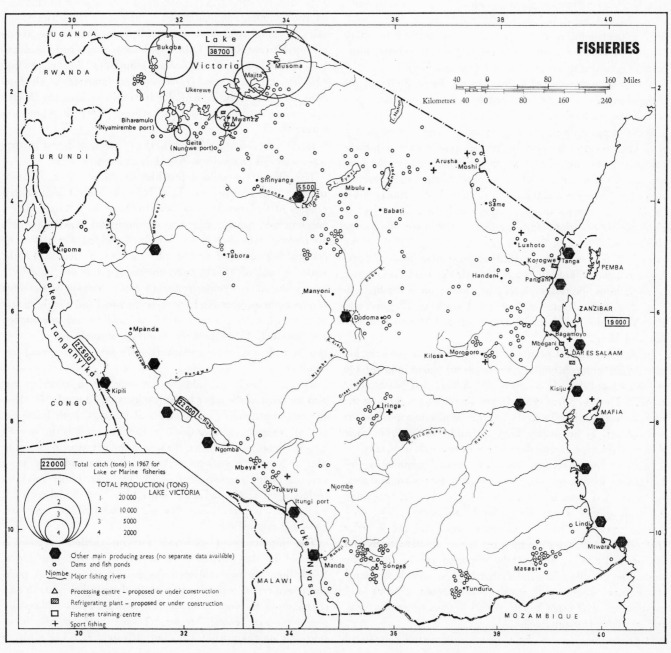

As may be seen from the map of vegetation associations (Map 10) closed forest now occupies a relatively insignificant area of Tanzania. The permanent forest estate does, however, include large areas of miombo woodlands which, although they are potentially less productive per unit area than closed forest, do provide the greater part of the national output of timber and other forest products.

By 'permanent estate', here, is meant those woodland and forest areas reserved by the state. These amount to some 128 000 sq. km. (50 000 sq. miles) divided as shown in Table 26, p. 164.

Most of this (113 920 sq. km. or 44 000 sq. miles) is administered by the central government, the remainder by local authorities. In addition there are about 307 000 sq. km. (120 000 sq. miles) of unreserved forest and woodland which are freely accessible for fuel and building materials, except that charges are made for commercial exploitation. The area of forest on private estates is small, comprising some 614 sq. km. (240 sq. miles).

The aims of forestry as outlined in the *Forest Policy of the Tanzanian Government* published in 1963 are two-fold: protection and production.

Some 13 590 sq. km. (5650 sq. miles) are regarded as protective. Their purpose is to protect the soil from erosion and, more particularly, to control the run-off of rainwater over the land surface. The former is relevant not only to the local conservation of soil resources but also to the control of sediment loads in the lower courses of rivers where irrigation dams, hydroelectric power stations and domestic water-supply works are sited. Run-off control is significant in the regulation of the amount of flow in rivers, especially in preventing floods and giving a reliable volume of water through the year. As a result of these aims, protection forests are found on watersheds in wet, steep upland areas such as the Usambara, Uluguru and Pare Mountains, the Southern Highlands and Mounts Kilimanjaro and Meru.

In addition natural protective forests aid in the conservation of wild-life with concomitant benefits to the tourist industry. On the other hand there is no empirical evidence that forests affect rainfall. They do affect groundwater supplies by regulating the interception of rainfall and the infiltration of rainwater into the soil, as well as by storing large quantities of water in their tissues. The importance of these effects is, however, uncertain.

Many of the protection forests are natural communities of indigenous species, but since most of these forests are also used for production there is a tendency to replace natural vegetation by exotic species where the former is uneconomic. The indigenous softwoods, podo (*Podocarpus* spp.) and pencil cedar (*Juniperus procera*), for example, regenerate unsatisfactorily and are gradually being replaced by imported species, especially pines. On the other hand some hardwoods, notably muninga (*Pterocarpus angolensis*), mvule (*Chlorophora excelsa*) and camphor-wood (*Ocotea usambarensis*) regenerate satisfactorily and are therefore maintained.

In production forestry the trees are systematically exploited for timber. The approach towards the forests is again dependent, in part, on the rate of regeneration and the economic productivity of indigenous species. Where these are uneconomic, destructive felling is carried out and the areas are replanted with more suitable trees. Afforestation is also carried out to increase forest resources in previously unforested and unproductive areas.

Of the permanent forest estate 111 838 sq. km. (43 686 sq. miles) are accessible for production of sawn timber and of this area 83 085 sq. km. (32 455 sq. miles) are in use.

The production forests may be divided into five main types, namely natural closed forest, miombo woodland, softwood plantations, hardwood plantations and mangrove swamp.

Natural closed forests are largely restricted to the humid upland areas mentioned earlier. The principal economic species are podo and camphorwood, but loliondo (*Olea welwitchii*) is produced on Mount Meru. Mvule is locally important and, with *Antiaris* spp., was the dominant species prior to clearance for the Longuza teak plantations in the eastern Usambara Mountains. Natural mvule forests are also maintained in the Rondo area of Mtwara Region. Other significant species include mtambara (*Cephalosphaera usambarensis*), muhuhu (*Brachylaena hutchinsii*) and blackwood (*Dalbergia melanoxylon*), all low-montane forest trees. In the Kilombero valley mahogany (*Khaya nyasica*) occurs in strips of riparian forest where it regenerates naturally.

In all a total of 7404 hectares (18 437 acres) of forest in 1966 was under systematically managed natural regeneration.

The miombo woodland provides the largest area of forest reserve. Most reserved woodland is in the central and western regions of the country, especially in the Tabora Circle. There are, however, considerable areas of unreserved woodland which are commercially exploited and, in 1966, yielded over half of the national log output of 237 861 cubic metres (2·8 cubic feet) of the national total of 388 155 cubic metres (4·7 million cubic feet). The principal economic timber in forest reserves is muninga (*Pterocarpus angolensis*). In unreserved woodland a wide variety of species is exploited for export, for building and construction and for fuel. In addition to muninga, mtunda (*Brachystegia spiciformis*) and mperamwitu (*Combretum schumannii*) are significant.

The woodlands are valuable not only for their timber but also for most of the other forest products of Tanzania. Of these the most outstanding are honey and beeswax, both being exported in significant quantities. In fact Tanzania is the world's largest exporter of beeswax. Tabora is the principal beekeeping area and research stations at Arusha, Tabora and Songea are devoted to the improvement of the industry. Other products include gum arabic, raffia and other fibres and sandalwood oil. Fuelwood – especially for charcoal – and building poles are harvested everywhere.

The importance of softwoods for construction purposes is reflected in the increasing interest in softwood plantations. While there are two valuable indigenous coniferous trees, podo and pencil cedar, both of which are exploited, their growth and regeneration are slow. Consequently they are being replaced by plantations of exotic species. These developments occur primarily on the upland areas but attempts are being made to establish suitable species, especially *Pinus caribaea*, on hotter lowland sites such as Bana. There are seventeen softwood projects as shown in Table 27, p. 164.

The dominant plantation species are pines, especially *P. radiata*, *P. patula* and *P. elliottii*, and cypress (*Cupressus lusitanica*). At Kawetire *Eucalyptus* spp. are grown while in Njombe, the western Usambaras, Kilimanjaro and Mbulu areas black wattle (*Acacia mollissima*) is grown for tannin extraction from the bark. Wattle is grown both on local authority plantations and by peasant farmers as a cash crop. Many district councils also establish *Eucalyptus* spp. plantations for building poles and fuelwood.

Hardwood plantations cover a smaller area. Both utility and fine timbers are grown. There are a number of hardwood projects, namely Longuza–Kwamkoro, Loliondo, Mtibwa, Rondo and Sanya Juu, but hardwoods are also planted in many softwood plantation areas. The most important species are teak (*Tectona grandis*), loliondo (*Olea welwitchii*), *Gevillea robusta* and muzizi (*Maesopsis eminii*), the first three being fine timbers, the last mentioned a utility timber. Of these, teak is the most extensively planted, particularly at Mtibwa and Longuza–Kwamkoro, while *Grevillea* and *Olea* are predominant in Loliondo and Sanya Juu.

Along the coast, particularly on the Rufiji delta, there are mangrove swamps which are important sources of building poles for the coastal area, which is otherwise lacking in suitable

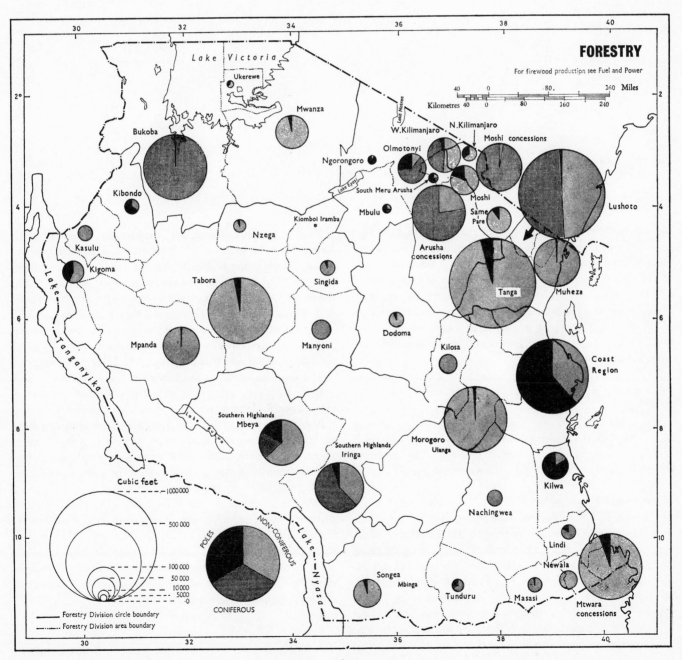

forest or woodland. The mangroves (*Rhizophora mucronata, Bruguiera gymnorhiza, Ceriops tagal*) are sources of tannin.

In addition to administering the forest estate of Tanzania the Forest Division of the Ministry of Agriculture and Co-operatives is responsible for forest protection, particularly from fire, agricultural encroachment, animal pests and diseases. Re-search stations at Moshi and Lushoto (with a sub-section at Mbeya) are concerned respectively with timber utilization and sylviculture studies as well as advisory services. There is a Fores-try Training School at Olmotonyi and extension work amongst beekeepers is carried out by the Beekeeping section.

JOHN E MOORE

29 FOREST PRODUCTS

In 1967 the total output of logs was 132 268 cu. m. (4 670 958 cu. ft.) of which 37 211 cu. m. (1 328 969 cu. ft.) or 28.5 per cent was coniferous timber (see Table 28, p. 164). Marketed output of poles was 16 131 cu. m. (576 121 cu. ft.) and of firewood 418 000 cu. m. (14.9 million cu. ft.). The latter two figures do not, however, truly reflect the total harvest of poles and fuelwood which is estimated to be 616 000 and 10 220 000 cu. m. (22 million and 365 million cu. ft.) respectively and is largely derived from unreserved land.

The division of log production between reserved and un-reserved forest is indicated by the production figures for 1966 (see Table 29, p. 165).

The importance of unreserved land for hardwood production in contrast with the almost wholly reserved output of softwoods is clearly discernible. This is further emphasized by the distri-bution of production between species in 1966 (see Table 31, p. 165).

The regional distribution of output is closely related to the distribution of forest reserves. Most exploitation is carried out, on a concession basis, by private loggers. The importance of co-operative ventures was emphasized in the 1965–69 National Development Plan and the exploitation of blackwood, for ex-port, is now handled exclusively by co-operative societies. Some blackwood is also exploited by casual concessionaries for the carving industry. Other co-operatives have been formed, for example the Usambara Timber Trading Co-operative Society, to harvest timbers other than blackwood.

Most of the harvested timber is consumed within Tanzania for construction and a range of industries. There are two ply-wood factories, one in Moshi and the other in Tanga, using podo and *Grevillea*. The Kibo match factory at Moshi is testing the use of local timber, especially *Croton megalocarpus*. In addi-tion there are large numbers of small-scale furniture works.

Exports of forest produce in 1966 were valued at 37 948 940 shillings, the principal commodities being as follows: logs and lumber, plywood and wood carvings. See Table 30, p. 165.

The most important of the minor forest products in the same year were: honey, palm nuts, gum arabic, beeswax and wattle extract. See Table 32, p. 165.

Although exports of forest products are relatively insignificant, the timber resources of Tanzania are of vital importance in the domestic economy. Despite the exports outlined above there were imports of forest produce valued, in 1966, at 52 662 740 shillings, considerably more than exports. Further developments are therefore necessary to make Tanzania self-sufficient in these products, hence an allocation of 79.5 million shillings to the Forest Division in the 1969–74 National Development Programme.

Note. Except where otherwise stated tables are drawn from the 1966 *Annual Report of the Forest Division*, Ministry of Agriculture and Co-operatives.

JOHN E MOORE

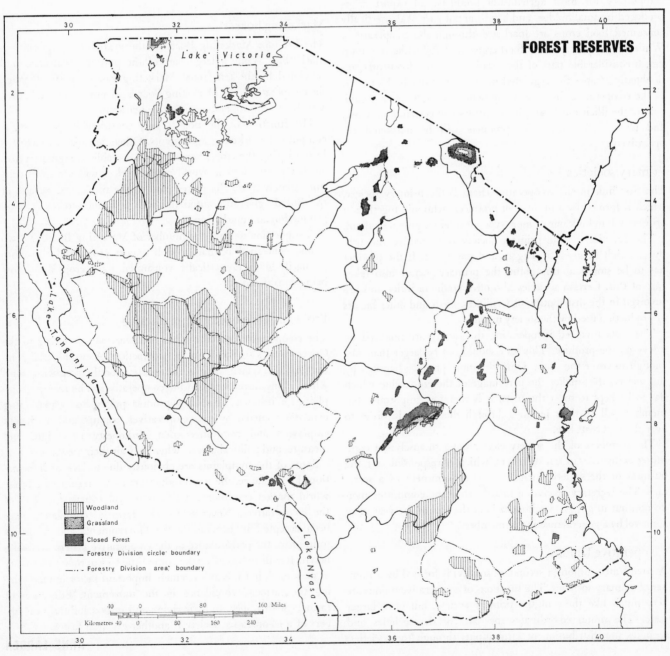

FOREST RESERVES

Lake Victoria

Lake Tanganyika

Lake Nyasa

Woodland

Grassland

Closed Forest

———— Forestry Division circle boundary

—·—·— Forestry Division area boundary

40   0   80   160 Miles

Kilometres 40   0   80   160   240

The Tanzanian Government puts heavy emphasis on co-operative marketing as a means of achieving economic independence in the sense that the economy should be controlled by 'the indigenous people rather than by expatriates and others non-African in origin'. Hence, the Co-operative Movement has been greatly expanded since Independence in 1961. In 1961 there were 857 registered co-operative societies; by 1967 the number had increased to 1650. During this period the tonnage handled by co-operatives increased more than four times.

The Government is actively engaged in the development of co-operatives: it has a division for co-operative development, and all co-operative societies are registered with and controlled by the Government. Marketing through the co-operatives is compulsory for most agricultural products; all export crops produced by smallholders and a substantial part of domestically consumed food crops are marketed through the co-operatives. While officially only a few food crops are left for the free market, a considerable part of the locally marketed foodstuffs undoubtedly escapes the regulated marketing channels. However, as the co-operatives become strengthened through better organization, the illicit marketing in foodstuffs will certainly decrease, and almost all smallholder products will be marketed co-operatively.

Primary societies

The first link in the co-operative chain is the primary society, which is formed by a number of producers who join together in order to sell in bulk one or more types of produce grown by them.

The function of the primary society is to receive the produce, weigh it, grade it, bag it, and pay for it. If the product has to be stored at this point, the primary society also takes care of this. Certain societies also offer credit facilities and are involved in the distribution of fertilizers, seeds and other factors of production used by the society members.

The costs involved in operating the society are financed by a levy on the produce. This levy should not be larger than just enough to cover the costs. Thus, the more produce handled by the society, the smaller the percentage of the crop value which has to be kept to meet the costs. It is therefore important that members sell all their produce through the society in order to keep the unit costs low.

The members of the society elect among themselves a committee with four to ten members, which is responsible for the business of the society, including the appointment of a secretary. The secretary receives a salary, while the committee men do not, but might receive honoraria at the end of the year after approval by a general meeting of members.

Co-operative Unions

A co-operative union (a secondary society) is formed by a number of primary societies. The functions of co-operative unions are very much like those of the primary society, but on a larger scale. The union co-ordinates the sales of the societies and arranges the distribution of farm inputs through the societies.

The unions usually arrange local transport, containers or bags, loans, insurance, etc., with the suppliers.

The costs connected with the union activities are also financed by a levy on the produce handled. Some of the unions have accumulated considerable surpluses, which have not in all cases been distributed to the members. Instead, the union has invested in processing facilities or other activities related to local development. Thus, in some cases, the unions have taken over the processing functions. For example, in the Sukumaland area the Nyanza Co-operative Union, the largest union in Tanzania, owns a large part of the cotton-processing plants (ginneries and oil-mills). Other unions own coffee pulperies, tobacco and pyrethrum driers, maize mills, rice mills, etc.

All the unions (thirty-three in 1968) are united in the Co-operative Union of Tanzania (CUT). The purpose of CUT is administrative and political rather than marketing.

Marketing Boards

The Produce Marketing Board is the next step in agricultural marketing. While a large part of the produce controlled and regulated by the ten (1968) Marketing Boards passes through the co-operatives, the Marketing Boards are governmental bodies, which also control non-co-operative marketing.

The function of the Boards vary considerably. Some make compulsory marketing agreements. Others are directly involved in marketing the crops. Some Boards are able to regulate prices so that fluctuations in world market prices will not necessarily immediately affect the prices paid to the producers. Several of the Boards give substantial financial assistance to research on production and marketing.

A suggestion to limit the number of Marketing Boards to two – one concerned primarily with export crops and the other primarily with domestically consumed food crops – is now being considered.

Problems in co-operative marketing

The co-operative movement has been far from working to the Government's or the farmers' satisfaction. A presidential committee has revealed some of the reasons for the scepticism with which many farmers regard the co-operatives. The farmers complain, for instance, about low product prices, heavy marketing expenses incurred by the co-operatives, corrupt and inefficient employees and committee men, dishonesty in weight and measure, and political threats when they air their views.

Some of the complaints are obviously due to lack of information. For instance, the low product prices are results of adverse world market conditions, which is not, of course, the fault of the co-operatives. Nevertheless, the farmers' complaints have been accepted in general by the Government, and measures to improve the performance of the co-operative system are being taken. It will necessarily take some time to improve the quality of personnel, but it is an extremely important factor in maintaining the farmers' confidence in the movement. Education of farmers with respect to their rights and responsibilities as members of a co-operative society is another essential factor.

ARNE LARSEN

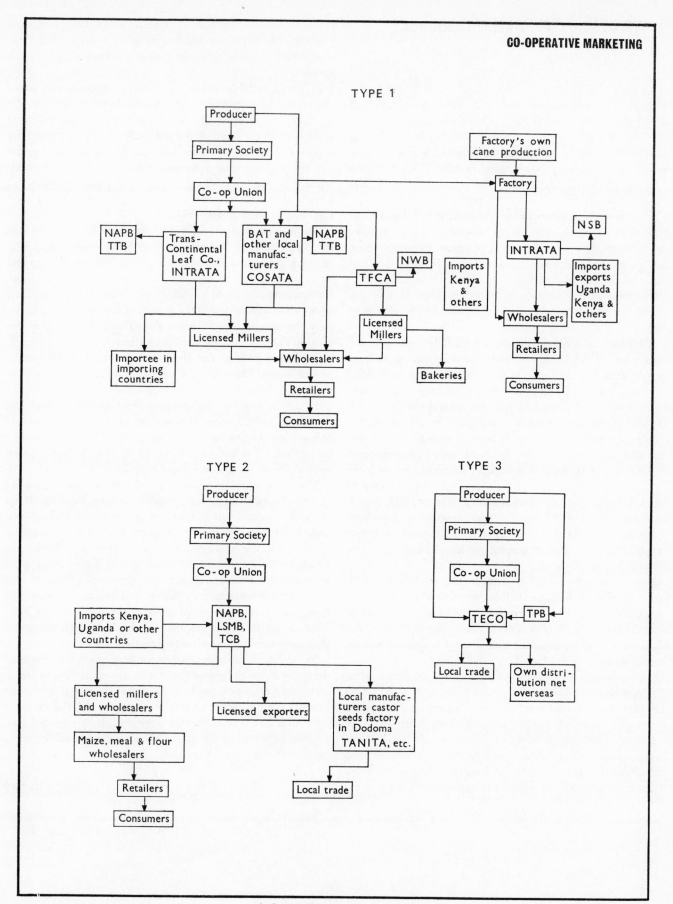

TYPE 1

TYPE 2

TYPE 3

The key to this diagram is on page 172

Although Tanzania extends close to the equator, only a small part of the country can be said to have adequate supplies of water for crop growth. The rainfall probability map (Map 15) indicates that only 21 per cent of the country has a 90 per cent probability of receiving over 750mm. of rain. There is thus a major need for storage and conservation of water for human and animal use, and in some areas for crop production.

The aim of the Government of Tanzania is to bring a clean drinking water supply to as many of the population as possible, and the map shows a wide variety of inputs into rural water supplies, most of which have been carried out by the Ministry of Water and Power. Most private installations are not included.

The greatest concentration of effort has been in the dry, central part of the country and in the more densely populated areas.

In Dodoma and Singida Regions rainfall is uncertain, and water resource development is therefore essential. In the past the emphasis has been on the provision of cheap earth-filled dams across the ephemeral streams of the area to hold wet-season water for human and animal consumption during the rest of the year. These have been successful in some areas, but in general problems have arisen because of high evaporation rates and soil erosion in the catchment areas and consequent silting up of the reservoir. For example, silting has now reduced the capacity of Ikowa reservoir, constructed in 1957, by over 50 per cent. Dams and hafirs are common in this area and, despite these problems, they still provide the major source of dry-season water. In a few places the stored water is also used for irrigation, but this is a secondary purpose and has seldom proved very successful.

More recently there has been a major effort to tap the ground-water supplies of the area and the town of Dodoma is now supplied from a series of boreholes reaching a well-defined water-body in a basin of weathered granite north of the town. Plans for the future focus on underground water, rather than surface storage.

Sukumaland is another area of concentration on rural water development and a variety of approaches have been made. Small dams are more effective here, though silting remains a problem. There are no known extensive underground reservoirs.

Around Meru and Kilimanjaro Mountains the local people have long used the surplus water from the high rainfall zone and channelled it to lower ground for a variety of purposes. There are also good local supplies of underground water in the volcanic rocks, although around Meru mineral impurities are a problem. Modern water use has adopted and modified these traditional practices, often by using pipelines or improving furrows.

In Tanga and Morogoro Regions, large quantities of water are needed to supply the sisal decorticating factories, and the concentration of boreholes and other storage means in these areas is mainly a result of the sisal industry, though many are private and not shown on the map. In Tanga, boreholes generally tap a good water reservoir in the local limestone rocks, while in Morogoro small dam storage and pipelines from small streams are the usual methods. However, boreholes have proved successful in the area east of the hills.

The major towns provide a new dimension in water-use both for people and for industry. Dar es Salaam with its rapidly growing population (7 per cent a year in the last decade) and its growing industrial base uses over 36 million litres (8 million gallons) a day, over 7 million litres (over 1½ million gallons) of which reflect the industrial growth of last two years, particularly the opening of the Friendship Textile Mill. Eighty per cent of this comes from the Ruvu River through a pumped, piped supply and the rest from reservoirs to the south of the city at Mtoni. There are plans to expand the Ruvu supply to over 36 million litres (8 million gallons) a day by 1970. As other towns expand, water-supply may become a problem, though at present most of the regional centres of Tanzania are not meeting major water difficulties. However, Dodoma in particular has had to attempt to develop various sources, now relying on good underground supplies.

The water resources of the major streams are now beginning to be developed. Plans for irrigated farming from the Ruvu are well advanced, and work is being carried out on the Wami basin to determine irrigation prospects there. The development of the Rufiji for hydro-electric power would also provide the possibility of large-scale irrigation in the lower flood plain area, and the development plans for the Kagera River include a long-term programme of drainage and irrigation. Some ideas have also been put forward about the possible use of Lake Victoria waters in the irrigation of the Malagarasi basin, but these must remain projections far into the future.

In the near future the policy is to complement the long-term development of the major rivers with the utilization of small-scale water resources, particularly in the dry central areas, and in those parts of the country as yet poorly served. For example, the south has been relatively neglected. It is expected that priority in water-supply will be given to ujaama village settlements where they are being set up.

LEN BERRY

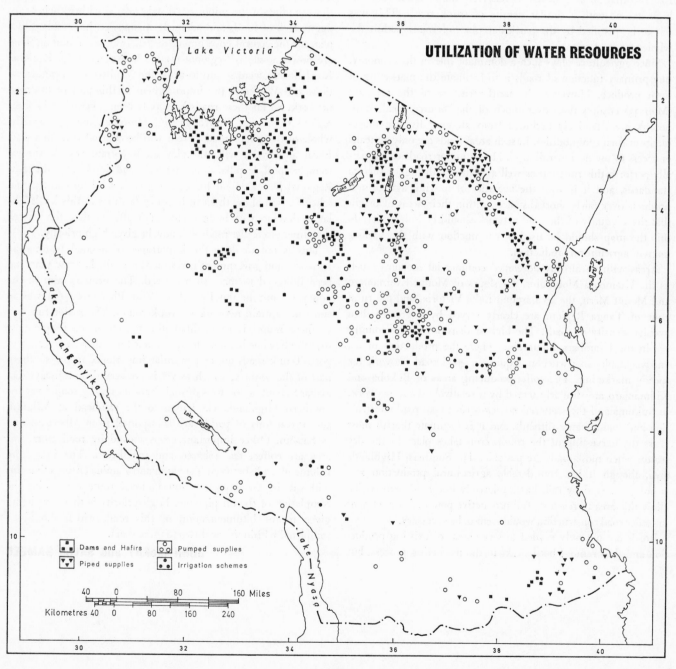

UTILIZATION OF WATER RESOURCES

Lake Victoria

Lake Tanganyika

Lake Eyasi

Lake Natron

Lake Manyara

Lake Rukwa

Lake Nyasa

■ ■
■ ■ Dams and Hafirs

▼ ▼
▼ ▼ Piped supplies

o o
o o Pumped supplies

● ●
● ● Irrigation schemes

40   0   80   160 Miles

Kilometres 40   0   80   160   240

As Tanzania moves from a predominantly subsistence economy to one in which external and inter-regional trade are increasingly important, the road network has become a vital agent of development. The map opposite is an attempt to depict how adequately each part of the country is served by motorable roads. The density of main and secondary roads was calculated by measuring the length of such roads in each fifteen minute square (approximately 740 sq. km. or 289 square miles) using a 1:500 000 map base. The appropriate length was then assigned to the centre point of each square, and isolines drawn to join places of equal density. No extra weight was given to trunk roads so that an area served by relatively minor roads ranks as high as one with a similar density of trunk roads. This was felt to be justified by the particular place of roads within the whole transport sector.

Since agriculture plays such a dominant role in the economy, one primary function of roads is to facilitate the marketing of farm produce. However, the tariff structure of the railways (Map 33) ensures that, over much of the country, road transporters are effectively excluded from all long-distance movements of such commodities. In such areas roads are only a means of access to the nearest rail-head. Hence minor roads can generally perform this function as well as routes with higher surface standards, and it is with the necessity of moving agricultural products over fairly short distances within their areas of origin that the adequacy of the road network should be judged. To do this the map should be used in conjunction with the various maps of agricultural production.

Areas with an already developed commercial economy, such as the Usambara Mountains, the slopes of Mount Kilimanjaro and Mount Meru, the area around Lake Victoria, and the rural zone of Tanga Region, are clearly served by a greater than average density of roads. The highest densities in the country are in the Usambara Mountains, where the production of tea and vegetables in particular requires a good road network for speedy marketing. The coffee-producing areas of Bukoba and Kilimanjaro are similarly served by a relatively dense network. In Sukumaland the scattered *mbuga* areas make road construction and maintenance difficult, and it is fortunate that in most years the harvesting of the cotton crop takes place in the dry season when most roads are passable. The Southern Highlands area, though it has considerable agricultural production and is not yet served by rail, has a relatively low road density. To allow this area to reach its full productive potential, investment in feeder road construction would seem to be necessary.

Roads are not only needed to serve areas of existing production and thus remove bottlenecks in the marketing process, but they can also be a powerful means of opening up areas which are at present under-utilized. The movement of population to the newly constructed Chalinze–Segera road amply demonstrates the attractive power of such a facility. The existing areas of most advanced agricultural growth are also, on the whole, areas of high population densities, and here shortage of land is already becoming a major problem. To relieve this pressure, resettlement in new areas must take place. This can only be done if a number of the areas which appear in the map opposite as having poor access to the road network are given connections to a wider market, and hence can play their part in increasing agricultural production.

The Tanzanian Government has become increasingly aware that the marketing of agricultural commodities must receive as much help as possible, and efforts are being made to improve transport at the local level. The inability of the district authorities to maintain the minor or 'district roads' within their areas, due to lack of funds and adequate manpower, has resulted in a plan for the central government to take over and maintain what are now known as 'regional roads'. In August 1967, Regional Road Boards were set up to assist the Ministry of Communications and Works in the improvement of this part of the road network. So far these roads have only been taken over in three regions (Mwanza, Shinyanga and Musoma), but by 1972 the whole of the minor road system will be controlled in this way. Local authorities will still play an important role at the extremely local 'capillary' or 'feeder' road level, and the new Regional Development Fund, along with self-help construction schemes, will allow them to improve facilities at this level. The latest development budget (1968–69) affirms that the overall investment in feeder roads will now be given high priority.

This is not to deny the importance of a good trunk road network, and government investment over the last few years has been designed to meet such a need. The primary aim of the policy set out in the First Five Year Plan (1964–69) was to construct a main network of trunk routes. The major function of these routes is to facilitate the movement of people now that the bus has become the dominant form of passenger transport. Trunk roads are of particular importance in the southern part of the country, which as yet is not served by railways. On average about 30 000 tons of maize are moved by road from the Southern Highlands via Iringa to the rail-head at Mikumi, and 12 000 tons of paddy are transported from Mbeya to Dar es Salaam. Other important crops moved by road from this area are coffee, tea, tobacco and pyrethrum. The increasing volume of trade between Tanzania and Zambia ensures that this will still be an important international route even with the completion of the oil pipeline. High priority is therefore being given to the bitumenization of this road, which should be completed within the next two to three years.

JOHN McKAY and SALIM HAMEER

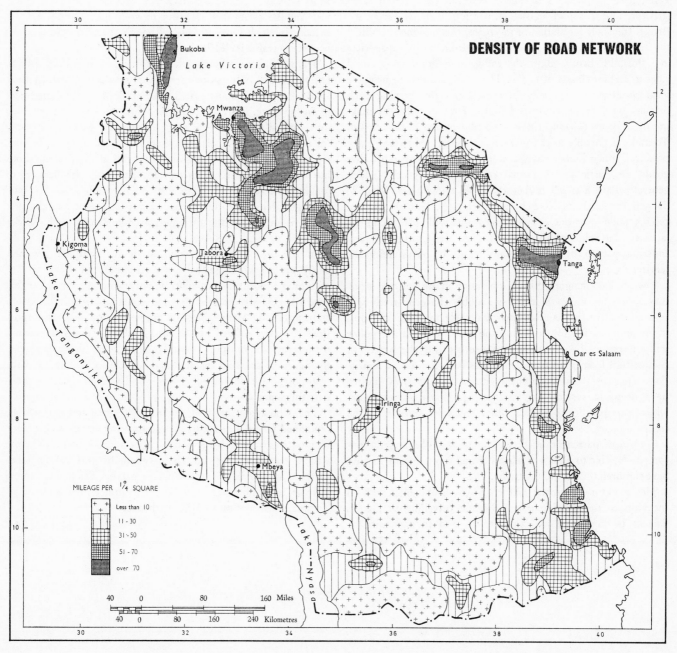

DENSITY OF ROAD NETWORK

Lake Victoria

Bukoba

Mwanza

Kigoma

Tabora

Tanga

Lake Tanganyika

Dar es Salaam

Iringa

Mbeya

Lake Nyasa

MILEAGE PER ¼° SQUARE

Less than 10
11 - 30
31 - 50
51 - 70
over 70

40   0   80   160 Miles

40   0   80   160   240   Kilometres

33 RAILWAYS

It is in many ways unfortunate that in this volume, as in so much of transportation planning, roads and railways have had to be considered in separate sections. Many current problems have arisen from the separation of two modes which should supplement each other in the transportation of goods and passengers. While steps are being taken to integrate transport planning, the current division of administration of the railways, controlled on an East African basis, and roads, planned on a national basis, makes an effective solution difficult.

The 'problem of the railways', which is in fact the problem of planning the most effective allocation of traffic between the railways and the roads, has faced East Africa for a number of years, and generated a sizeable literature. The present tariff structure and transport legislation, much of it derived from the British transport legislation of the 1930s, was designed to shield the railways from undue competition from road transporters and thus, in theory, allow the railways to grant preferential rates to certain classes of traffic. The basic aim was to promote local production, especially in agriculture, by carrying such primary products as cotton and sisal at low rates, thereby making these goods as competitive as possible on the world market. To make it possible to charge such low rates for carrying these products, much higher charges were set for a number of other goods. In particular, imported manufactured goods, which generally have a much higher value per unit volume than do the primary products, were charged high rates. Thus the general pricing policy was one of 'what the traffic will bear', being related to the value of the goods carried, rather than in any conscious way to the actual cost to the railways of providing the service.

The obvious danger with the operation of such a rate structure is that the more valuable, and highly charged, traffic will seek alternative means of transport, notably by road, and thus the finance needed for operating the cross-subsidization policy will disappear. In an attempt to prevent this the extent of competition from road transporters has been limited by legislation. The operations of all haulage firms are severely limited by a licensing system, and this is particularly so on routes which run parallel to railway lines and offer most potential competition.

Control of passenger traffic has been less severe and the bus companies, able to offer a much faster and more flexible service, have captured the bulk of the traffic.

The pattern of railway traffic shown in the map, reflects the aims of this pricing policy. Freight travelling to Dar es Salaam is dominated by export crops, and in particular by cotton moving from the Lake Victoria area. The traffic of the sample station of Malampaka clearly shows the importance of cotton. The problems faced by the railways in carrying such traffic are considerable. For example, the cotton traffic is highly seasonal, with some 300 000 bales having to be moved within a matter of weeks. The Lint and Seed Marketing Board frequently points to the lack of a sufficient number of wagons during this period to move the cotton. The railways, on the other hand, point out that it is uneconomic to buy large numbers of wagons for this traffic when demand lasts for such a small part of the year. Similar problems are faced with other agricultural products. Considerable numbers of cattle are sent by rail to Dar es Salaam from the Lake Victoria area, and from Dodoma, Tabora and Shinyanga Regions and this is an important potential year-round traffic. However, there are considerable problems of feeding and watering the cattle en route, which must be solved before a satisfactory livestock transporting service can be established. Traffic moving inland from Dar es Salaam is much more diverse, although the importance of the petroleum traffic is clearly shown.

The aim of any efficient traffic allocation policy should be to encourage the railways to carry those products to which their kind of service is most suited, and allow the road transporter to do the same. Railways can most efficiently carry bulky traffic over long distances, while road transport is generally cheaper for moving smaller loads over short distances. There have been signs over the last few years that this kind of division of labour has been developing. Between 1963 and 1967 the number of ton/km. on the railways grew at a faster rate than the total tonnage carried, and the increasing importance of long-distance traffic is shown by the increased average length of haul. See Table 33, p. 165.

At the time of writing, consultants are completing a new study of the whole railway rate structure, with the aim of obtaining a more efficient allocation of traffic. It seems clear that road hauliers are destined to play an increasing role in freight transportation. Many shippers prefer the quicker and more flexible service offered by the road hauliers, even if this means an increase in transport costs. However, it is also certain that the railways are able to offer a much cheaper service for the transport of cotton and other crops and will continue to dominate this market.

The whole operation of the railways in Tanzania will be replanned in the near future. Large investments are being made to modernize the existing routes. It is hoped that dieselization will be completed for the whole system by 1976. Much more spectacular will be the construction of the Tanzania–Zambia railway, an important step in the complete realignment of Zambia's transportation outlets to the sea.

JOHN McKAY

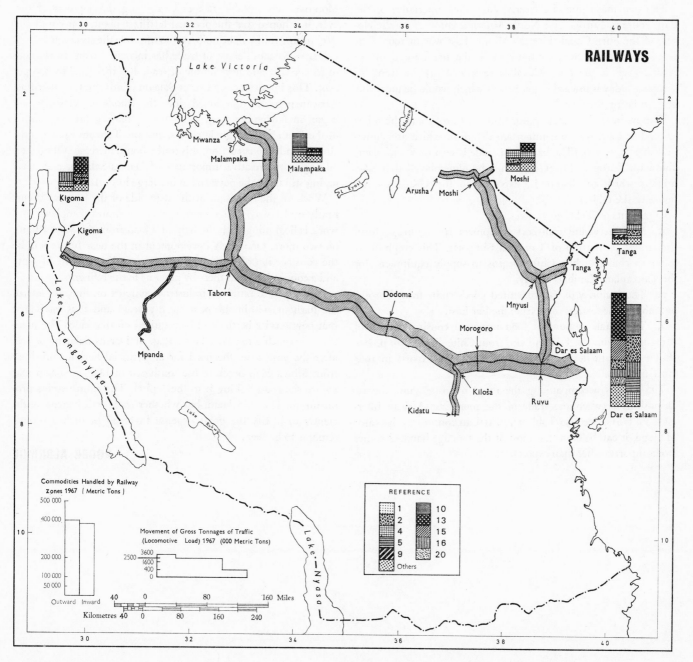

Key to numbers on map

1   Live animals
2   Maize
4   Sugar
5   Animal feed
9   Fertilizer
10 Agricultural products: mainly cotton/sisal
13 Petroleum
15 Cement
16 Iron and steel
20 Paper

RAILWAYS

Lake Victoria

Mwanza

Malampaka ← Malampaka

Kigoma

Kigoma

L. Eyasi

Arusha Moshi

Moshi

Tanga

Tanga

Lake Tanganyika

Tabora

Dodoma

Mnyusi

Morogoro

Dar es Salaam

Mpanda

Kiloŝa

Ruvu

Kidatu

Dar es Salaam

Lake Rukwa

Commodities Handled by Railway
Zones 1967 (Metric Tons)

500 000
400 000
200 000
100 000
50 000

Outward Inward

Movement of Gross Tonnages of Traffic
(Locomotive Load) 1967 (000 Metric Tons)

2500 3600
1600
400
0

Lake Nyasa

REFERENCE

1   10
2   13
4   15
5   16
9   20
Others

40 0   80   160 Miles
Kilometres 40 0   80   160   240

The major part of Tanzania's trade is by ship, as revealed by the sizeable totals of imports and exports through the major ports. Trade with the East African Community and other African countries is excluded both from the maps and the total values, as most of the trade is by land or inland water routes. Virtually all other imports arrive by sea, but two sizeable features of the export trade are omitted:

1. Diamonds, transported to the UK by air.
   (£6·8 million)
2. Petroleum, re-exported to Zambia by pipeline.
   (£6·5 million)

The two maps opposite clearly show the importance of the Cape route to Europe and North America, enforced by the closure of the Suez Canal since the Middle East war in 1967. It is probable that this will continue to be the main route in the future, even if the Suez Canal is re-opened, as the trend in shipping today is toward larger vessels which would be incapable of negotiating the Canal.

Two main trade routes appear: one to Europe and the other to the Far East, the most important details of which are shown in Table 35, p. 166. (The balance of trade is seen to be unfavourable with Europe. However, it must be remembered that £6·8 million worth of diamonds, exported to the UK, does not figure in the table.)

Comments on Table 36, p. 166.

1. Machinery and transport equipment from Europe form the largest proportion of Tanzania's imports. This emphasis is liable to change when China begins to supply equipment for the Tanzanian–Zambia railway.

2. The majority of manufactured goods come from Europe, but most of the textiles come from the Far East.

3. The small amount of food imported consists mainly of dried milk from the UK and rice from China. Table 36, p. 166, shows the main destinations of major shipped exports in 1968 (in £ million).

The graphs accompanying the maps opposite show the relationships between the trade of the four East African international ports. See also Table 37, p. 166. In contrast to the value of cargo, it can be seen that most of the tonnage handled comes from imports rather than exports.

Mtwara's share of East African trade has remained at about 2·5 per cent although its trade has increased by about 150 per cent during the last decade. This is a considerable achievement allowing for its undeveloped, inaccessible hinterland and the various adverse economic factors which have hampered its growth. Originally developed for the groundnut scheme in 1948, Mtwara's trade today depends upon sending cashew nuts to India for shelling and cassava to Europe for starch manufacture. World demand for cashew nuts is increasing and this crop should provide the mainstay of trade for Mtwara in the future.

Tanga's share of trade has decreased from 6 per cent to 3 per cent and the total tonnage handled at the port has only increased by 30 per cent during the last decade. Its future seems to be less bright than Mtwara's. The shallow harbour, requiring lighterage facilities rather than direct off-loading at the quayside, the rapid decline of sisal in world markets, and competition from Mombasa are sizeable factors hampering development. However, it is hoped that the planned fertilizer plant, paper mill and steel rolling mill will be built and so improve the situation.

Dar es Salaam's share of trade has increased from 20 per cent to 26 per cent and her volume of trade has increased by 200 per cent. This importance of Dar es Salaam relative to the other East African ports has developed since the Rhodesian crisis, which began in November 1965. With the decreasing use by Zambia of the Beira and Benguela routes, and the Tanzam railway line, already under construction, this trade should increase still further, adding to the relative importance of Dar es Salaam, and developing still more the potential of her large hinterland.

Work on the extension of the west side of the harbour is currently under way. Three extra berths are almost completed and work is beginning with the help of a loan from the World Bank on two more. One likely development in the near future will be the construction of a terminal for supertankers at Mji Mwema and a connection from there by pipeline to the refinery.

It is hoped to build an industrial complex on the east side of the harbour within the next twenty years and it is envisaged that new service berths will be required on that side. The planners responsible for the Master Plan of Dar es Salaam foresee, after the year 2000, the need for an artificial harbour off-shore from Mbwa Maji beach to the south-east of Dar es Salaam and an arterial road linking it to the capital. The future seems promising for Dar es Salaam, but whether trade will increase sufficiently to justify the great expense involved in such a project remains to be seen.

ROGER ALDRIDGE

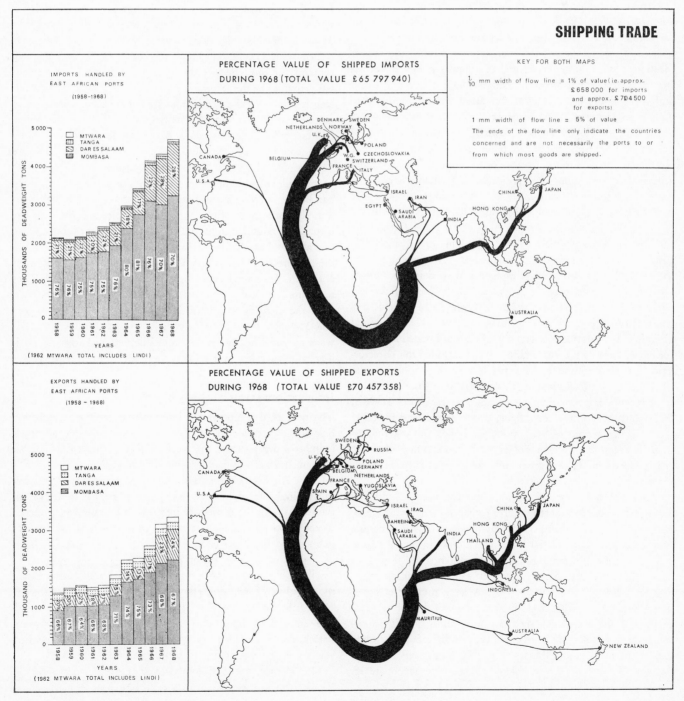

IMPORTS HANDLED BY EAST AFRICAN PORTS
(1958–1968)

THOUSANDS OF DEADWEIGHT TONS

- ☐ MTWARA
- ▦ TANGA
- ▨ DAR ES SALAAM
- ▩ MOMBASA

YEARS

(1962 MTWARA TOTAL INCLUDES LINDI)

PERCENTAGE VALUE OF SHIPPED IMPORTS
DURING 1968 (TOTAL VALUE £65 797 940)

KEY FOR BOTH MAPS

$\frac{1}{10}$ mm width of flow line = 1% of value (ie. approx. £658 000 for imports and approx. £704 500 for exports)

1 mm width of flow line = 5% of value

The ends of the flow line only indicate the countries concerned and are not necessarily the ports to or from which most goods are shipped.

EXPORTS HANDLED BY EAST AFRICAN PORTS
(1958 – 1968)

THOUSAND OF DEADWEIGHT TONS

- ☐ MTWARA
- ▦ TANGA
- ▨ DAR ES SALAAM
- ▩ MOMBASA

YEARS

(1962 MTWARA TOTAL INCLUDES LINDI)

PERCENTAGE VALUE OF SHIPPED EXPORTS
DURING 1968 (TOTAL VALUE £70 457 358)

35 AIR TRANSPORT

Three distinguishing characteristics set aside air transport in Tanzania from most other African countries. First, the national airline is owned in partnership with the two neighbouring countries of Kenya and Uganda and as a result the three countries can afford to have a well developed and viable airline system. Secondly, the value of aircraft and air transportation was realized fairly early and the national airline was established before the proliferation of African airlines as national symbols. Thirdly, there is a sizeable domestic traffic.

Historically, during the early days of commercial aviation the country benefited from its location along the London to the Cape route. For over a decade after the first aircraft landed at Tabora in 1920, pioneers tried many types of aircraft and several locations in the country were used as stopping points. Local flying enthusiasts could therefore maintain their interests in flying and realized the advantages of operating aircraft in the Tanzanian environment. The large area of the country with its pockets of developed areas separated by enormous tracts of barren and sparsely populated land, gives aircraft a relative advantage over surface forms of transport. In addition, atmospheric conditions are favourable for flying over most parts of the country. Fortunately too, one flying enthusiast was in a sufficiently high official position to demonstrate effectively the potentialities of using aircraft. In 1928, Mr P E L Gethin, the Director of Surveys, made Tanganyika the first British Dependency to own an aircraft. Over the next few years he piloted the departmental Avro *Avian* biplane and used it experimentally for aerial photographic purposes. On the basis of this experience, more aircraft were ordered, a network of airfields was constructed and an air survey division created. Departmental aircraft were also used for carrying officials to isolated areas and for emergencies. By 1929, Gethin's duties included the Directorship of Civil Aviation and he was largely responsible for the 'Air Navigation Direction, 1931'. Aircraft have since been used in Tanzania for mapping, geological and ecological surveys, locust and pest control, for a flying doctor service and for relief work during periods of food shortages, floods and other disasters. The country became dotted with rudimentary airfields, only a few of which have grown into commercial airfields which are maintained and used regularly.

Dar es Salaam is the only International Class airport with full facilities. In addition there are three categories among the classified airfields. Airfields inspected daily (category A) are generally used for normal commercial traffic while those inspected once a week (category B) carry light aircraft on unscheduled flights. In 'C' category, the airfields are generally used for special services, and there are no inspection reports. A large number of emergency landing strips are also found throughout the country (see map). All the airfields inspected daily can handle *Dakotas*, which were until recently the main type of aircraft used locally in East Africa. Tanga, Mtwara, Mwanza, Moshi and Zanzibar are suitable for the larger Fokker *Friendships* which are replacing the *Dakotas* on the busier routes.

Internal traffic

During the 1930s several airways, including Imperial Airways, kept up infrequent but regular services. Scheduled services to facilitate mail and despatches were maintained, largely by government aircraft. The Second World War interrupted all development, but soon after, in 1946, the East African Airways Corporation was formed by the three East African countries. The corporation with a capital of Shs. 1 000 000 operated mainly on Dragon *Rapide* biplanes hired from the British Government. Over 9000 passengers were carried on the twenty-one scheduled services during the first year, netting over Shs. 1 700 000. As more aircraft became available more planes were bought, mainly the versatile *Dakotas*. The first routes to be inaugurated were from Dar es Salaam to Zanzibar, Tanga and Mombasa in the north and southwards as far as Lindi. By the early 1950s Tabora Mpanda, Mombo and other centres in the interior were connected with Dar es Salaam. The coastal route, however, still remains the most heavily used passenger route. Tanga airport has grown to be the second largest in the country and is a minor transit centre for the Pemba and Zanzibar traffic as well as for most domestic incoming flights from Kenya. There are several flights daily along this route. Since the Independence of the three countries a fast inter-city jet service connects Dar es Salaam with Mombasa, Nairobi and Entebbe. Arusha and Moshi have made considerable headway in the last few years and handle over 15 000 passengers per annum. Mwanza is a centre of some importance locally. The airport handles a sizeable volume of passengers and freight and in addition to scheduled services operated by East African Airways, Caspair Ltd operates a 'round the lake' route. Along the other routes traffic is light and transportation of freight is more significant. The pattern of the internal routeways is likely to remain the same for some time. However, the airfields at Mbeya, Bukoba, Iringa, Tabora, Mtwara and Mwanza are being enlarged. At present East African Airways operates nearly 16 000 route kilometres (10 000 miles) in Tanzania covering over 1 600 000 aircraft kilometres per year.

International traffic

The pace of development of international air traffic at Dar es Salaam has increased at a greater rate than post-war air traffic in most other parts of the world. Initially, most of the international traffic was handled by British airlines. In 1957 East African Airways Corporation opened a once-a-week service to the United Kingdom and twice-a-week service to India and Pakistan. With the growth of international passenger traffic the Corporation purchased jet aircraft beginning with the *Comet* 4 in 1960 and five years later, the larger *Super VC* 10. The larger jets are used for the European and Far Eastern routes. The smaller *Comets* are more profitable on the inter-city routes and those within Africa, connecting East Africa north with Ethiopia, west with Nigeria and Ghana, and south with Zambia. Currently there is a daily jet service to London. Eastwards the routes stretch as far as Hong Kong; westwards New York has been added as a new terminal.

The opening up of diplomatic and trading relations has increased the number of airlines calling at Dar es Salaam and seventeen foreign airlines now provide regular services to the city (See the map below).

The number of passengers handled at Dar es Salaam has greatly increased since 1961. At that time 91 000 passengers passed through Dar es Salaam. In 1964 it was 145 000 and in 1967 over 170 000. With the continued increase in tourist traffic and the potential growth of freight, international traffic is likely to continue to grow rapidly. As part of the development of the tourist industry a new international airport will be constructed between Moshi and Arusha.

Major freight traffic was first generated during the Rhodesian UDI crisis when large amounts of petroleum were airfreighted to Zambia, and copper brought back on the return flights. Under present conditions it is profitable to bring machinery and delicate goods into the country by air freight. There is also a strong possibility that the export of fresh tropical produce will be expanded.

Measured by any yardstick the national airline has been a success. The fleet has been built up from six small, hired planes to nine *Dakotas*, four jet-propped Fokker *Friendships*, three *Comets* and four *Super VC* 10s. Aircraft mileage has increased from the initial 800 000 km. to over 16 000 000 km. in 1968. It is generally accepted that the development of air communication is an important part of national progress.

ADOLFO MASCARENHAS

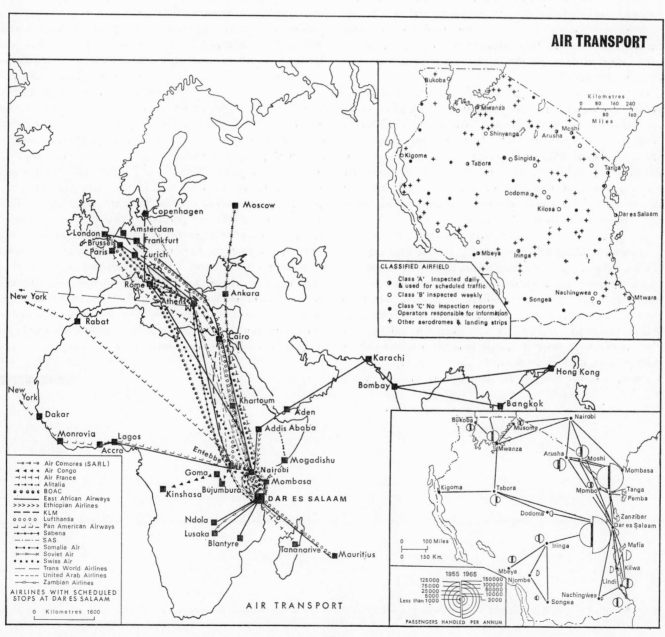

83

Policy and pattern

Like most developing countries Tanzania is actively concerned with the promotion of manufacturing industries. During the colonial period the economy depended heavily on subsistence agriculture, the export of raw materials to Western Europe and the import of manufactured goods from Europe and also Kenya. For many years to come Tanzania's economy will be firmly rooted in its agricultural resources, but its industry will be of growing importance in providing employment in urban areas, and in saving foreign exchange by import substitution. Since Independence there has been considerable industrial activity, associated firstly with the processing of the major agricultural crops. A second phase has been the growth of repair, maintenance and assembly facilities for the machinery and vehicles used in agriculture. Current activity is concentrated upon self-sufficiency in the vital building construction industry, and in the manufacture of consumer goods, particularly those that make use of local materials.

The Arusha Declaration has determined the future industrial pattern of Tanzania, and the major means of production are now under the control of para-statal bodies such as the National Development Corporation, the Tanzania Sisal Corporation and the National Milling Corporation. The Government has delineated the fields of industrial production in which the money and skills of the private investor will be welcomed, but through its state monopoly of commercial banking and insurance it is clearly in control of the economy.

By 1967, there were over 6500 registered factories in Tanzania, employing over 90 000 people, but the large majority of these comprise sisal-processing plants, flour mills, cotton ginneries, woodworking shops and tailoring establishments, each employing a small number of workers. In the same year, there were 131 manufacturing or power establishments with more than 100 employees and only 15 with more than 500 workers. The categories of these industrial establishments, employing more than ten workers are shown in Table 38, p. 167.

Tanzania is not rich in raw materials for industry, but it does have adequate power supplies for its present level of industrial development, an expanding communications network and a rapidly expanding consumer market in Eastern Africa. About thirty million people live in the territories that make up the East African Community, and under the treaty for East African Co-operation, signed in 1967, the respective countries are committed to rectifying the former imbalance in trade between Kenya and the other two partners. In a bid to ensure Community self-reliance in certain manufacturing activities, without destructive international competition, member countries have been given exclusive rights for the development of certain industries for the wider market. Tanzania has the exclusive right of establishing industries for the assembly and manufacture of four-wheel-drive vehicles, the assembly and manufacture of radios and the manufacture of motor vehicle tyres and tubes. The radio factory opened at Arusha in 1968, and work on the building of the tyre factory also began at Arusha in 1969.

In constant price terms, manufacturing industry net output has recorded an average annual growth of over ten per cent during 1960–67. An objective of the government's industrial strategy is to maintain this rate. A substantial start has been made on import substitution, based on local raw materials, in such varied fields as textiles, cement, soap, cooking oils and sugar-refining. In recent years processing plants have been established or expanded for cashew nuts, instant coffee, canned meat and meat extract, pyrethrum extract, sisal twine and tobacco. In the chemical sector, there are now factories producing oxygen and other gases, the common drugs and insecticides, cosmetics and industrial paints. Recent metallurgical industry development includes the manufacture of bicycle parts, aluminium hollowware and enamelware whilst there are industries manufacturing plastic and rubber products. Table 39, p. 167, gives an indication of the rapid growth in some of the major industries.

Industry depends for its power upon the para-statal Tanzania Electric Supply Company. Much of the power is generated at three hydro-electric stations on the River Pangani, but extensive use is still made of diesel generating plants. Indicative, however, of the rapid growth in demand for power by industrial and other users, is the increase in local sales from 122 million kilowatt hours in 1960 to 240 million kilowatt hours in 1967.

JOHN WHITE

INDUSTRIAL PRODUCTION

Lake Victoria

DAR ES SALAAM

Lake Tanganyika

Lake Rukwa

Lake Nyasa

NUMBER OF EMPLOYEES PER
DISTRICT IN INDUSTRIES

1
     (1) Agricultural
     (2) Non – Agricultural

2

ESTABLISHMENT BASED ON
  1   2
  o   ●   100 – 499 employees

  O   ●   500 and more employees

35 000 27 000

40   0   80   160 Miles

Kilometres 40   0   80   160   240

Location and trade

Industrial enterprises ancillary to agricultural production, or engaged upon the primary processing of produce, are usually sited close to the growing areas. Hence, not located on the map, are over two hundred sisal-decorticating factories in Tanga, Coast and Morogoro Regions, eighteen ginneries around the shores of Lake Victoria, and numerous coffee-pulping plants in the coffee-growing areas of Kilimanjaro, Arusha, West Lake and Mbeya Regions. Many of the industries that diversify Tanzania's economy and generate wealth are very small, and include traditional activities such as copra-drying, wood-carving, furniture-making, stone-crushing, fish-curing and salt-manufacturing. Such industries are naturally located where the raw materials and markets are in close proximity. Most modern manufacturing industries, however, are concentrated in Dar es Salaam and its suburbs or close to the towns of Tanga, Mwanza, Moshi, Arusha and Morogoro. In each of these towns the Government has allocated land for industrial development, and provides such services as surfaced roads, rail line facilities, water and electricity.

As Dar es Salaam offers the best industrial location in terms of consumer market, port facilities, communications and labour supply, over half of the real manufacturing industry is sited there. The major industrial concentration is along the railway line that links the port to the upcountry area. (see Map 36). Minor industries in this industrial area, other than those shown on the map inset, include the manufacture of neon signs, alumunium goods, galvanized sheets, block flooring, bricks and tiles, wire nails, screws and blankets.

Just outside the present city boundaries of Dar es Salaam, towards Morogoro, another industrial zone is being developed and already contains a large textile mill, a farm implements factory and a brewery that specialises in local millet beer. When the proposed railway link from the port to the new Wazo Hill cement factory is completed, this industrial area will be well served with both road and rail communications to upcountry areas. The cement factory worked very close to its full capacity of 150 000 tons in 1967, and is now being further developed for a capacity of 400 000 tons per annum.

A new 100 000 000 Shs. oil refinery was opened in Dar es Salaam in June 1966, and is now connected by pipeline to the Zambian Copperbelt, over 1600 kilometres away. With major improvements now being made to the main Dar es Salaam–Zambia Road, and the proposed railway now a firm commit-ment, the industrial strategy of the capital city is very much linked with that of Zambia.

At Arusha, the capital of the East African Community and the centre for a prosperous farming area, some twenty-three square kilometres (nine square miles) of land have been allocated for industrial development. Already developed industries include a textile mill, a dairy, a pyrethrum extract factory, a plastic and foam-rubber factory, a brewery and a radio-assembly works. Nearby is an important specialist industry that makes pipes for smokers from the locally obtained meerschaum.

In the Moshi area, there are factories producing matches, sisal bags and mosquito-coils. Twenty-five kilometres from the town at Arusha Chini is one of the two large sugar refineries in Tanzania, sugar being a commodity in which the country is now self-sufficient.

Tanga, the second port and town of Tanzania, has suffered an economic recession in recent years, following the contraction in the sisal industry. In a bid to combat the recession, recent industrial development includes a shirt factory, a plywood-manufacturing plant and a sisal cordage factory. Important new projects under development include a fertilizer factory and a 200 000 000 Shs. industry for the manufacture of wrapping paper, liner board and corrugated cardboard from sisal pulp.

Mwanza, linked to the Tanzania mainland market by road and rail and to the lake ports of the three East African countries by railway wagon ferries, is extremely well sited for industrial development. Although the area of land suitable for new factories is restricted by the rocky terrain behind the lake shore, there is a fairly prosperous local consumer market, and adequate water-supply as added attractions. Recent developments include a fish-net manufacturing industry, a soap factory, a large textile mill, and a vegetable oil factory which manufactures cooking oil, cooking fat and margarine.

The growth in industrial production has resulted in significant changes in the total pattern of Tanzania's trade with other countries. With the rapid growth of local processing, manufacturing and service industries, intermediate inputs, transport equipment and capital goods imports have risen significantly. See Table 40, p. 167. With successful import substitution in consumer goods the percentage share of this class of item has declined from forty-eight per cent to thirty-four per cent. In recent years there has been a substantial reduction in the import of iron and steel manufactured goods and capital machinery. The export market for Tanzania's industrial production is extremely limited, and she has a sizeable trade deficit with the partner states of Kenya and Uganda. Zambia is her best customer, particularly as the purchaser of refined petroleum products from the Dar es Salaam refinery.

JOHN WHITE

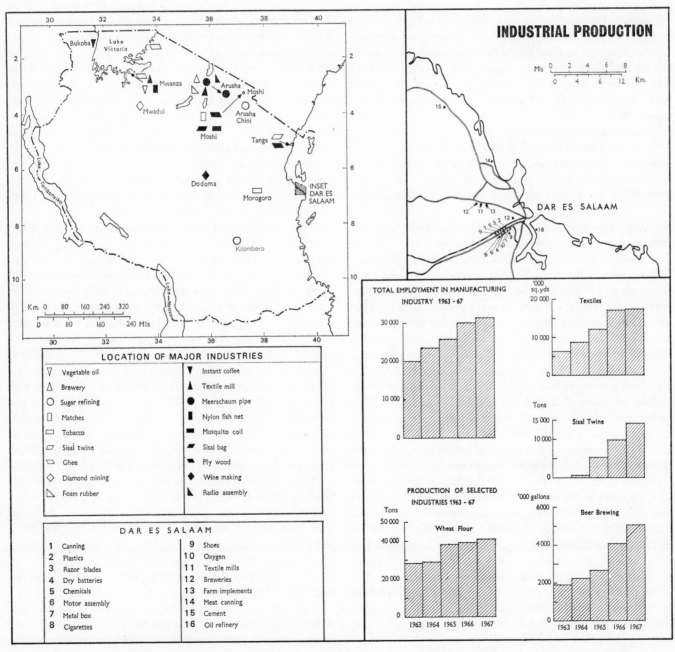

INDUSTRIAL PRODUCTION

LOCATION OF MAJOR INDUSTRIES

▽	Vegetable oil	▼	Instant coffee
△	Brewery	▲	Textile mill
○	Sugar refining	●	Meerschaum pipe
▯	Matches	▮	Nylon fish net
▭	Tobacco	▬	Mosquito coil
▱	Sisal twine	◥	Sisal bag
▱	Ghee	◣	Ply wood
◇	Diamond mining	◆	Wine making
◿	Foam rubber	◤	Radio assembly

DAR ES SALAAM

1	Canning	9	Shoes
2	Plastics	10	Oxygen
3	Razor blades	11	Textile mills
4	Dry batteries	12	Breweries
5	Chemicals	13	Farm implements
6	Motor assembly	14	Meat canning
7	Metal box	15	Cement
8	Cigarettes	16	Oil refinery

TOTAL EMPLOYMENT IN MANUFACTURING INDUSTRY 1963 - 67

'000 sq. yds — Textiles

Tons — Sisal Twine

PRODUCTION OF SELECTED INDUSTRIES 1963 - 67

Tons — Wheat Flour

'000 gallons — Beer Brewing

38 MINERAL OCCURRENCES

The history of mineral exploitation is described in section 39. Before 1945, except for the three-year period 1926–9, the most important mineral was gold, but since then the value of diamonds has outstripped that of all other minerals, and diamonds currently account for over 80 per cent by value of mineral production. Also important at present are tin, salt, mica, gemstones and cement. Potentially important for the future are iron, coal, gypsum and phosphates.

Mineral areas and occurrences are widely distributed over the country though only a limited number of these occurrences have, or have had, economic significance. Consequently a selection of the occurrences has been made and only the more important are shown on the map. This distribution pattern is superimposed upon a background shading showing the extent of detailed geological mapping. The relationship of these two patterns suggests the close link between systematic field survey and mineral finds. However, as geological investigations have been concentrated upon areas holding promise of minerals, it does not follow that the unmapped zones hold equivalent promise. Nonetheless, more minerals will almost certainly be found as systematic mapping is extended.

The type of mineralization is clearly related to the geology. Few mineral occurrences are associated with the Archaean rocks of the central plateau except corundum (an abrasive; in gem form, ruby). Much more significant in terms of mineralization is the Nyanzian occupying that part of northern Tanzania to the south and east of Lake Victoria. The Nyanzian forms host rocks to extensive gold mineralization. The South-west Mwanza, the Musoma and the Iramba-Sekenke goldfields, often collectively termed the Lake Victoria goldfields, are all located within areas of Nyanzian rocks: gold is frequently concentrated near the edges of the Nyanzian outcrop close to the contact with the surrounding granite, often in banded ironstones and associated tuffs, either as sulphide-impregnation deposits, mineralized shear zones or, less importantly, in quartz reefs. The Kavirondian system is similar to the Nyanzian but less significant in terms of mineralization. The Mozambiquian rocks, making up much of central and eastern Tanzania, contain a wide variety of economic minerals, but the most significant is muscovite mica associated with pegmatite dykes; these dykes also contain a variety of other minerals. Also found associated with these rocks are garnets (an abrasive and gemstone), kyanite (a refractory or fusing agent) and graphite. Ubendian metamorphic rocks of the south and south-east of the country have been affected by intrusive igneous activity and with this has been associated important economic mineralization as, for example, the titaniferous magnetite segregations in Njombe District; the lead-copper-silver-gold deposits associated with fissure veins, disseminations and replacements in shear zones of chalcopyrite and galena at Mpanda; and the gold of the Lupa field. In the Lupa field well-defined quartz veins contain gold, silver, chalcopyrite and galena, but it was initially alluvial gold which caused exploitation of the field.

Tin and tungsten mineralization of the Karagwe area is the main feature of economic interest in the rocks of the Karagwe–Ankolean system in north-western Tanzania; both tin as cassiterite and tungsten in the form of wolfram are, however, genetically connected with intrusive granites, rather than the Karagwe-Ankolean host rocks. Cassiterite and wolfram occur in quartz-mica veins found in the floors and walls of areas adjacent to this granite contact, but most of the present production derives from a stockwork exploited by opencast mining at Kyerwa, although, in the past, detrital deposits in addition to small, patchily mineralized veins were the main sources. Bukoban rocks are largely unmetamorphosed and are typically poor in minerals, while the only mineral of economic importance occurring in the Karoo rocks is coal. This occurs principally in the Ruhuhu coalfields of the south-west, though there are other deposits.

Significant in relation to the Jurassic and Cretaceous rocks of the coastal belt are limestones (used for lime, building stone and road metal) and an evaporite series comprising gypsum, anhydrite and rock salt. Large reserves and huge thicknesses of the latter have been proved north of Lindi but unfortunately in an area badly served by land communications. Of the Kainozoic rocks, most important are high-grade coralline limestones used for cement, as at Wazo, lime, building stone and aggregate. These materials are most intensively exploited around Dar es Salaam. Large easily-workable reserves of kaolin occur in association with Miocene sandstones in the Pugu Hills. Inland lacustrine deposits of mbugu limestone (road metal), rock phosphate at Lake Manyara (fertilizer), diatomite in the Kagera valley (abrasive) and meerschaum in Lake Amboseli (pipes) contribute a further range of mineral occurrences from rocks of this system.

By far the most important non-metalliferous deposits and mineral occurrences in the country are the kimberlite pipes and kimberlite bodies of post-Karoo age and their associated detrital materials at Mwadui, for these deposits are the source of diamonds, the most valuable of all minerals. Though more than one hundred kimberlite pipes are now known in Tanzania, most do not carry diamonds. The pipes occur in well-defined clusters in the Shinyanga, Nzega and Iramba–Singida area bordering the depressed Eyasi–Wembere basin. Associated with carbonatite volcanic centres are deposits of pyrochlore and niobium (an additive for high-temperature-resistant steel) notably near Mbeya. The saline springs at Uvinza may be related to comparable volcanic centres but this is so far uncertain. These springs are important as they supply most of Tanzania's salt.

There are thus at present six important mineral areas: (1) at Mwadui (2) at Uvinza (3) around Kyerwa in Karagwe (4) at Buhema in the Musoma goldfield (5) in Masailand, based on gemstones, and (6) the Ulugurus. Other areas, e.g. the Geita and Lupa goldfields, the Mpanda lead and copper mines, were once of major significance but are now no longer important. New mineral areas, based on at present unexploited reserves, may develop later, for example the Ruhuhu coalfield.

Other mineral occurrences of significance but not so far mentioned include iron ore (a titaniferous magnetite, 50 per cent iron) in large deposits south of Njombe; also titanium in the same area. Other iron ores occur south and south-west of Mpanda. The good-quality coalfield east of Lake Nyasa is close to these deposits and there are other comparable, though smaller, ore deposits to the north-west of the lake. Bases for potential chemical industries exist in the phosphate deposits near Lake Manyara and the gypsum/anhydrite (sulphate of lime) deposits south of Kilwa. Most other mineral occurrences are of little significance. Recent prospecting for petroleum along the coastal zone has been unsuccessful up to the present.

PAUL TEMPLE

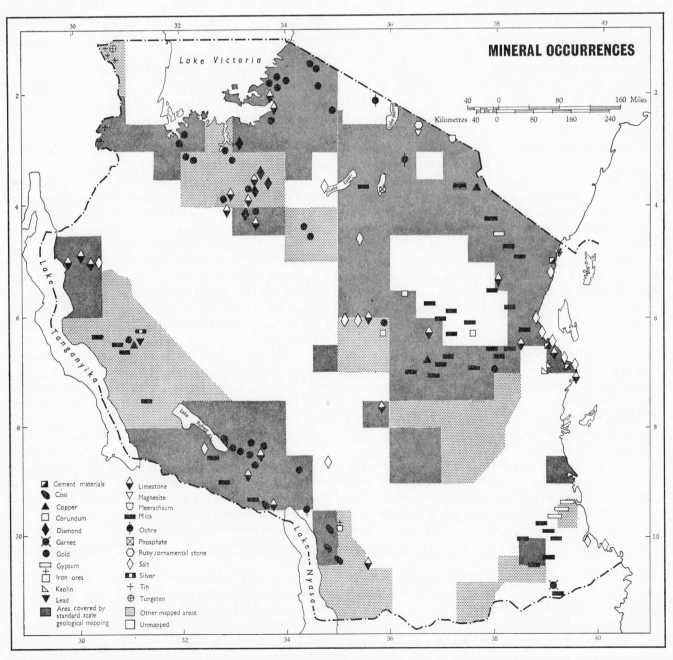

MINERAL OCCURRENCES

Cement materials
Coal
Copper
Corundum
Diamond
Garnet
Gold
Gypsum
Iron ores
Kaolin
Lead
Area covered by standard scale geological mapping

Limestone
Magnesite
Meerschaum
Mica
Ochre
Phosphate
Ruby/ornamental stone
Salt
Silver
Tin
Tungsten
Other mapped areas
Unmapped

Mining and mineral production were relatively unimportant during the 34 years of the German administration of Tanzania. Following the First World War the country was only re-opened in 1921 for prospecting after the enactment of mining legislation by the British administration. This date marks the real beginning of the mining industry. From this time, despite problems resulting from underdeveloped communications, World depression and supply shortages during the Second World War, the value of mineral production progressively increased up to 1967. Since then, mineral production has shown a decrease of 31 per cent by value, this reflecting the closing in 1966 of the country's two major gold mines and the declining throughput of diamonds from the Mwadui plant in 1968. With the prospect of the Mwadui deposit being exhausted within 10 years, it would seem that mining will make a progressively reduced future contribution to the economy unless new and viable occurrences are vigorously exploited.

However, mining contributed only 1·9 per cent of the gross monetary domestic product in 1968 and even less in terms of employment. Most of the mining output, with the principal exception of sands, gravel and cement for construction and some of the salt production, is currently exported and mineral exports made up approximately 9 per cent of total export value in 1968. Gross mineral sales were valued at £8·2 million in the same years. This total was broken down as shown in Table 41, p. 167 (1966 and 1967 figures given for comparison. Thus four minerals accounted for 96 per cent by value of the country's mineral production in 1968, an unfortunate situation in view of the future prospects of gold and declining output of diamonds. It seems clear that a marked overall decline in mineral production will result at least in the short-run. Forward estimates put this decline in the total value of mineral production over the next 5 years at 21 per cent.

The history of mining in Tanzania, as of such exploitative industries elsewhere, has always shown marked fluctuations. Before 1921 mining was a very small-scale activity, concentrating on gold from the Iramba–Sekenke plateau and mica from the Uluguru Mountains.

A relative decline in the importance of gold and mica in the late 1920s resulted from the discovery of the small but rich deposits of diamonds at Mabuki, south-east of Mwanza in 1922. Production of diamonds began in 1925 and the deposits were practically worked out by 1931. Gold then replaced diamonds as the major mineral product; this was associated with the opening up of the Lake Victoria and Lupa goldfields in the early 1930s. Gold production rose to a peak in 1940 when it comprised over 89 per cent by value of the country's mineral production.

An important turning point in another direction was the discovery by Williamson, in 1940, of the diamond deposits at Mwadui. Production of diamonds began at once and expanded to a peak production in 1967, when diamond sales comprised nearly 90 per cent of total mineral sales and realized over £11 million (see table). This growth in diamond production much more than offset the declining gold output at least up to 1967.

Gold production declined initially due to the effects of wartime (1940–45) supply restrictions upon small workings, such supply difficulties being particularly important in reducing output and enforcing closures in the Lupa goldfield. Most of the post-war production of gold has in fact come from medium-sized units, such as the Saza (operating 1939–56) and Ntumbi (1937–60) mines in the Lupa goldfields, the Mukwamba mine (1950–60) in the Mpanda area, the Geita (1930–66) and Mawe Meru (1930–52) mines in the South-west Mwanza field and the Kiabakari (Tangold) (1953–66) and Buhemba (1939–present) mines in the Musoma goldfield. Small workings are still in operation but their total contribution to mining output is very small. Gold production in fact fell drastically between 1965 and 1967 and although extensive resurveys of the Lake Victoria goldfields have been carried out recently, no important new occurrences have been discovered. One small site at Buck reef is currently under detailed investigation.

Development of the Mpanda field led to some diversification in mineral production over the period 1950–60: lead, copper and silver were produced together with some gold. Now this field is abandoned. Since then diamonds have assumed an unchallenged dominance while other minerals have declined in relative significance (see Graph 2). Diamonds presently rival sisal for the third place among the nation's exports.

Virtually all diamond production and exports since 1940 have come from the Mwadui deposit located 16 miles north-east of Shinyanga. It is worked by the Williamson Diamonds Limited group, jointly owned by government (through the agency of NDC) and De Beers (through the Willcroft company). The company works one kimberlite body and its associated detrital material. The Mwadui plant came into full operation in 1956 and production has rapidly increased since then, rising to an all-time record in 1967 (25 per cent increase between 1965 and 1967). The average grade of the diamonds is exceptionally high: stones of gem quality account for half the total value of diamond exports and several of the most famous stones in the world have been won from this deposit. After sorting and valuation in London by the De Beers Consortium, most gemstones are sawn and sorted in Amsterdam. Some are returned to Tanzania to be cut and polished in Iringa.

Tanzania's diamond production in 1966 placed her approximately eighth among world producers in terms of metric carats and seventh in terms of value of production (after Southwest Africa, South Africa, Sierra Leone, Angola, USSR and Congo) with just over 6 per cent of the world production by value. Intensively organized prospecting for diamonds may conceivably ensure some future for the industry, but no major new deposits have been located after 18 years of intensive prospecting.

Future mining developments are difficult to predict. The prospects for tin, with the revival of the Kyerwa syndicate and the re-opening of the Kaborishoke mine have recently improved. The expansion of the coloured gemstone industry has been spectacular (400 per cent growth between 1964 and 1968) but it is still relatively unimportant and can never expand, because of its nature, to take the place of declining diamond sales. Salt production is being expanded, both at Uvinza on the Central railway line and on the coast north of Bagamoyo, but it is still insufficient to satisfy internal demand.

New possibilities are currently under investigation. A number of these do not figure on the accompanying map because their extent and significance are not yet proven. The enormous reserves (2000 million tons) of kaolin which have been proved in the Pugu Hills close to Dar es Salaam could be utilized by separating the material into pure silica and kaolin. This separation would provide the raw materials for glass manufacture, as well as sanitary ware, crockery and possibly, if the quality were good enough, for paper and rubber products or for export

in an unprocessed form. Dawsonite (a basic carbonate of sodium and aluminium) is present in the volcanic tuffs of the Olduvai–Serengeti area. This occurrence, which may be widespread but is largely unproved at present and thus not shown on the figure, could assume a great importance as a source of alumina for an aluminium industry if the planned large-scale hydro-electric development at Stiegler's gorge on the River Rufiji is ever built, though the long distance between the deposits and the source of power would create difficulties. Along the Indian Ocean coast, particularly between Dar es Salaam and Bagamoyo, rich workable deposits of black sands exist, containing ilmenite, rutile, garnet and zircon. The full extent of these deposits is unknown and they are therefore not shown on the map, but with the present steady market for titaniferous

concentrates, the easy road access to many of the deposits and the high prices per ton being offered, this possibility seems particularly promising. Ilmenite and rutile are used in white pigment, in titanium metals and in welding rods. Ilmenite currently fetches Shs.170 and rutile Shs.1550 per ton. Zircon, used in steel-making, fetches Shs.550 per ton.

Older possibilities, recently revived by the construction of the new road and rail links through the south to Zambia, are the Ruhuhu and Songwe–Kiwira coal and the Liganga iron ore deposits. The reserves of iron ore at Liganga exceed 80 million tons, but the high titanium content of the ore precludes conventional blast furnace methods, because of the high melting temperature of the non-ferrous part of the mineral. The reserves of hard coal in the economically-exploitable coalfields have been proved at 200 million extractable tons, but the presence of five times that amount has been inferred.

Mineral development prospects are clearly therefore not simply a question of occurrence and discovery. Economic and geographical factors exert determining influences. World market prices for many minerals fluctuate widely. Existing established competitors prevent mineral exploitation, which in their ab-sence would have gone ahead. For example, the inexhaustible salt and soda ash deposits of Lake Natron might well have been developed if ICI had not already opened up the Magadi deposits in Kenya. Isolation of deposits from power sources or from transport routes pose further difficulties as, for example, with the dawsonite deposits, or up to the present, with the coal and iron ore fields. Technological difficulties, for example the special properties of the southern iron and coal deposits or the yellow colouration of local kaolin, have retarded exploitation. Existing industrial plants may need modification to use local materials. For example, the Tanga fertilizer factor is designed to use imported sulphur for sulphuric acid manufacture and not the pyrites deposits of the Geita-Samena area, low-capital availability is a constraint upon the expansion of the salt industry despite an unsatisfied local demand and abundant sources. Some of these problems may be resolved in the future if the government effectively implements a policy of import substitution aimed at stimulating local production and it if pursues an active policy of research and exploration. Both oil and uranium may be long-term prospects.

PAUL TEMPLE

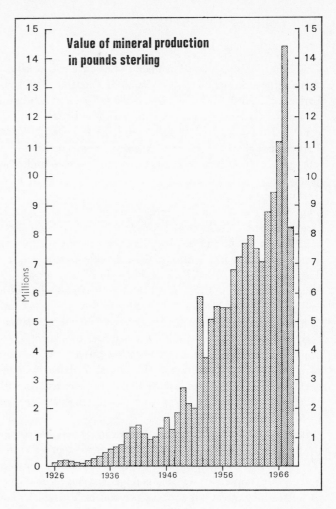

Value of mineral production in pounds sterling

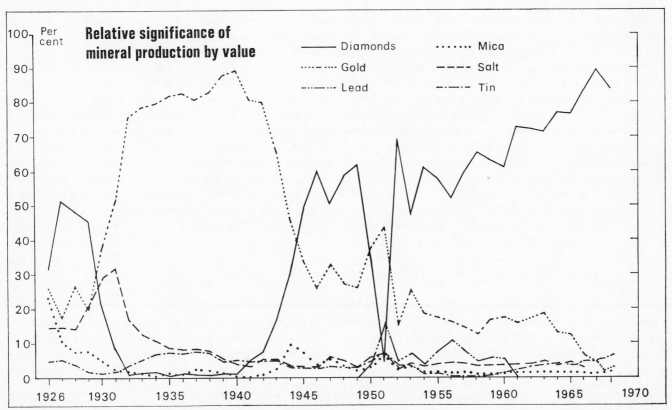

Relative significance of mineral production by value

Diamonds .... Mica
Gold .... Salt
Lead .... Tin

Few countries in the world can boast of a range and wealth of tourist attractions equal to those found in Tanzania. The game parks in the north of the country possess the greatest concentration of wild life found anywhere in Africa and have justly become world famous. It is estimated that the Serengeti National Park contains within its area of about 13 000 sq. km. some 350 000 wildebeest as well as large numbers of zebra and other plains game, and the seasonal migrations of these great herds attract visitors from all over the world. The Ngorongoro Crater, some 16 km. in diameter and almost 700 m. deep, also contains large numbers of wildebeest and zebra, as well as rhinoceros, elephant and lion, and has been described as one of the new wonders of the world. Added to these are the attractions of the Lake Manyara National Park, a thin strip of land attractively situated between the Lake and the foot of the Rift Valley scarp, and the Mt Meru National Park. Also in this area is Africa's highest peak, Mt Kilimanjaro. Less famous but equally attractive, are the fine beaches of the coast near Dar es Salaam. There are also a number of places of historical interest, such as the rock paintings of Kondoa, the old part of Zanzibar and the small town of Bagamoyo, which has many connections with nineteenth century explorers such as Livingstone, Speke, Burton, Stanley and Emin Pasha.

It is not surprising therefore, that a considerable tourist industry has developed. In the year 1967-8, 31 860 tourists visited Tanzania, and the industry as a whole earned Shs. 90 million. Particularly important was the foreign exchange component of this earning, accounting for 2.5 per cent of Tanzania's total foreign exchange earnings. On average, each visitor stayed for 6.6 days in the country and spent between Shs. 200 and 250 per day on transport, accommodation and other small items such as curios. The number of visitors to the National Parks has shown a considerable increase in the last few years. In 1967 there was a total of 86 000 visitors, compared with 26 700 in 1964. Lake Manyara and Ngorongoro had the largest number of visitors, with 29 000 and 25 800 respectively, followed by Serengeti with 16 200. The information available on the number of nights spent by visitors in hotels in various centres is not sufficiently detailed to supplement our information on average length of stay of tourists, since returns from all the game lodges are presented in a single total. A total of 66 000 bed nights were spent in the game lodges in 1967, of which 6 000 were spent by Tanzanian residents. Some 48 000 were spent in the northern tourist centres of Arusha and Moshi, of which 19 000 were Tanzanian residents. The largest total was recorded by Dar es Salaam with 224 000, but about half of these were spent by Tanzanians, and of the rest many were business visits.

However, the present contribution made by tourism to the economy represents only a small development of the huge potential, and there are now ambitious plans to greatly expand the industry. The 'northern circuit' taking in the Serengeti, Ngorongoro, Lake Manyara and the Arusha National Park will continue to be the major tourist attraction. Large investments are being made to expand hotel accommodation in the Serengeti, at Ngorongoro and at Arusha. Of even more importance to the area will be the construction of the news Shs. 70 million international airport at Sanya Juu between Arusha and Moshi. In the past, most of the tourists visiting northern Tanzania have been based on Nairobi, even though Ngorongoro and Serengeti are the most attractive tourist areas in the whole of East Africa. Most tours start and end in Nairobi, with only two or three days being spent in Tanzania. This is especially true of the rapidly growing 'package tour' traffic. The basic problem from Tanzania's point of view has been the lack of an airport and tourist centre with many hotels close enough to the game parks to be a tour start and finish point, Dar es Salaam being rather too far away. The aim is now to develop such a centre at Arusha. Apart from the airport, numerous hotels must be built.

It is also hoped to develop a 'southern circuit' which can also make a significant contribution to earnings from tourism. This circuit will be based on Dar es Salaam, with its fine beaches, on Zanzibar, the Mikumi National Park and the deep-sea fishing off Mafia Island. It is also hoped to open up parts of the massive Selous Game Reserve, now mainly used for hunting safaris, to game-viewing tourists. In this southern area there are also a number of interesting historical sites, notably at Bagamoyo and Kilwa. An ambitious hotel-building programme is planned to cater for this development. A number of new beach hotels are already under construction, as is a new game lodge at Mikumi.

Since the tourist trade depends so heavily upon the presence of a rich wildlife, it is obviously of great importance to ensure that the animals are preserved. An important early step was the creation of the national parks, and the area reserved for game has been gradually increased. However, this shielding of the animals has brought about a great change in the environment and has resulted in a series of new problems. The population of some species has risen quite rapidly and there are fears that the available food supply will not be sufficient. At the same time, animals, seeking refuge in game controlled areas, have moved into ecological zones in which they are not normally found, and this has caused some problems. A good example is the movement of large numbers of elephant into the Serengeti, an area where they were not normally found. The damage caused by these elephant threatens the whole ecological balance of the area. Research work now under way at the Serengeti Research Institute is intended to make sure that wildlife is preserved, and also to ensure that animal populations, in the absence of former controls, do not become so large that they threaten the environment of the national parks. At the same time, work is going on at the Ngorongoro Research Unit on the possibilities for the future development of mixed wildlife and agricultural land-use systems. It is important to remember that people do live in areas also occupied by animals, and the welfare of these farmers must be ensured.

Thus the future of tourism appears very promising, with large investments being made to tap the growing market. It is now estimated that by 1974 the number of visitors will increase threefold to some 120 000 bringing in Shs. 120-160 million in foreign exchange.

JOHN McKAY

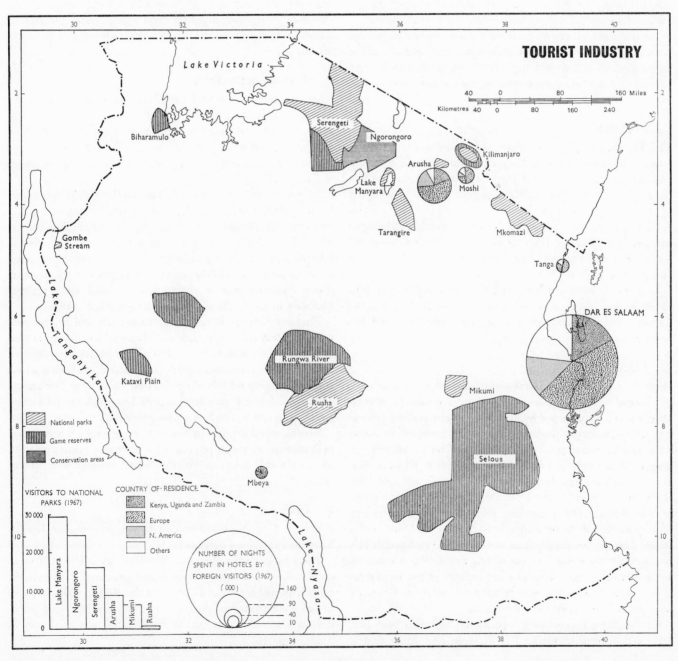

TOURIST INDUSTRY

Lake Victoria

Biharamulo

Serengeti

Ngorongoro

Arusha

Kilimanjaro

Moshi

Lake
Manyara

Tarangire

Mkomazi

Gombe
Stream

Tanga

DAR ES SALAAM

Lake Tanganyika

Katavi Plain

Rungwa River

Ruaha

Mikumi

Selous

Mbeya

Lake Nyasa

40   0   80   160 Miles
Kilometres 40 0   80   160   240

National parks

Game reserves

Conservation areas

VISITORS TO NATIONAL
PARKS (1967)

COUNTRY OF RESIDENCE

Kenya, Uganda and Zambia

Europe

N. America

Others

30 000

20 000

10 000

0

Lake Manyara

Ngorongoro

Serengeti

Arusha

Mikumi

Ruaha

NUMBER OF NIGHTS
SPENT IN HOTELS BY
FOREIGN VISITORS (1967)
(000)

160

90

40

10

The consumption of fuel and power in Tanzania in 1967 was as follows:

Electricity . . . . 240.4 million units
Petroleum products . . . . 446 million litres (98.1 million gall.)
Coal . . . . 1668.0 tons
Fuelwood/Charcoal (estimate) . 30.7 million cu. m. (365.0 million cu. ft.)

The *United Nations Statistical Yearbook for 1967* estimates a total energy consumption of 0.87 million metric tons of coal equivalent, being approximately 70 kilograms per head of population. The greater part of this, however, must be based on estimates of wood fuel consumption, since the corresponding approximate coal equivalents of the other sources of energy are: electricity 30 000 metric tons and petroleum products 28 000 metric tons. Although only approximations, the figures do serve to indicate the relative importance of the various forms of fuel and power.

1. Fuelwood

The map (top l.h.) opposite shows the production of fuelwood returned by the Forestry Division of the Ministry of Agriculture and Co-operatives. The total marketed output of 1.25 million cu. m. (14.9 million cu. ft.) is negligible compared with the estimated total consumption of 30.7 million cu. m. (365.0 million cu. ft.) (Sangster, 1962). The distribution of revenues accruing to the Forestry Division from fuelwood in 1967 are given in Table 42, p. 167, but show the relative rather than the absolute pattern.

Largest sales occur either in areas of heaviest demand, such as Coast Region, or in areas of maximum production, such as Tabora Circle. No data are available on production from unreserved land.

2. Electricity

Since the map of power installations was completed a number of changes have been made. In 1969 the Nyumba ya Mungu Dam was officially opened by President Nyerere and the generation of hydro-electric power began. Of the proposed 30 megawatt thermal power station at Ubungo in Dar es Salaam 13.2 megawatts are now in production. Capacities at Kigoma, Singida and Mtwara have been increased to 720, 360 and 1365 kilowatts respectively and an extension of 150 kilowatts is proposed at Nachingwea. The major new proposal is the development of a hydro-electric power station at Kidatu on the Great Ruaha River. The site has already been surveyed through Swedish aid, and the first stage development of 100 megawatts, at a cost of 271 million shillings, rising to a full capacity of 200 megawatts is proposed. Studies are also being made of hydro-electricity potential at Gonja in the Pare Mountains.

Of the current generating capacity of Tanzania over half (48.0 out of 87.0 megawatts) is derived from hydro-electric power. This proportion will increase sharply when the Kidatu scheme is commissioned. The Pangani River is the principal source of this power, providing for the Nyumba ya Mungu, Pangani Falls and Hale stations. Transmission lines from these stations supply power as far as Tanga, Kilosa, Dar es Salaam and Arusha. As yet the Nyumba ya Mungu power is not linked to that of Pangani Falls and Hale, though this is planned. The thermal stations are run exclusively on diesel fuel. The largest capacity is, as might be expected, in Dar es Salaam at the Kurasini and Ubungo stations. Despite their output, however, the city must draw additional supplies from the Pangani River stations.

Consumption in 1967 was 240.4 million units and in 1968 266.2 million units. The main increases were in Dar es Salaam and in Arusha, where industrial developments added to the demand. Electric power is restricted largely to the major towns and very few rural areas are supplied other than by private individual generators. Regional variations in sales correspond, naturally, to the generating capacity, and to the size of the towns served.

3. Petroleum products

There are five oil companies in Tanzania whose total sales in 1967 amounted to 446 million litres (98.1 million gall.). This figure excludes oil products exported to Zambia and diesel oil serving thermal electric power stations. The types of petroleum product and their corresponding consumption in 1967 are shown in Table 43, p. 167.

All petroleum products are distributed through fifteen depots in the major towns (Tanga has two). From the depots the products are distributed throughout their corresponding market areas. The sales in Dar es Salaam are inflated by supplies to East African Railways and by the direct distribution of petroleum to upcountry selling points, so by-passing the regional depots. However there is a heavy industrial and bunkerage consumption in the city, as well as normal domestic demand.

The petroleum is imported in crude form and is processed at the TIPER refinery in Dar es Salaam which has an annual capacity of 660 000 metric tons. The oil companies all draw their stocks from this refinery. Tanzania exports oil to Zambia whose supplies were cut off following Rhodesia's Unilateral Declaration of Independence. Formerly transported by road, the oil is now carried by a 1728 km (1080 mile) long pipeline.

No natural oil deposits of economic value have yet been found in Tanzania, although prospecting is currently taking place on the continental shelf and in the coastal area of sedimentary rocks.

4. Coal

Although Tanzania is not entirely lacking in coal, her deposits have not, as yet, been developed.

There is only one colliery, the Ilima colliery, which is situated on the Kiwira–Songwe coalfield and produced 1688 tons in 1967. The coal measures all occur in the Karroo series of rocks in the southern half of the country, that is in the Nyasa-Ufipa-Rukwa zone. Reserves of the major fields are as shown in Table 44, p. 168.

Of these fields, that with the best quality is Ruhuhu, which has a medium grade non-coking bituminous coal. The measures are not interrupted by faulting and could be easily worked. In most other fields, however, there is extensive faulting and the coal measures have a high shale content.

A technical mission from the People's Republic of China is currently investigating the possibilities of utilization of local coal. This could be considerably enhanced by the building of the Tanzania–Zambia rail link.

JOHN E MOORE

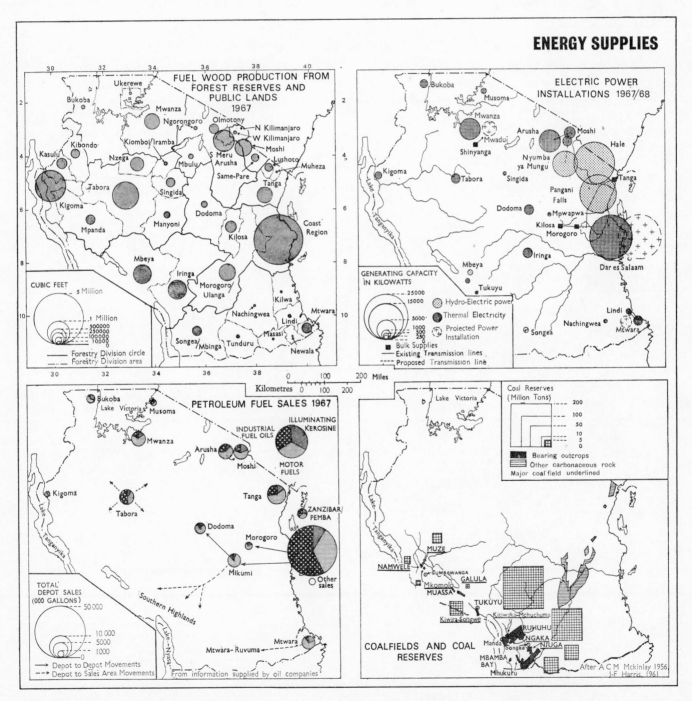

ENERGY SUPPLIES

FUEL WOOD PRODUCTION FROM FOREST RESERVES AND PUBLIC LANDS 1967

ELECTRIC POWER INSTALLATIONS 1967/68

GENERATING CAPACITY IN KILOWATTS
- 25000
- 15000
- 5000
- 1000
- 500
- 250

- ⊙ Hydro-Electric power
- ● Thermal Electricity
- ⊕ Projected Power Installation
- ■ Bulk Supplies
- — Existing Transmission lines
- --- Proposed Transmission line

CUBIC FEET
- 5 Million
- 1 Million
- 500000
- 250000
- 100000
- 10000
- — Forestry Division circle
- --- Forestry Division area

Kilometres 0 100 200
Miles 0 100 200

PETROLEUM FUEL SALES 1967

INDUSTRIAL FUEL OILS
ILLUMINATING KEROSENE
MOTOR FUELS
ZANZIBAR/PEMBA
Other sales

TOTAL DEPOT SALES (000 GALLONS)
- 50 000
- 10 000
- 5000
- 1000
- → Depot to Depot Movements
- --→ Depot to Sales Area Movements

From information supplied by oil companies

Coal Reserves (Million Tons)
- 200
- 100
- 50
- 10
- 5
- 0
- Bearing outcrops
- Other carbonaceous rock
- Major coal field underlined

COALFIELDS AND COAL RESERVES

After A C M Mckinlay 1956,
J-F Harris, 1961

Archaeology is the study of man's material remains – of his bones and tools and broken pots, his abandoned living-places and his art: in fact of any trace of former life and work that has survived the processes of erosion and decay. As such it is a means of discovering history, of the recent as well as of the distant past. Archaeological knowledge depends, of course, on how thoroughly the land is surveyed and how diligently suitable sites are excavated: as the map shows, there are large parts of Tanzania that remain virtually unexplored. This, therefore, is not a map of the early history (or 'prehistory') of Tanzania, but merely of the most impressive and important sites that are

known. The fact that more sites are marked in some regions than in others does not necessarily mean that those regions were more favourable for human settlement at certain periods in the past. It may equally indicate that relics of the past are better preserved or more conspicuous in those regions, and have hence received more attention from archaeologists.

Fossils of early man

The archaeology of Tanzania spreads over two million years, from the earliest men to the present day. Of world-wide fame are the fossilized bone remains of early men or 'near-men' (known as *australopithecines*) found at Olduvai Gorge and two other sites between Lakes Eyasi and Natron. The australopithecines were the first two-footed beings in the evolutionary line leading to modern man. They roamed the grasslands and

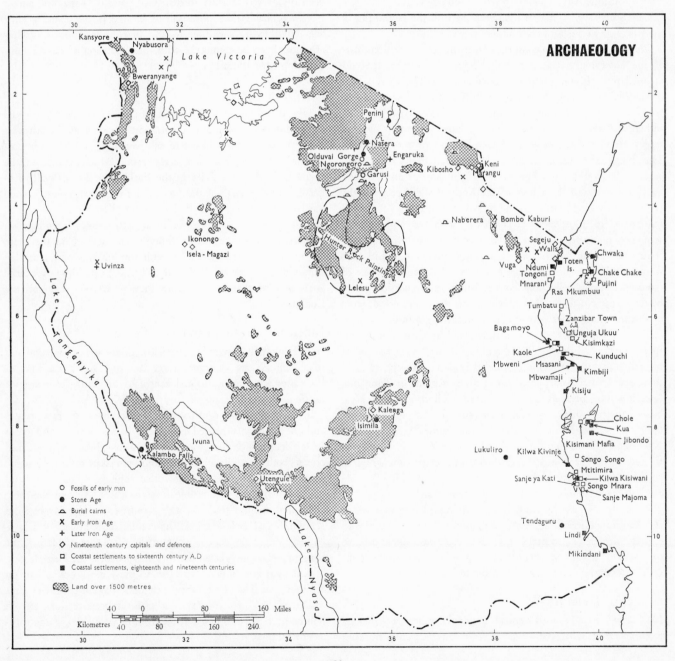

ARCHAEOLOGY

Legend:
- ○ Fossils of early man
- ● Stone Age
- ⌂ Burial cairns
- ✕ Early Iron Age
- ✛ Later Iron Age
- ◇ Nineteenth century capitals and defences
- □ Coastal settlements to sixteenth century A.D
- ■ Coastal settlements, eighteenth and nineteenth centuries
- ▨ Land over 1500 metres

savannas of eastern and southern Africa between about two million and half a million years ago. The Olduvai specimens are among the earliest found, being dated by potassium-argon to one and three-quarter million years. They belong to two distinct types of australopithecines that lived side by side, the one *Australopithecus boisei* (also called *Zinjanthropus* and 'Nutcracker Man'), the other, which was apparently more advanced, named *Homo habilis* (or 'Handy Man'). With them were crude stone tools of the earliest types recognized. It remains uncertain whether the austropithecines in general or only *Homo habilis* made the tools.

Stone Age

In sub-Saharan Africa the Stone Age is divided for convenience into three parts:

Early Stone Age: about two million to 50 000 years ago.

Middle Stone Age: about 50 000 to 10 000 years ago.

Late Stone Age: about 10 000 years ago till the beginning of the Iron Age in the last two thousand years.

The *Early Stone Age* comprises both the 'pebble-tool culture' of the australopithecines, and the 'hand-axe culture' that developed from it some half million years ago. The early stages of the 'hand-axe culture' are apparently connected with *Homo erectus*, a type of man intermediate between the australopithecines and modern man; but its later and more evolved stages are the work of early *Homo sapiens* or modern man. The 'hand-axe culture' includes cleavers and many other tools besides the well-known hand-axes. Technological and cultural evolution through the whole of the Early Stone Age from the earliest recognizable tools to the most beautifully manufactured hand-axes is illustrated at Olduvai with its unparalleled sequence of archaeological layers. Another site with a long sequence, but one that has not been studied in detail, is Lukuliro in the south. For the later part of the 'hand-axe culture', one of the world's finest collections is from Isimila, a big erosion gulley by the Great North Road near Iringa. All these sites are situated by former lakes, which provided ideal hunting grounds.

The *Middle Stone Age* is distinguished by further improvements in the techniques of tool-making, as well as expansion of human settlement into more wooded regions. Though tools of this period have been picked up in many regions of Tanzania, few sites have been examined in detail. Collections from Nyabusora in the north-west and Tendaguru in the south-east belong to the beginning of the Middle Stone Age, while at Kalambo Falls on the Zambia border there is a sequence from the end of the Early Stone Age through to recent times. Nasera rockshelter (Apis Rock) in the northern grasslands has Middle Stone Age overlain by Late Stone Age occupation.

Rock shelters are the most typical living-sites of *Late Stone Age* hunter-gatherers. They are very numerous in some regions: it is not practicable to mark individual examples. Diagnostic of this period are much smaller and more intricate stone tools, indicating more accomplished hunting techniques.

Hunter rock-paintings

In a broad area of north-central Tanzania, many rockshelters are decorated with paintings of wild animals and hunting scenes. Many of these paintings are the work of Late Stone Age hunter-gatherers who camped under these rocks; but some of them may be very recent.

Burial cairns

A *cairn* is a mound of stones; and in the grasslands of northern Tanzania (as also in Kenya) they were built to mark burials at the end of the Late Stone Age by early pastoral-agricultural peoples. They have not been well investigated, but some of them may date as early as 1000 BC. Others probably continue into the Iron Age.

Early Iron Age

The first iron-working peoples in eastern and southern Africa are recognized by distinctive types of pottery known as 'dimple-based', 'channelled' and related wares. A number of sites have been discovered recently in dispersed parts of Tanzania, and it is very probable that more will be located in due course. They are dated by radiocarbon to the first millennium AD. They are thought to be connected with the expansion of early Bantu-speaking agriculturalists.

Later Iron Age

Few sites of the second millennium AD. have been excavated in the interior. Ivuna and Uvinza, in the west and south-west respectively, are both places of salt-working, and hence important for the development of early trade. (At Uvinza, it will be noticed, there was activity in the Early Iron Age as well.) Engaruka, in the north at the foot of the rift escarpment, has extensive dry-stone remains of old homestead-enclosures and fields. It was a concentrated agricultural settlement, dependent on irrigation. Also noteworthy, though not marked on the map, are numerous old house sites with foundations of burnt clay (sometimes incorrectly described as 'bricks') extending over large areas of central Tanzania from Pare to Unyamwezi and the Ruaha.

Nineteenth century capitals and defences

In pre-colonial Tanzania, large kingdoms were few, and old royal capitals are therefore rare. But one worth marking is Bweranyange, the traditional centre of the kings of Karagwe in the north-west.

In the nineteenth century, the development of trade routes and the insecurity caused by Ngoni bands, slavers and other raiders led in several regions to greater consolidation of political power, both by traditional chiefs and by upstart military leaders. They established forts and defended capitals, whose walls and embankments are still visible in some cases. Among the most important are the *Ikulus* of the Nyamwezi leader Mirambo at Ikonongo and Isela-Magazi; the capital of Kimweri of Usambara at Vuga; the rubble walls of the *Utengule* of Merere, the Sangu chief, near Mbeya; the fort of Mkwawa, the Hehe leader, at Kalenga; and Sina's stone fort in the Kibosho chiefdom on Kilimanjaro. The last two were defended against the Germans as late as the 1890s. A larger and more impressive stone fort on Kilimanjaro is Horombo's at Keni, built very early in the nineteenth century.

Other peoples found it necessary to defend their villages. In Ufipa in the south-west a number of earthen embankments are still visible; in the mountains east of Lake Nyasa the Pangwa people tried to avoid the Ngoni by siting their villages on hill-tops; while on the coast north of Tanga several Segeju villages were surrounded by walls of stone and mortar against Masai or 'Kwavi' attacks. A different device used on Kilimanjaro and North Pare was underground tunnels where people took refuge with their livestock at times of strife with neighbouring tribes or chiefdoms. The most accessible of these 'dug-outs' are at Marangu.

Coastal settlements, to the sixteenth century AD.

In contrast to the interior, the coast has for long had overseas contacts through the Indian Ocean trade-routes. Harbour towns gained in prosperity by exchanging African products, notably ivory and gold mined in Rhodesia, for cloth, pottery and other imports. Pottery in the lowest levels at Kilwa Kisiwani, and from certain other sites on the Tanzania and Kenya coast, date the beginning of this trade to about the ninth century AD. In time, there developed a distinctive Swahili-Islamic civilization, through the intermingling of immigrants from Arabia and the Persian Gulf with the Bantu population of the coast. Stone architecture began on a small scale in the twelfth century; but it was in the period from 1300 to 1500 that the coastal towns reached their greatest prosperity. This is shown not only by the increasing volume of pottery and other imports, but also by the more numerous and splendid stone buildings – mosques (both flat-roofed and domed) and tombs (sometimes with pillars), as well as houses and palaces. All have of course suffered damage, and domestic structures have often been robbed of their stone by later builders. The most important town was Kilwa Kisiwani. It contains the finest mosques on the coast and the great palace of Husuni Kubwa built about 1300. The best surviving examples of domestic architecture are on the nearby island of Songo Mnara. Of the more easily accessible sites, Kaole by Bagamoyo and Tongoni near Tanga contain the most impressive ruins.

Coastal settlements, eighteenth and nineteenth centuries

The prosperity of the coast declined sharply in the sixteenth century, mainly owing to the activities of the Portuguese, who not only seized or stifled the Rhodesian gold trade, but also tried to control the whole Indian Ocean trading network. However, from the seventeenth to the nineteenth centuries, there was a gradual revival of coastal fortunes, especially with the increasing commercial and political interest that the Omani Arabs took in East Africa. Stone architecture was resumed, in styles somewhat different from those of the earlier period, both on some of the old sites, and at new towns, such as Kilwa Kivinje and Bagamoyo. These harbours developed in the nineteenth century as termini for the caravans from the interior bringing ivory and slaves to be shipped to Zanzibar and elsewhere.

JOHN SUTTON

43 PATTERNS OF PORTS AND TRADE-ROUTES IN DIFFERENT PERIODS

The eastern coast of Africa is also the western shore of the Indian Ocean. The continental and the oceanic worlds were linked through history by population movements on the one hand and by trade on the other. The numerous ruins of the Swahili ports studding the entire length of the coast are a symbol of such links and exhibit their dual parentage and their commercial function. This essay and the accompanying maps seek to demonstrate the spatial and economic factors which led to the development of the Swahili ports and the trade-routes which linked them with the African interior and the lands across the Indian Ocean.

The coast, however, has not always been in intimate contact with the interior. A thick belt of meagre rainfall intervenes, particularly marked in Kenya, where it is graphically known as the *nyika* or wilderness. Southwards through Tanzania it is more broken and recedes progressively into the interior. However, lack of navigable rivers and the presence of the tsetse-fly combine to impose a heavy burden on human shoulders for any transportation of goods between the coast and the interior. This tremendous barrier is broken only by the River Tana near whose mouth the prosperous port of Ungwana was located; and by the corridor formed by the River Pangani and the Usambara-Pare range of hills. The earliest known East African port, Rhapta of the second century A.D., may have been located on this part of the Mrima, while the numerous ruins of the later Swahili settlements underline its rich hinterland. By far the most important corridor into the interior, however, was that between Sofala and the ivory and goldfields of the Zambezi region on which was based the prosperity of many of the Swahili ports.

The north-east south-west alignment of the *nyika* belt seems in general to favour the growth of ports in the southern half of the coast of eastern Africa where the hinterland is more expansive. The *nyika*, however, was not an insuperable obstacle. Rather it must be seen as the price to be paid for commercial communication with the interior. Before the nineteenth century, world demand for African commodities was readily satisfied through the corridors outlined above so that the hazards of traversing the *nyika* were not justified. The focus for the economic history of East Africa is the attempt to discover less well-known corridors and the economic forces which led to their exploitation at particular times.

The land factor discussed above finds its natural counterpart in the monsoonal system of the Indian Ocean. Dhows sail from Arabia and India with the north-east monsoon between November and February. The season for the homeward journey with the south-west monsoon, however, suffers a long interruption between mid-May and mid-August when the seas are too boisterous. There are, therefore, two seasons for the return voyage, in April (*Musimu*) and in August (*Demani*). The former is preferred if commercial transactions can be completed in the short trading season as dhows then avoid the long idle wait in East Africa.

The second and related consideration is that East Africa is at the fringe of the monsoonal system. Since the monsoons are established later and break up earlier southwards, the length of the trading season in East Africa decreases proportionately. As far south as Zanzibar a trading season of up to three months could be expected, which would still allow dhows to sail home in April. At Kilwa the trading season is appreciably reduced unless dhows can await the *Demani*. Those dhows which passed to the south of the Ruvuma had no alternative to spending the months of severe winds in East Africa. Thus sailing conditions, unlike the land factor, favour the northern coast, but the two factors appear to give the central part of the coast, roughly the Mrima, the advantage for trade with the northern rim of the Indian Ocean. The precise location of the ports was naturally influenced by more local considerations, such as natural harbours, especially between offshore islands and the mainland coast.

These two factors, the monsoonal 'pull' to the north and the hinterland 'pull' to the south, were perhaps the most important ones in the growth of East African ports before the European intervention. As late as the twelfth century the monsoonal pull was probably the stronger. Archaeological work and Arabic sources permit us to reconstruct the history of the Swahili city-states from about the ninth century. Most of them were located on the northern half of the coast on offshore islands which offered protection to the emerging class, composed probably of immigrants as well as of Africans who were being gradually Islamized. Ports to the south of Zanzibar may have been visited occasionally. As the hinterlands of these northern ports were limited, any increase in demand for African commodities was initially met by the expansion of their 'maritime hinterland'. More of the smaller 'outports' on the mainland opposite, each with a constricted hinterland, were developed and fell in the orbit of these larger ports.

By the tenth century most East African ivory was going to India, and a massive Chinese demand was also added as local supplies in China and South-east Asia diminished. During the twelfth century, therefore, the southern pull of the Sofala sources of ivory as well as gold began to make itself felt. Since Sofala lay beyond the limit of reliable monsoons, need arose for a full-blown entrepôt which could be visited by monsoonal dhows and which could act as a centre for the collection of African commodities and distribution of imports. As these entrepôt functions could be performed during the other seasons of the year, the length of trading season was no longer a crucial factor in the location of the entrepôt. Mogadishu is stated to have initially dominated the trade of Sofala, but as it lay too far to the north its lines of communication could be cut by an ambitious port lying closer to the source. Indeed the Shirazi royal family of Kilwa is now believed to have shifted their headquarters from the north, first to Mafia and then to Kilwa. The 'Husuni Kubwa', an ostentatious palace backed by a vast warehouse built in the early fourteenth century, bears testimony to Kilwa's success in capturing the trade of Sofala, and the effect of that trade in shifting the centre of economic power to the south.

So long as Arabs were virtually the sole carriers of trade, the

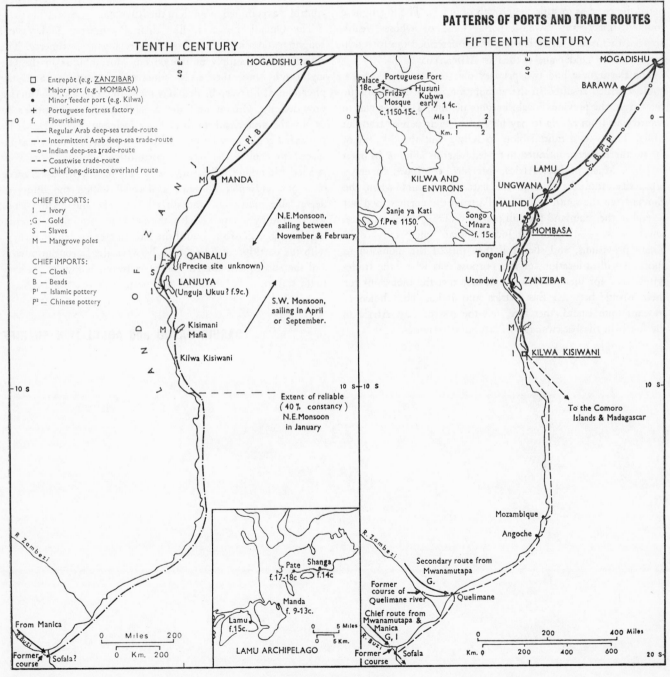

PATTERNS OF PORTS AND TRADE ROUTES

TENTH CENTURY

FIFTEENTH CENTURY

□ Entrepôt (e.g. ZANZIBAR)
● Major port (e.g. MOMBASA)
• Minor feeder port (e.g. Kilwa)
+ Portuguese fortress factory
f. Flourishing
―― Regular Arab deep-sea trade-route
―·― Intermittent Arab deep-sea trade-route
―o― Indian deep-sea trade-route
- - - Coastwise trade-route
―→ Chief long-distance overland route

CHIEF EXPORTS:
I — Ivory
G — Gold
S — Slaves
M — Mangrove poles

CHIEF IMPORTS:
C — Cloth
B — Beads
P¹ — Islamic pottery
P² — Chinese pottery

MOGADISHU ?

MANDA

QANBALU
(Precise site unknown)

LANJUYA
(Unguja Ukuu? f.9c.)

Kisimani
Mafia

Kilwa Kisiwani

N.E.Monsoon,
sailing between
November & February

S.W. Monsoon,
sailing in April
or September.

Extent of reliable
(40 % constancy)
N.E.Monsoon
in January

Portuguese Fort
Palace
18c.
Friday   Husuni
Mosque   Kubwa
c.1150-15c. early 14c.

Mls 1   2
Km.1   2

KILWA AND
ENVIRONS

Sanje ya Kati
f.Pre 1150.

Songo
Mnara
f. 15c

MOGADISHU

BARAWA

LAMU
UNGWANA
MALINDI
MOMBASA

Tongoni

Utondwe   ZANZIBAR

KILWA KISIWANI

To the Comoro
Islands & Madagascar

R.Zambezi

From Manica

R.Buzi
Former
course   Sofala?

0   Miles   200
0   Km.   200

Pate   Shanga
f. 17-18c.   f.14c

Manda
f. 9-13c.

Lamu
f.15c.

0   5 Miles
0   5 Km.

LAMU ARCHIPELAGO

R.Zambezi

Secondary route from
Mwanamutapa
G.

Former
course of
Quelimane river

Chief route from
Mwanamutapa &
Manica
G., I

R.Buzi
Former
course   Sofala

Mozambique

Angoche

Quelimane

0   200   400 Miles
Km. 0   200   400   600

hinterland pull could supersede the monsoonal one. They could leave home early and enjoy a sufficiently long trading season to be able to visit Kilwa. However, Kilwa's prosperity seems to have attracted other seafaring nations, especially Indians from Gujarat from about the thirteenth century. As suppliers of the primary imports, cloth and beads, and as consumers of African ivory, their role was crucial. Due to cyclones in the eastern half of the Arabian Sea during the early months of the monsoon, however, they could leave home only in December and so suffered from a shorter trading season in East Africa. Kilwa was beyond their convenient reach, and they seemed to have preferred Mombasa with its excellent harbour and, to a lesser extent, Malindi. When the Portuguese arrived they observed the gradual shift of economic power to the north, with Mombasa emerging as the main entrepôt. However, no one port so dominated the coast as to stifle the growth of others. The Portuguese counted thirty-seven Swahili ports, some of whose wealth amazed them; and an archaeologist has described the fifteenth-century as the 'golden age' of the East African coast.

The Portuguese had two primary objectives in East Africa, both of which resulted in the amputation of the Mozambique coast from the previous Swahili economic unit. The first was to divert gold from Sofala to pay for part of their pepper trade in India. This was a mortal blow to Kilwa, but the Swahili of the northern ports continued to trade, either as allies or in open defiance. Much of East Africa, therefore, continued to enjoy prosperity until the end of the sixteenth century when the Zimba from the south and the Galla from the north wiped out several of the mainland Swahili ports. Secondly, the Portuguese sought a way-station in the Indian Ocean where they could obtain provisions, and shelter if they missed the monsoon to India. An ideal location for this purpose was where the trade-winds used for their northward journey met the monsoons for their voyage between East Africa and India. The choice of Mozambique Island, therefore, put the rest of East Africa to the north in the backwaters of Portuguese activities.

While the Portuguese made a feeble attempt to resurrect the whole economic system of East Africa with Malindi as their northern entrepôt, it was not until the end of the sixteenth century that a real effort was made with the construction of Fort Jesus at Mombasa. The Swahili were ill-equipped to resist so soon after the catastrophes that they had suffered from the inland tribes. The northward extension of direct Portuguese rule, however, permitted the Swahili ports to recover a measure of their prosperity. Kilwa is believed to have become the terminus of an overland route from Lake Nyasa. Pate was an even greater beneficiary, and when the Portuguese, fearful of its power, sought to suppress the town, it became the focus of anti-Portuguese insurrection all along the coast. Pate solicited the help of the Omani who had just liberated their country from the Portuguese. With the loss of Fort Jesus in 1698 Portuguese control was confined to south of the Ruvuma.

The Omani, however, like their Portuguese predecessors, sought to dominate East Africa, especially its commerce. The collapse of the supply of ivory from Mozambique in the late eighteenth and the early nineteenth centuries, and the phenomenal increase in demand for it in Europe and America provided the Omani and the Swahili with opportunities to exploit the hinterland north of Cape Delgado. The price set by the *nyika* could now be paid with dividends. Mombasa was ill-placed to exploit the new opportunities because of its constricted hinterland. The stage was thus set for the emergence of a new entrepôt. Zanzibar is located within the limits of dependable monsoons, and directly opposite the Mrima from where trading relations with the interior were most promising. Zanzibar flourished until the late nineteenth century when, with the partition of East Africa between the European powers and the subsequent contruction of railways, it lost its primacy to the rail termini of the mainland coast.

BASHIR DATOO and ABDUL M H SHERIFF

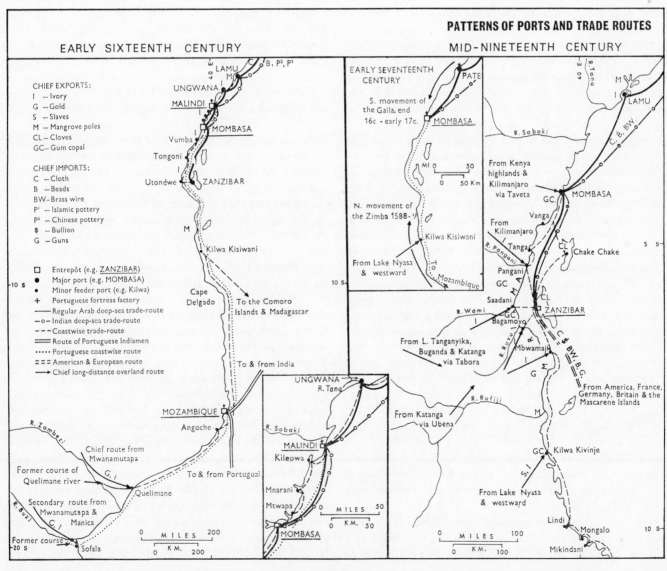

EARLY SEVENTEENTH CENTURY

CHIEF EXPORTS:
I — Ivory
G — Gold
S — Slaves
M — Mangrove poles
CL — Cloves
GC — Gum copal

CHIEF IMPORTS:
C — Cloth
B — Beads
BW — Brass wire
P¹ — Islamic pottery
P² — Chinese pottery
$ — Bullion
G — Guns

☐ Entrepôt (e.g. ZANZIBAR)
● Major port (e.g. MOMBASA)
• Minor feeder port (e.g. Kilwa)
+ Portuguese fortress factory
— Regular Arab deep-sea trade-route
-o- Indian deep-sea trade-route
- - - Coastwise trade-route
≡ Route of Portuguese Indiamen
······ Portuguese coastwise route
=== American & European route
→ Chief long-distance overland route

S. movement of the Galla, end 16c - early 17c.

N. movement of the Zimba 1588-9

From Lake Nyasa & westward

From Kenya highlands & Kilimanjaro via Taveta

From Kilimanjaro

From L. Tanganyika, Buganda & Katanga via Tabora

From Katanga via Ubena

From America, France, Germany, Britain & the Mascarene Islands

From Lake Nyasa & westward

Chief route from Mwanamutapa

Former course of Quelimane river

Secondary route from Mwanamutapa & Manica

Former course

Prior to the 1880s German interest in East Africa was largely confined to the exploitation of the interior and to commercial activities based on Zanzibar. The questionable activities of Dr Karl Peters in 1884–5 on behalf of the Society for German Colonization subsequently resulted in a formal Imperial Charter of Protection being granted over territories supposedly relinquished to him by chiefs. A reconstituted company – Deutsche Ostafrikanische Gesellschaft or the German East Africa Company – was able to lay extensive claims over territory in Sambaa, Pare, Chagga, Zaramo, Uhehe and Ngindo country. The tenuous claims of the Sultan of Zanzibar over these mainland territories were largely ignored. Violent opposition to the Company's activities by the inhabitants along the coast and the inability of the Company to cope with the situation resulted in the intervention of the German Government. In 1891 company rule was formally transferred to the German Government, but indigenous opposition to colonization came from many areas and people and culminated in the 1905–6 Maji Maji Uprising. The cruelty with which the Uprising was put down resulted in the death of thousands of inhabitants. The full impact of this destruction on the demography, settlement and social life have yet to be studied. Although after the Uprising, subjugation of the country was almost complete, the German colonial administration reappraised and toned down their policies. Civilian rule was established over most of the country but military posts were established throughout the country (top l.h. map opposite).

Despite the upheavals during the establishment of German rule, a considerable amount of fundamental development took place. Since there was a paucity of German administrators, governing the vast territory of 992 000 square kilometres was a major problem. At the height of the administration in 1914 there were only 79 administrators so that without the assistance of indigenous people there would have been little chance of governing the country. In a typically colonial situation the administration was heavily centralized. Generally, at the lowest level of the administration there were village headmen or *jumbes*, several of whom came under the jurisdiction of an *akida*. The *akidas* in each district were under a German executive officer, the *Bezirksamtmann* who in turn was responsible to the Governor stationed at Dar es Salaam. Initially, four administrative districts were created along the coast and by 1903 there were 12 civilian and 16 military districts. By 1912, after the Uprising, nineteen of the districts were under civilian rule. Mahenge and Iringa were under military administration, while Bukoba, Ruanda and Urundi were indirectly administered as residences with chiefs holding a comparatively high degree of power. The larger districts or *Bezirke* were divided into subdistricts. Each major administrative unit had a district capital. The majority of district capitals have grown to become the major towns of Tanzania.

The value of good communications was realized fairly early. In 1890 a cable line was laid connecting Dar es Salaam with overseas countries through Zanzibar. Soon after this the main coastal ports were linked by telegraph. In 1902–3 a telegraph line was established between Abercorn and Ujiji. Subsequently three main telegraphy systems evolved, two of which radiated from Dar es Salaam and one based on Tanga followed the Usambara Railway. The postal agencies closely followed the opening of military stations. Wireless stations were eventually established at Dar es Salaam, Bukoba and Mwanza. A regular steamship service had been started between Hamburg and Dar es Salaam in 1890 but there was little trade. In addition to the sea links between the coastal ports, the sole means of transportation of goods to the interior was by head porterage. Improvement in transportation to the interior was therefore urgently needed. Construction of a railway line from Tanga towards the interior was started in 1893 but did not get to Moshi, 406 km. (220 miles) away, until 1911. Progress on the construction of the other major railway – the Central Railway Line – was much more rapid and Kigoma was reached in 1914. It took only nine years to span over 1260 km. (700 miles) of territory. At least eight other railway lines were contemplated and construction work had begun on a line from Tabora to Mwanza and Lake Kivu. Emphasis was also given to lake transportation and boats plied on Lakes Victoria, Tanganyika and Nyasa. Although a considerable amount of road construction had been undertaken and maintained through enforced local authority tasks, it was too early a stage in the development of motorized vehicles for much advantage to accrue, especially as disease restricted animal-drawn vehicles.

The exploitation of the resources of the colony, which was one of the main reasons for acquiring the territory, was not easy to undertake. However, notable advances were made in the understanding of the potentialities of the environment. Under Dr Franz Stuhlmann the Department of Surveying and Agriculture was set up in 1893. He encouraged the collection of information, especially on the topography, and this resulted in the colony being the best mapped country in East Africa. The agro-biological institutes – especially the one at Amani – paved the way for future development, and numerous crops were tried and even introduced. By the end of German administration large plantations of sisal, rubber and coffee were in production. By 1910 there were 250 rubber plantations, 54 sisal plantations and 17 coffee plantations. European settlement took valuable land in the highlands, especially in the Usambaras, Pare and Kilimanjaro regions, and to a lesser extent in the south-east and north-west. Considerable land was also alienated around Dar es Salaam and the Ulugurus, and ranches were established at Bukoba, Moshi, Langenburg, Dodoma and Kondoa–Irangi. As a result of these developments, European plantations increased from 180 in 1905 to 758 in 1912. Although indigenous people were incorporated into the monetary economy, the methods were coercive and the benefits were largely incidental. The extent of German development can partly be gauged from Table 46, p. 168. The role of the missionaries probably had a greater effect on the welfare of the people. By 1909 there were over 150 mission centres, most of them located in remote areas. Their contribution to health and education were significant. The extent of their assistance in education can be measured by the fact that by 1911 the administration was responsible for the schooling of

6000 children compared with 30 000 pupils in mission schools. The outbreak of the First World War curtailed all developments, and there was once again widespread destruction of property and lives. Following the peace treaty between Germany and Britain, Britain was granted a mandate over the former German colony. However, in recognition of the Belgian participation in the war fought in East Africa, the north-west sector comprising mainly the districts of Ruanda–Urundi were excised

and given to them. The twenty-three years of German rule had ended, but their influence lasted for several more decades. Remarkable as the developments were, they were largely possible through the massive exploitation of indigenous labour and the almost complete suppression of the values and wishes of the majority of the people.

ADOLFO MASCARENHAS

THE GERMAN ADMINISTRATION

45 EVOLUTION OF THE ADMINISTRATIVE FRAMEWORK, 1919-61

The conflict between Britain and Germany from 1914 to 1918 extended to East Africa. By the Treaty of Peace signed in June 1919 Germany renounced all rights over its overseas possessions. Arrangement was made for former German territories to be administered by mandatories on behalf of the League of Nations, and Britain agreed to administer German East Africa with the exception of Ruanda and Urundi. The office of Governor was constituted by the Tanganyika Order in Council, 1920, and Tanganyika remained under British rule until 1961. Zanzibar had been a British Protectorate since 1890 but the mainland territory and off-shore islands remained administratively separate until 1964, by which time both had independent governments.

At the inception of British rule Tanganyika was divided for administrative purposes into twenty-two districts which were based principally on the German administrative units of the area. The geographical network was noticeably finer along the coast where contact had been greater (especially in the centre and north), and reflected the significance attached to concentrations of population in the mountains. The framework was significantly coarser in the north and west: in part this reflected variations in population density (a common determinant of the areal extent of administrative areas) but it also reflected the limited penetration of the interior.

With a country as large and as varied geographically and culturally as Tanganyika, it was only to be expected that the administrative structure would not remain stable but would need to be modified to suit changing conditions and in the light of increasing experience. Administration is the management of human affairs: it is, therefore, a set of relationships between people and does not intrinsically require the precise definition of geographic boundaries. Nonetheless the colonial administrations imposed a system of administrative areas whose boundaries were given legal definition. Whereas administrative practice is dynamic and can undergo constant modification, administrative areas are essentially static, and if they change they do so sequentially. Important stages in this sequence are shown by the four maps which depict the areas at the opening of the period of British administration (1922), the results of the major period of reform from 1925-32 (1933), the post-Second World War situation (1948), and the relatively stable pattern (1957) before the reorganizations immediately preceding Independence (Maps A, B, C, D opposite). See also Table 47, p. 168.

The first districts of Tanganyika were in the charge of administrative officers who were the executive authority and carried out the policies formulated by the government. They were empowered to hold courts, administer justice and collect revenue. In areas where there were strong tribal chiefs it was a matter of financial and manpower expediency for the central government to recognize and support the indigenous administration. In areas where this was less well developed the political officers of the central government necessarily took a more positive and executive role in the day-to-day administration. The interests

of expediency and a new emphasis on the value of local self-government were instrumental in encouraging a major administrative revision during the years 1925 to 1932. Having taken over the German districts in 1920 and having maintained this form of administration, the mandated territory had a somewhat different framework from that operating in other British-governed territories in tropical Africa where a two-level hierarchy existed with provinces sub-divided into districts. The first change, therefore, was effected in 1925 when the districts were grouped into eleven provinces each in the charge of a Provincial Commissioner who was responsible to the Governor for the administration of his province, the district administrative officers in turn being responsible to the Commissioner for their districts. An attempt was made to make the provinces meaningful in terms of geographical characteristics and tribal distribution:

This re-organization initiated a period of change in the number, location and extent of the districts. These changes were made in order to rationalize the existing system but also as an instrument of policy in attempting to put into effect the administrative system of 'indirect rule' associated with the name of Sir Donald Cameron, Governor, 1925–31. Districts were re-formed to take account of tribal affiliations and what were believed to be historically natural groupings of the people. The policy was 'uniting as far as possible separated units of a tribe under one chief and placing the tribal entity so formed within one administrative district'. As a result the number of districts was increased from the initial 22 to 37 in 1926, 42 in 1928, and 44 in 1930. At the close of this period of activity, in 1932, the number of provinces was further reduced – this time to eight. Within districts legal recognition was given to the status of chiefs, and they together with the native authority were authorized to enact by-laws. Secondly, native courts were established, and thirdly native treasuries were created. These three institutions were the main instruments of the policy of indirect rule.

Subsequent modifications to the system of administrative areas were less fundamental. They represented attempts by the administration to solve the difficulties met with in imposing a uniform system on a large and diverse country; to take account of changing economic fortunes; and to adjust to population growth and urbanization. Response became more of a possibility as the civil staff grew and the network of communications was improved.

It was not easy to unite all sections of a tribe in one administrative district. In Central Province the area occupied by the Gogo was administered as Dodoma District in 1921–5 and 1937–46, but at other times was divided between various combinations of Manyoni, Kongwa, Mpwapwa and Dodoma District. Certain sections of the country were inaccessible or insufficiently viable. Mafia Island, for instance, was part of Rufiji; Pangani was linked with Tanga; and Kasulu and Kibondo (Buha from 1947 to 1949) were incorporated in Kigoma.

Economic developments often made new administrative arrangements desirable, feasible and necessary. The increase in activity on the Lupa Goldfield in the 1930s was directly responsible for the formation of Chunya District in January 1942, and Chunya settlement, the goldfield township since 1937, became the district headquarters. The headquarters of the Southern Highlands Province (until 1936 Iringa Province) was moved from Iringa to Mbeya adjacent to the mining area in 1936. In 1948 Mpanda in the south-west of Western Province was given separate status following the development of lead and silver mining. The ill-fated groundnut scheme gave rise to the ephemeral districts of Kongwa and Ruponda. The former (1948–51) disappeared completely, Ruponda (1948–52) was renamed Nachingwea and still exists.

Population growth together with economic development was responsible for the creation between 1948 and 1958 of numerous new districts by sub-division of the former units (for example, Lushoto–Handeni in 1948, Geita–Ukerewe in 1950, Karagwe–Bukoba and Singida–Iramba in 1958). Urbanization also led to the creation of new units. As early as 1938 the urban area of Dar es Salaam was separated from the surrounding rural area, and while the former remained as Dar es Salaam District, the latter was styled Temeke District (later Uzaramo and finally Kisarawe). From 1954 until 1961 Tanga and Mwanza were each separated into urban and rural districts.

IAN THOMAS

EVOLUTION OF THE ADMINISTRATIVE FRAMEWORK

With the exception of small numbers of recent immigrants of Arabian, Indian and European origin, the people of Tanzania are all of the Negroid physical type. Linguistically, however, there is no such uniformity. Of the four main African language families, each is represented in Tanzania; and the Kondoa area contains the most diverse collection of languages to be found in the whole continent. However, as the map shows, it is only the northern and north-central part of Tanzania that is linguistically complex: the rest of the country — and ninety-five per cent of the Tanzanian population — is Bantu-speaking.

Bantu languages cover the larger part of Africa south of Cameroun, Lake Victoria and the Kenya coast. They number several hundreds. In Tanzania alone about a hundred Bantu tongues are distinguishable. (For individual names and location see Map 47 and Table 45, p. 168.) Neighbouring dialects are often mutually intelligible, but more distant ones are not. Nevertheless, the basic similarity is easily recognized, indicating that all Bantu languages derive from a common origin.

Of the non-Bantu languages, the biggest group in Tanzania is *Nilotic*. Nilotic languages extend from the southern Sudan through Uganda and Kenya to central Tanzania. There are three branches:

Highland Nilotic has two sub-branches. The first consists of the Kalenjin of Kenya and certain 'Dorobo' groups, of which one or two are to be found in northern Tanzania. The second comprises the Tatoga groups (also known as Mangati and Taturu) of north-central Tanzania. The largest of these groups are the Barabaig living near Mount Hanang.

Plains Nilotic has several sub-branches, of which two are represented in Tanzania. The first is very small — the Ngassa of East Kilimanjaro. The other is Masai, which includes the Arusha, Baraguyu and other groups sometimes called 'Kwavi' or 'Loikop'.

The third group, *River-lake Nilotic*, consists in East Africa of the Lwoo-speaking peoples. Their only representatives in Tanzania are the Luo who have expanded from Kenya along the lake-shore into North Mara District.

Cushitic languages are mostly found in Ethiopia and Somalia, but one division of them — *Southern Cushitic* — is confined to north-central Tanzania. It comprises the Iraqw (or Mbulu), and to their south the Gorowa (or Fiome), Burungi, Alawa and Ngomvia, as well as the Mbugu of Usambara and the small bands of Asa-Aramanik in Masailand.

Khoisan (or 'click') languages are spoken by the Sandawe in the centre, and probably by the Hadza (or Tindiga) hunters by Lake Eyasi. (A contrary view would classify Hadza as Cushitic.) Apart from these East African examples, Khoisan languages are spoken only by the Bushmen and Hottentots of southern Africa.

Despite this linguistic diversity, with four unrelated families and some ancient divisions and numerous tribes within those families, it would be wrong to imagine the people of Tanzania as belonging to a series of completely separate and mutually hostile ethnic groups. Neither in Tanzania — nor anywhere else in the world — are there 'pure' tribes or races. Rarely has one group exterminated or expelled another. Rather, the history of Tanzania has been a process of intermingling and intermarriage between tribes, with later settlers and invaders assimilating, or being assimilated by, the resident populations. In this way tribes have been altered and new ones formed; and likewise, some languages have been maintained and developed, while others have been abandoned. However, sometimes a language lingers on among a small unassimilated remnant group (of which several examples are shown in northern Tanzania); or a few words of an extinct language are preserved through being borrowed and incorporated into the language of the assimilating group. These provide the historian with valuable clues about former populations.

By combining this linguistic evidence with that derived from archaeology, anthropology and — for recent centuries — from oral traditions, a tentative outline of the peopling of Tanzania can be reconstructed as follows.

During the Late Stone Age, Tanzania, like most of southern Africa, was inhabited by bands of hunter-gatherers of Bushman-type, from whom the Khoisan language of the modern Sandawe is descended. Then, about 1000 BC., Southern Cushites, with cattle and goats and grain agriculture, began expanding from Ethiopia into Kenya and the highlands and Rift Valley of northern Tanzania. Here they absorbed some of the hunter-gatherers; but they did not penetrate the southern and western parts of the country. These regions remained the domain of hunter-gatherers until the coming of Bantu-speakers mainly from the west or south-west, beginning early in the first millennium AD. and continuing into the second millennium. The Bantu from the start were not only cultivators: they also worked and used iron. Thus they opened up the land and increased in numbers. Hunter-gatherers, being fewer and technologically inferior, were either absorbed or forced to retreat into less desirable areas. In the north, however, the Bantu have encountered larger and more settled non-Bantu populations, consisting not only of the long-established Southern Cushites, but also of Nilotic groups. Of the latter, the Tatoga may have been in the northern Tanzania grasslands for over a thousand years, whereas the Masai arrived from the north only about two centuries ago. The Masai have tended to confine the Tatoga, many of whom have been forced to assimilate themselves among other peoples, notably the various Bantu tribes that have been pressing into this non-Bantu region from all sides. The Khoisan-speaking Sandawe and many of the smaller Southern Cushitic groups have been undergoing similar processes of 'Bantuization'. However, assimilation has not been all one-way. For instance, while several Bantu tribes have taken in numbers of Masai (especially Masai who have lost their cattle or been forced off the grasslands by other Masai), certain Masai-speaking groups (the Arusha, for example) have absorbed considerable elements of Bantu origin. On the eastern shore of Lake Victoria, moreover, the recently expanding Luo have absorbed and intermarried with local Bantu. And, within the Bantu regions, there has, needless to say, been continual intermixture between one Bantu tribe and another.

Among the Bantu languages is one of immense importance for modern Tanzania – Swahili. This has developed over the centuries on the East African coast. While it has borrowed from Arabic and other foreign tongues, it remains in its structure and basic vocabulary entirely Bantu. As trade-routes began to link the coast and the interior in the nineteenth century, and as the two have become more fully integrated in the twentieth century to form the Tanzanian nation, so Swahili has become increasingly adopted, first as a lingua franca and now as a national language, overcoming the linguistic divisions of Tanzania's past.

JOHN SUTTON

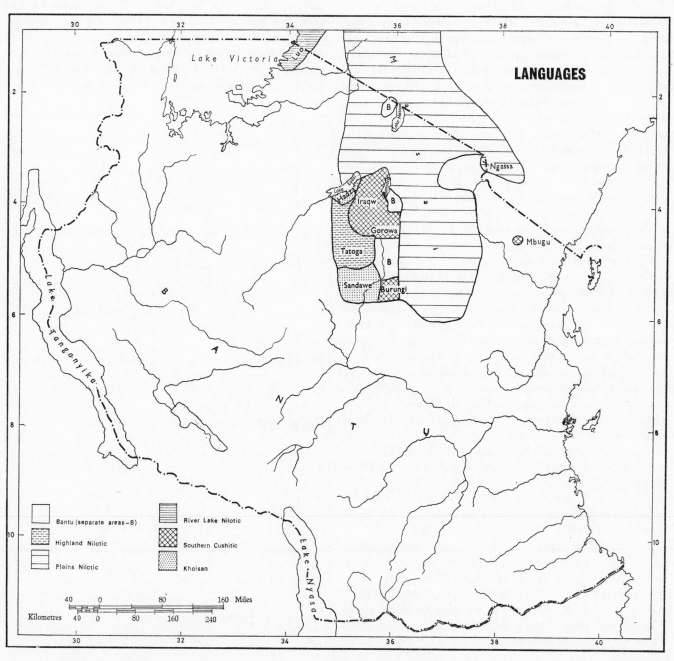

The map of tribes is an historical map: to some it may even seem to be an anachronism in a book of this type. Certainly contemporary discussion of 'tribes' is likely to be controversial not only because there are considerable difficulties of precise definition but also because the term has come to have pejorative connotations. 'Ethnic group' is not an entirely satisfactory substitute in Tanzania for its suggests something more fundamental than the loose associations of people which are customarily designated tribes, whereas, as Dr Sutton shows, the great majority of the people are similar in language and racial origin. However, more than one hundred separate tribes of Tanzania are recognized. Attempts have been made to create a middle-level classification between the general term *Bantu* and the multiplicity of local names. The early censuses grouped the tribes according to a supposed chronology of migration with Elder and Younger Bantu groups. Later attempts, while taking note of traditional and cultural affinities, have been basically geographical classifications with Coastal, Interlacustrine, Western and Ruvuma Bantu sub-groups. This is essentially an academic exercise and no one system has been widely accepted or adopted. By contrast the relevance of the tribal classification is clear, for Tanzania has a great variety of peoples whose modes of life, customs, traditions, and habitats are diverse. There has been debate as to the extent to which all the peoples of Tanzania can readily be allocated to one tribe or another, but when used with due caution a division of the population into tribal categories can be useful both as an aid to understanding past events and as a guide to the complexity of the present.

The map showing the distribution of tribes is based on the work of Dr P H Gulliver. The figures in the tables are derived from the 1957 census reports. To a large extent both sources reflect the sub-divisions the people themselves recognize. Although there have been many cases of administrative interference, the tribal groupings are essentially indigenous. Early travellers to East Africa also quickly distinguished between various peoples occupying the area. Because of differences in their appearance, economy, and customs, the Wadigo, Wasambaa, the people of Chagga, the Masai, the Wanyamwezi, the Hehe and the Nyakyusa soon came to be recognized and differentiated. Varieties of social organization, religious belief, language, agricultural practices and house types were described and discussed. In addition to the travellers: scientists, historians, ethnographers and administrators organized their writings in terms of tribes. It is for this reason that the tribal map has value for historical studies. Anthropological accounts are still being written on this basis.

Secondly, from 1925 the administration was organized spatially with reference to the distribution of peoples with a supposed ethnic, cultural, and economic homogeneity. These groups were uniformly called 'tribes', but there was little structural and functional uniformity in the character of the group. The Sukuma, Chagga, and Hehe, for instance, represent amalgamations of people who among themselves recognize many sub-groups. The sense of overall tribal identity has increased only in the twentieth century as they have been incorporated in a national territorial framework and been made increasingly aware of their distinctiveness. The hierarchy of local government was also based on that of the local people, though again the imposition of a uniform system throughout the country did considerable injustice to indigenous governmental forms. Until 1963 chief and sub-chief were important officials, and chiefdoms and sub-chiefdoms were official units of organization.

Thirdly, there are important variations culturally and economically between the groups of inhabitants of Tanzania. Day-to-day administration had to take account of differing autochthonous legal systems in settling disputes or in deciding the inheritance of land and property. The ceremonies held at birth, puberty, marriage, and death vary from one part of the country to another as do the usual forms of expression in song, dance, and handicrafts. More basically the subsistence activities range from hunting and gathering (Hadza) through the spectrum from nomadic pastoralists (Masai) to sedentary arable farmers without livestock (Luguru, Makonde), with many intermediate stages between. The accordance of form of political organization, cultural expression and economic foundation is

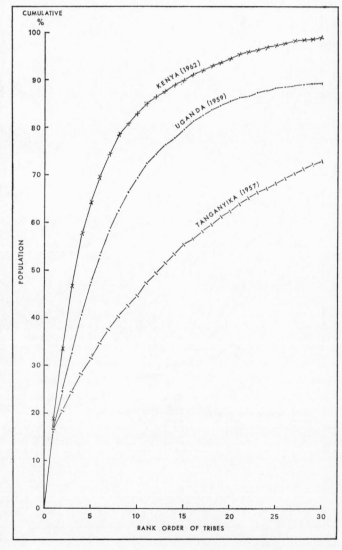

not perfect, nor can variations in life-style be simply related to particular physical environments. However, any attempt to deal with small regions of Tanzania – whether to describe settlement, characterize agriculture, or analyse variations in fertility, mortality and migration – is likely to find *tribe* a significant variable for consideration and a useful indicator of a wide range of inter-related characteristics.

Two contemporary issues will serve to illustrate the continuing relevance of tribal classification and awareness. In a country with a firmly-established natural unity, the development of the national culture will draw on the rich regional variations in artistic forms and is likely to foster local pride. Conversely, the maintenance of natural unity to some extent depends upon the success with which sectional interests within the country are prevented from polarizing. If the recognition and encouragement of tribal distinctiveness reinforces differences in political and religious alignment, degree of economic development, provision of welfare of educational services, etc., this convergence of regional interests may be nationally divisive. However, this does not appear to be a special danger for Tanzania, so that the variety of local organization and the recognition of regional affinities is not likely to weaken the nation. In this respect we may note the size of the largest tribes in Tanzania, Kenya and Uganda (Tables 48 and 49, p. 168) and the extent to which a few tribes dominate the distribution. The distribution of peoples among the tribes is much more even in the case of Tanzania, but the number of tribes is greater. This fact together with the pattern of population distribution, the existence of a lingua franca, and the presence of capable leaders has contributed to the strength and stability of Tanzania.

IAN THOMAS

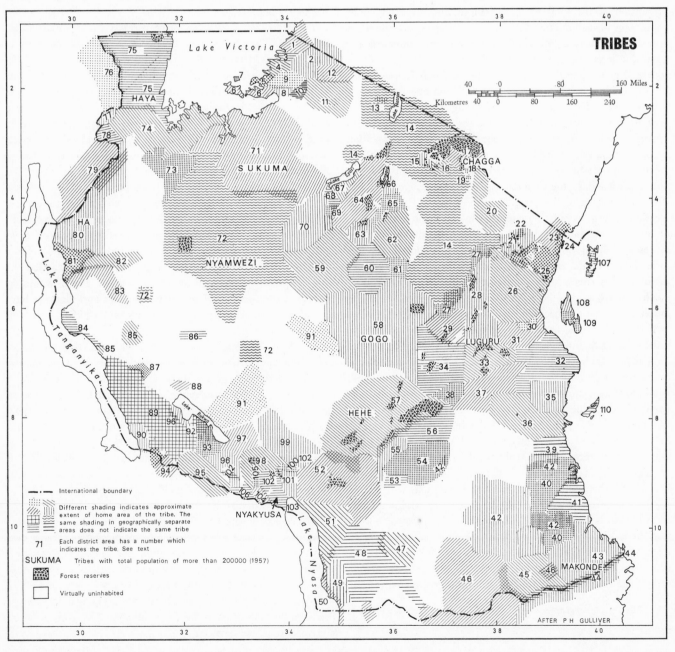

As early as 1936 C Gillman, in a study of the population of Tanganyika which is a classic of the population geography of Africa,[1] noted that the well-watered parts of the territory contained two-thirds of the whole population on roughly one-tenth of the total area. Regional variation in water-supply was a major explanatory factor. It has been demonstrated that in addition to these ecological determinants (among which should be included the nature of the soil), historical experience, regional demographic trends, differential economic development, and urbanization – all contribute to the evolution of the population pattern. That the people of Tanzania are still very unevenly distributed throughout the country is illustrated in Table 50, p. 169, which gives the proportion of the total population and proportion of the total national area in districts grouped by population density. The accompanying map gives the rural population density by divisions. There are three hundred and sixty divisions which were mapped for the first time in the course of geographical planning for the 1967 population census. They provide a better basis for the calculation and mapping of population density than the districts, though they vary considerably in size and in a number of cases incorporate different ecological zones so that important variations in population density remain unrevealed by division mapping.

Dominant features of the pattern of population distribution and density within the national area are: the fragmented and dispersed pattern of the areas of high density, the peripheral location of large population clusters, and the relative emptiness of much of the interior. If the population density were to be represented by a three-dimensional surface, population peaks located around the edge of the country would be linked by discontinuous ridges with south-east/north-west or north-east/south-west alignments, between which would be extensive population depressions. The main axis, or ridge of higher density population, extends from Dar es Salaam in the south-east, north-westwards through Morogoro, Kilosa, Mpwapwa, central Dodoma, Singida, Iramba, Nzega and Shinyanga, and thence to the well-populated country around Lake Victoria. A second, continuous axis, crosses the first at right angles and runs from the lands at the north end of Nyasa north-east through north Njombe, the uplands of Mufindi and Iringa, meets the Dar es Salaam–Lake Victoria belt at Kilosa and Mpwapwa, and links with the north through Handeni with the agglomeration inland of Tanga. This population cluster in Tanga, Lushoto and Korogwe is the south-east end of a developing axis which runs north-west through Pare to the high density and populous areas of Arusha and Moshi. A similar line of separated concentrations is discernible in the north-west and includes parts of Kigoma, Kasulu, north Kibondo, Ngara and Bukoba. This has a south-west to north-east alignment. In the extreme south-east of the country is the isolated but populous agglomeration

[1] C Gilman, *A population map of Tanganyika Territory*. Government Printer, Dar es Salaam, 1936; also in *Geographical Review* 26 3 1936, pp. 353–75.

which extends from the coast at Mtwara–Mikindani and Lindi to Newala district where, on the Makonde Plateau, there are very high densities of rural population. Adding to the fragmented nature of the population pattern of the coast, where the population clusters which focus on the three main ports are separated by areas of low population density, are the offshore islands of Mafia, Zanzibar and Pemba.

Three large tracts of the country are sparsely inhabited. East of Lake Victoria, from eastern Maswa and Musoma south-east through Masai to Handeni and south Pangani is an extensive area which separates the Tanga–Kilimanjaro axis from that running inland from Dar es Salaam. In the south, much of Kilwa, Lindi, Nachingwea, Ulanga, Songea and Tunduru are sparsely populated, and this zone separates the south-east cluster from that inland of the capital. Finally, almost the whole of the western plateau extending south of Sukumaland and north of Mbeya, and west of Dodoma and east of Lake Tanganyika is sparsely populated.

Three ecological situations are marked by population concentration. These are: mountain lands – the volcanic cones of Kilimanjaro, Meru and Rungwe, and the fault-bounded blocks of Pare, Usambara, Uluguru, Poroto and Safwa; lakeshore zones – especially those of Victoria and Nyasa; and restricted parts of the coastal belt, including the offshore islands. Certain upland and plateau areas support fair densities of population, but in general the plateau and hill country is characterized by population densities of less than 15 per square kilometre. Table 50 summarizes the population data for landform categories: The mountain category contains only 10.9 per cent of the national area but carries more than twenty per cent of the population. However, by sub-categories the upland lakeshore group has the highest average population density, followed by the coastal areas and then the non-volcanic and volcanic mountain lands. These are rural densities: if the urban populations were added the total population and density in the coastal group would be increased considerably. The upland and lowland plateaux have the lowest overall population densities and cover almost half the country.

The level of population density is affected by a variety of circumstances. Urban areas show particularly high population densities because large numbers of people find employment in industrial and service activities whose location is highly concentrated. The food supplies and other requirements of these people are gathered from a wide surrounding area. In rural areas small population clusters can occur where there is some concentration of non-agricultrual activities. The location of a mining community as at Mwadui, Kiabakari, or formerly at Mpanda and on the Lupa goldfield explains certain local clusters. Others, more numerous in their occurrence, mark the site of service centres where trade goods can be obtained, welfare and community services are located, and marketing is carried out. However, the major determinant of the level of population density in the rural area is the system of agriculture practised. The lands occupied by nomadic pastoralists carry markedly different population densities from those occupied by maize/beans/cattle agriculturists or those inhabited by coffee-banana cultivators and rice farmers.

It has been noted earlier (Section 6, p. 20), that Tanzania is, overall, experiencing population growth, and that the increment of people per unit area is great in areas of high rural population density. The pattern of population density largely reflects the prevailing systems of agriculture. The stability of the pattern suggests the difficulty of changing current agricultural systems in areas which face environmental problems, and changing them sufficiently rapidly to permit a more uniform distribution of people among the regions of the country. This situation which is likely to continue for some time has rather important consequences for the areas of high density. It means that unless standards of living are to be permitted to decline or the agricultural land is seriously exploited with consequent declines in yield and eventual soil erosion, ways must be found of supporting large numbers of extra people. This can be done by: (a) increasing the production and income derived from cash crops, which has the same effect as providing non-agricultural employment and wages, since material requirements can then be purchased from elsewhere; (b) increasing the production of food, which can be done by cultivating more land if this is available, or increasing the yield from currently farmed areas; (c) providing non-agricultural remunerative employment in small industries, or service industry. Alternatively, out-migration can be encouraged, and the migrants directed to potentially productive areas at present under-utilized. Tanzania is attempting to do all these. The latter would change the pattern of rural poulation density, and might result in an increase of density on some parts of the plateau and river basin areas.

IAN THOMAS

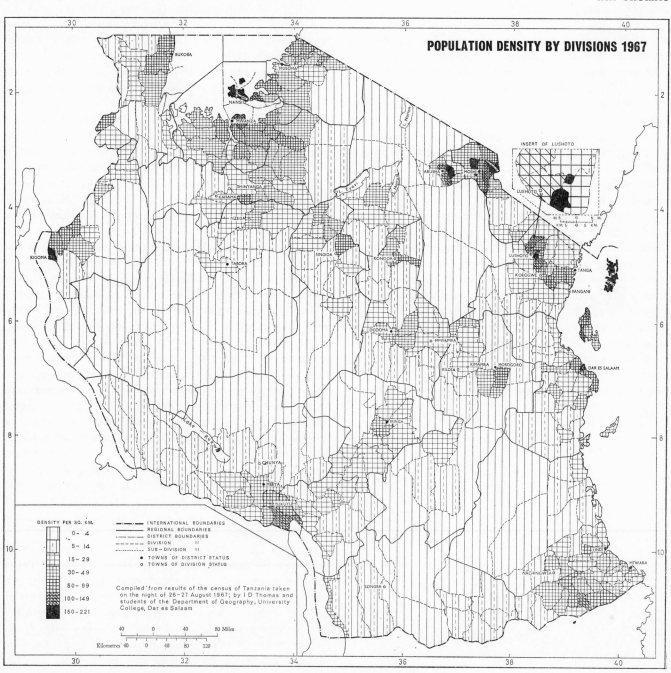

POPULATION DENSITY BY DIVISIONS 1967

DENSITY PER SQ. KM.

0 – 4
5 – 14
15 – 29
30 – 49
50 – 99
100 – 149
150 – 221

INTERNATIONAL BOUNDARIES
REGIONAL BOUNDARIES
DISTRICT BOUNDARIES
DIVISION   "
SUB – DIVISION   "
• TOWNS OF DISTRICT STATUS
○ TOWNS OF DIVISION STATUS

Compiled from results of the census of Tanzania taken on the night of 26–27 August 1967; by I D Thomas and students of the Department of Geography, University College, Dar es Salaam

The population of any area has inherent and acquired characteristics. The sex of individuals, their racial origin, and place of birth, for instance, are determined at birth, and their age are determined at birth and later by their ability to survive. Other characteristics are not fixed in this way. The health, educational level, type of occupation, religion practised, and language spoken, etc. can be modified to a greater or lesser extent both for any single individual or for a group of persons over time. It is one of the objects of development to change the acquired characteristics: to improve the health, level of literacy, and standard of living of the national population. Thus the quality of the population can be improved. Though fixed at birth for a single individual, the inherent characteristics of the total population or geographic segments of the total can vary. The sex, age, and racial composition of populations vary from country to country, alter within one country at different times, and differ from place to place within a single national area.

Developing countries have to rely almost entirely on the data collected in population censuses for information on the age and sex composition of the populace in the absence of country-wide systems of vital registration. There are particular difficulties in gathering data on ages in many parts of Africa because it is not a customary practice to keep a careful record of date of birth or years lived. Many people are ignorant of their exact age; some estimate to the nearest five or ten years; while disproportionate numbers choose an age ending in the digits two or eight. This introduces distortions into the age distribution for a country. Other distortions common in census records in tropical Africa include unexpectedly large proportions in the age group 5 to 9 years, and between the ages 20 and 30; relatively small proportions in the age groups 10 to 14, and 15 to 19 years; and more males than females at the higher ages. These features were apparent in the age data of the 1967 census of Tanzania and affect the appearance of the age-sex pyramid by five year age groups (see below). The triangular shape with a very wide base and sides which are in general concave upwards is charac-teristic of many developing countries in the world where birth rates are high and mortality is declining. With this age structure Tanzania has 44 per cent of the population aged less than 15 years old. (Table 51, p. 169). A considerable burden is imposed on the resources of the country because not only are nationals of this age essentially non-productive, but if the country is attempting to improve the quality of its population a large amount of capital and skilled effort must be devoted to health, welfare, and educational services for these young inhabitants. Nor is this, necessarily, a transitory feature. Unless the level of fertility falls rapidly, Tanzania will continue to have a large proportion of its population in the young age groups.

Tanzania has a low overall sex ratio and this has been one of the most permanent features of the population (Table 52, p. 169). The sex ratio expresses the number of males to females, or vice versa, in the population. The map presents the male sex ratio – that is, the number of males per hundred females – for the divisions of Tanzania. The male sex ratio at birth is normally above one hundred, that is, rather more males are born than females. In western countries the ratio is usually of the order of 106, but data becoming available from African countries suggest that it might be lower for African populations and the current estimate for Tanzania is 102 to 103. Thereafter at most ages males usually have a greater probability of dying so that in youth the proportions of males and females are approximately equal, and at high ages there is often an excess of females, i.e. the male sex ratio is low (see Table 51, p. 169). It is possible that the conditions in Tanzania result in rather higher mortality rates for adult females owing to the risks of maternity and the hard physical work which females undertake in the rural areas. This combination of differential birth numbers and differential mortality accounts in part for variations in sex ratios by age for Tanzania as a whole, and for the geographic distribution of sex ratios. However, the overall sex ratio of a country, and the pattern of sex ratios within the country, is also affected by the amount of migration, for this is commonly sex-differentiated. Usually more men migrate than females so that areas of in-migration have higher sex ratios, and areas of out-migration have lower sex ratios. A country which on balance serves as a labour reservoir can be expected to have a lower sex ratio than one which offers employment opportunities. The emigration of males has been suggested as the reason for the low overall sex ratio of Tanzania. A decrease in the amount of international labour migration from Tanzania since Independence may account for the change in the sex ratio between 1957 and 1967.

The male sex ratio for the country in 1967 was 95, but the range for districts was from 77 in Kasulu to 122 in Pangani, and the values for divisions ranged from 75 in Buhoro and Muyama (both in Kasulu District) to 150 in Amani (Tanga District) (Table 53, p. 170). The north-east has an especially marked excess of males with the three Districts of Korogwe, Pangani and Tanga each having more than 115 males per 100 females. There is a concentration of employment opportunity on the sisal estates of this part of the country, and in the town of Tanga, so that the area has been a focus of labour migration over a long period. Arusha, Mwanza, and Mtwara Districts and central Zanzibar similarly combine rural wage-earning possibilities with the

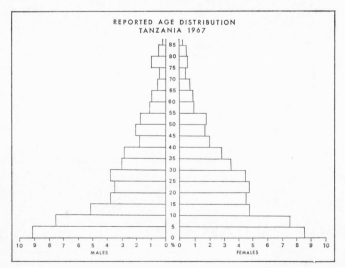

REPORTED AGE DISTRIBUTION
TANZANIA 1967

attraction of urban centres. Geita and Biharamulo, Mbulu, Kilosa and north Iringa have higher than average ratios and these are areas of cash crop production (cotton, wheat, sisal and tobacco and maize respectively), so that they are areas to which labourers and new settlers move. Mzizima and Dar es Salaam offer the attractions of city life and industrial and tertiary occupations. Extensive areas with a great deficit of males are found in the north-west in Kasulu, Kibondo and Ngara Districts and in western Biharamulo, and in the south-west in Njombe District. In the centre and south-east of the country there are also widespread areas of moderately low ratios: these include much of Nzega, Iramba, and Singida, Dodoma, south Morogoro, and the plateau country of the south in Nachingwea,

Ulanga, Songea, and Tunduru. Smaller but significant areas with an excess of females are found in Moshi, North Pare, Lushoto, and central Morogoro. These are mountain areas where population density is high. Finally, the coastal and coastal hinterland areas south of Dar es Salaam in Rufiji and Kiilwa have low ratios. Almost all of these areas are recognized centres of out-migration, though the casual factors vary. The two main situations, however, are: first, a relative lack of development as in Kasulu and Njombe, the central uplands, and the south-east plateaux; and secondly, population growth in excess of the population carrying capacity of the land even where, as in the mountain lands, the agricultural potential is high and the agricultural system relatively productive.

IAN THOMAS

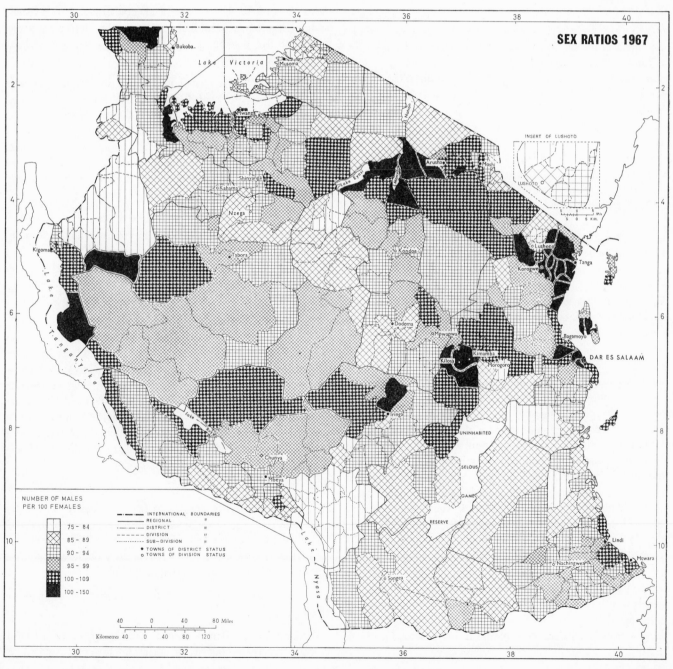

50 HEALTH SERVICES AND THE INCIDENCE OF DISEASE 1

Provision of public and private health measures for the widely dispersed population of Tanzania constitutes a formidable problem. Specialized health facilities and hospitals are restricted to the principal urban areas and district centres: extension of effective services throughout the rural population is an urgent need. Until recent years rural areas were served primarily by scattered, simple dispensaries: a network of more elaborate and better staffed Rural Health Centres is now being established. Each centre acts as a focus of preventive and clinical medicine for a large area (approximately 50 000 persons), supported by a number of small satellite dispensaries. The first Five Year Plan (1964–9) included an increase in the number of these centres from 30 to 113, with a concurrent increase in dispensaries from 1039 to 1339. In addition, national health provisions include basic medical research undertaken by the research institutes of the East African Community.

So little information is available that it is impossible to provide general accounts of the pattern of disease and the numerous pressing health problems which include protein deficiency and other forms of malnutrition. For a few diseases it is possible to delineate their broad geographical pattern and to indicate the local conditions under which they are prevalent. These are the parasitic infections in which the parasite or vector is restricted to particular physical conditions.

The data available are highly variable in completeness of coverage and in detail. In all cases, conditions favouring the disease can be outlined, but only for malaria can the distribution of endemic areas be mapped in any but the broadest manner.

Malaria

Although malaria is not commonly fatal in adults it exerts a considerable toll in infant and early-childhood mortality and in a high incidence of morbidity throughout the population.

1. *Vectors of malaria in Tanzania*

Major vectors in transmission of the malaria parasite are the anopheline mosquitoes, *Anopheles gambiae* and *A. funestus*. *A. gambiae*, the most dangerous and widespread, breeds in any fresh or brackish water not covered with dense vegetation. It is notorious for the rapidity of its population build-up even in short rainy seasons: its peak transmission periods occur during and immediately after rainy seasons. *A. gambiae* is present at some or all times of year over the whole country except very high, cool altitudes and very dry areas: its upper limit is at altitudes where temperature falls below 13°C., and it has never been found above 2000 m. in Tanzania. *A. funestus* is found in more shaded and permanent breeding sites, particularly the grassy margins of slowly moving streams: it is also widely distributed at lower altitudes wherever water in the form of rivers, swamps or lakes persists for long periods. As the temporary breeding places to which *A. gambiae* is restricted dry up after rainy seasons, so its numbers diminish and a second wave of transmission dominated by *A. funestus* occurs.

2. *Distribution of malaria*

With vectors present for at least part of the year almost throughout Tanzania, variations in malaria incidence depend in the first place upon the length of the transmission season (Map 50). Accuracy of detail in the map is limited by scale, particularly in broken country where local contrasts are marked.

a. Transmission for over six months in a year. Over forty per cent of the country most of the year is characterized by intense malaria transmission resulting in constant re-infection of the population. Much illness occurs among children, with mortality ten per cent or more among infants under one year. Those who survive to adulthood acquire natural immunity, and are generally free from clinical signs of malaria, although longitudinal blood tests reveal low levels of parasitaemia. Typically parasites are found in some seventy to one hundred per cent of the population in the absence of chemotherapy, the incidence being highest in early childhood (often one hundred per cent for the one to five year age-group) and declining rapidly to about fifty per cent in adults.

b. Transmission restricted to three to six months per year (just under forty per cent of the country). Malaria tends to be seasonal, occurring in mild epidemics. Where these are repeated annually some immunity is built up, but where they are less frequent immunity is lower and epidemics can be serious. Average parasite rates are commonly in the range fifty to seventy per cent, slight immunity giving rates of thirty per cent among adults.

c. Transmission for less than three months per year. The lack of permanent water bodies restricts transmission to those infrequent periods when the rainy season permits the build-up of *A. gambiae* populations. Little immunity is acquired by the inhabitants unless they visit zones of more intense transmission: brief occasional malarial attacks therefore affect all age groups.

Intensity of malaria transmission is not precisely reflected in malaria incidence, for population mobility commonly involves frequent movement between areas of different endemicity status. The practice of labour migration occasions peasant farmers to travel through or to areas of malaria transmission in order to find employment. In the wholly rural context many families work land in both malaria-free highlands and the malarious foothills and plains below. Local natural contrasts may also be modified by control of the vector population or the use of suppressive drugs.

3. *Malarial control*

Eradication of malaria appears to be a particularly intractable problem on account of the intensity of transmission, mobility of the population, and technical and administrative difficulties. Large-scale efforts have been concentrated on interruption of transmission by vector eradication or control.

a. Major breeding sites can be eliminated by drainage of creeks and swamps.

b. Drainage is often combined with the application of larvicides to the remaining water surfaces. However, coverage of all water surfaces, including the smallest and shortest-lived, is impracticable except in a few small, densely settled areas such as the major towns and certain institutions (map below).

c. Imagicidal measures to reduce the number of adults vectors have also been used. On the periphery of towns as an ancillary to larvicidal measures in the central areas it is effective in establishing a barrier zone to guard against introduction of infection. Used alone in rural areas, success is limited by technical problems and administration of drugs would be effective in eradicating malaria, but is operationally impossible in most areas. An exception occurs at Mto Wa Mbu near Lake Manyara, where universal medication was achieved through the sale of chloroquinated dietary salt to the exclusion of untreated salt.

Problems of insecticide and drug resistance have not yet developed to a serious stage. Resistance of the parasite *Plasmodium falciparum* (which accounts for about ninety per cent of infections) to pyrimathamine developed in Tanga District during 1953, and the resistant strain subsequently spread to locations up to 150 miles away. In the absence of further drug pressure the strain declined, and by 1965 formed only forty per cent of the incidence in the focus locality. Gross resistance to proguanil and other related drugs has been demonstrated. No species, however, has yet proved resistant to the 4-aminoquinolines as has occurred widely elsewhere. Controlled chemotherapy, therefore, continues to be effective: in view of the difficulties of vector control it is encouraging that surveys indicate that spontaneous use of suppressive drugs is becoming more widespread in some rural communities.

HILARY PAGE

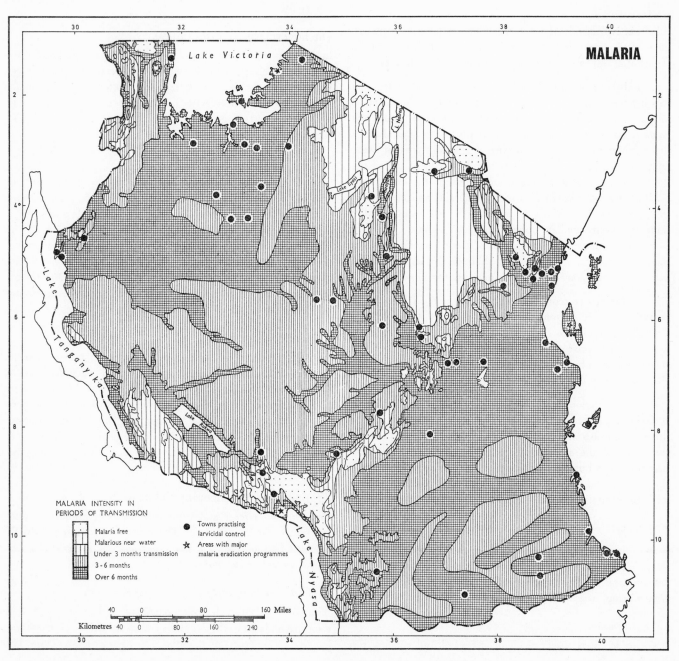

Schistosomiasis (Bilharzia)

Bilharzia probably ranks second only to malaria as a cause of human suffering and economic loss. Extensive treatment is not practicable due to the side-effects and toxicity of available drugs; moreover, cure is not always complete. In addition to parasitaemia, the disease is associated in its later stages with irreversible and sometimes fatal pathological conditions. A survey near Mwanza found fifty per cent of primary school children to be infected and twenty per cent to have already suffered irreversible damage.

1. *Distribution*

Bilharzia is transmitted when the bilharzia parasites penetrate the skin of persons in contact with infective water. Distribution of potential transmission areas is controlled by two factors:

a. Existence of suitable habitats for species of water snail which act as intermediate hosts for part of the parasite's developmental cycle. A number of species of both *Bulinus* and *Biomphalaria* act as hosts: each has a fairly distinct ecological range, the combination of these covering nearly all types of water bodies found in Tanzania. The overall pattern of the disease shows contrasts between the distributions of the two forms, *Schistosoma haemotobium* (urinary bilharzia) and *S. mansoni* (rectal bilharzia), which arise largely from contrasting distributions of the intermediate hosts. *S. mansoni* is found in a strip along the south-east and east shores of Lake Victoria almost to the exclusion of *S. haemotobium*, although the latter predominates in a broad zone of infection inland of the shore.

b. Temperature requirements of *Schistosoma* for successful completion of development from egg, through stages independent of the snail host to infective parasite. For *S. mansoni*, 27°C. for the preliminary stages and 24–27°C. for the final stages appear to be optimum, but a variation of some 10°C. on either side can probably be tolerated.

Potential develops into actual transmission through human behaviour. Firstly, water-use activities of a community determine the number and characteristics of suitable water bodies in the area and the amount of contact people have with them. Secondly, it is human contamination that initiates infection of the water: areas where people are crowded together without adequate sanitation facilities are almost invariably contaminated.

Filariasis

Bancroftian filariasis, an infection by the worm *Wurchereria bancrofti*, is transmitted by mosquito vectors, primarily *Culex fatigans* and the two anophelines responsible for most malaria transmission, *Anopheles gambiae* and *A. funestus*.

1. *Distribution*

Like malaria it is absent or slight at cool altitudes, being rare above 1000 m., and in very dry areas. Surveys of nearly 150 villages throughout the country showed a positive correlation between mean maximum and minimum temperatures and humidity on the one hand, and incidence and intensity of infection on the other. Infection covers one-fifth of the country: in the coastal areas, river valleys and other low-lying areas; also in the districts south-east and east of Lake Victoria; and in a small but intense focus on the northern shore of Lake Nyasa (lower r.h. map opposite).

2. *Control*

Curative treatment of parasitaemia is possible in individual cases, but the disabling deformities associated with acute cases – elephantiasis and hydrocoele – do not always respond well to treatment. As with malaria, mosquito control measures are effective in reducing transmission but are practicable in only a few areas.

Onchocerciasis (river-blindness)

In contrast to the other diseases considered here, the known distribution of infection by the worm *Onchocerca volvulus* (lower l.h. map opposite) is characterized by a pattern of several small, separate foci. Onchocerciasis has now been found to be more widespread and of greater medical importance than was formerly supposed.

1. *Distribution*

The vectors of onchocerciasis, *Similium* spp. flies, breed only in running water: topography and rainfall, therefore, are primary controls of its distribution. *Simulium damnosum* breeds in large rivers and small streams in both forest and savanna area. In the case of *S. neavei*, which favours dense vegetation, any deforestation may reduce transmission, but with *S. damnosum* thinning of forest as opposed to clearance may increase transmission. Development is markedly inhibited or absent at temperatures outside the range 18–28°C.

2. *Known incidence*

Established foci of infection (lower l.h. map opposite) are in the eastern Usambaras (Amani and the Sigi valley), Western Usambaras (Bumbuli area), Uluguru Mountains, Mahenge area, and Ruvuma Region. Other suspected foci include the northern shore of Lake Nyasa and Kilimanjaro District. In the well-established centres over one-third of the population is infected, incidence rates being considerably higher among the middle-aged.

Trypanosomiasis (sleeping-sickness)

Both the *rhodesiense* and *gambiense* forms of human trypanosomiasis occur in Tanzania. The former is transmitted chiefly by tsetse-flies of the *Glossina morsitans*, *G. swynnertoni* and *G. pallidipes species*, and the latter by *G. fuscipes*.

1. *Distribution of vectors*

Tsetse-fly are extremely widespread (upper r.h. map below), but each species is very selective in its choice of habitat. *G. morsitans* habitats are in tracts of miombo (*Brachystegia*) woodland. The distribution of *G. swynnertoni* relates to thorn (*Acacia-Commiphora*) woodland. It is confined to the northern part of Tanzania in two areas on either side of the Mbulu Highlands. *G. pallidipes* is more restricted, being found where thickets are plentiful or vegetation fairly dense, but not in continuous dense thicket.

2. *Incidence*

Distribution of infection is now more limited in extent. The major areas of *Trypanosoma rhodesiense* are in a block bounded by Lake Rukwa in the south, Tabora town in the east, Lake Victoria in the north, and a strip bordering Lake Tanganyika in the west (upper r.h. map below). There are also a number of smaller areas of transmission.

Within infected regions there occur 'islands' free from infection. In densely populated areas sustained modification of the natural vegetation through settlement and agriculture has eliminated tsetse habitats. In less densely populated areas partial clearance of the natural vegetation is often sufficient to destroy the particular conditions required.

Records show a marked decline in the disease over the last few decades, and actual outbreaks are now typically very localized.

HILARY PAGE

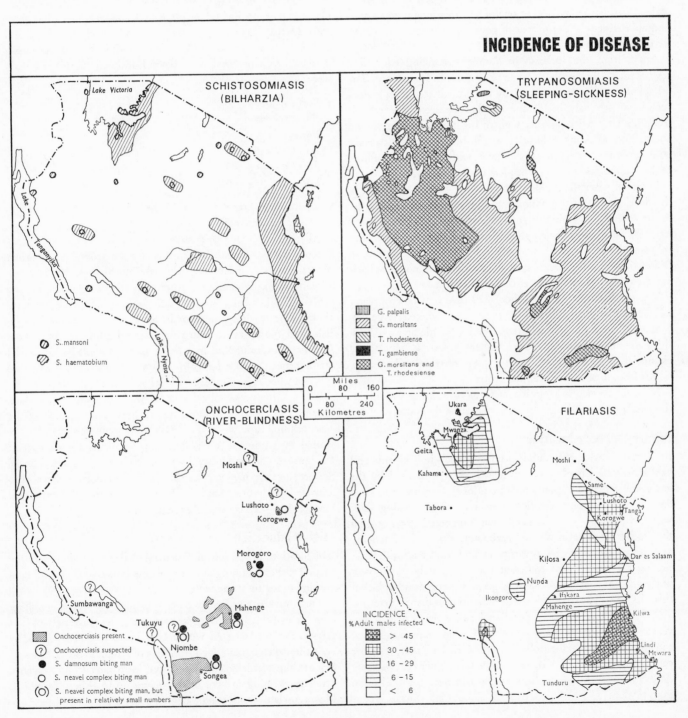

The first formal schools in Tanzania were established by the early German missions in the 1860s, but the present system reflects the educational background developed during the period of British control from 1919 to 1961. At Independence about 40 per cent of children received some schooling but fewer than 5 per cent received more than four years' education. Shortage of skilled manpower was such a grave problem that the development of secondary and higher education received maximum priority. The 1964–69 Development Plan gave self-sufficiency in trained manpower by 1980 as one of its three long-term targets, and approximately 20 per cent of government revenue has been devoted to education.

Apart from the increase in numbers receiving education, several major changes have taken place since Independence. The school system has become racially integrated, secondary school fees have been abolished, the number of secondary schools trebled, a University together with an Institute of Education and an Institute of Adult Education established and curricula have been made more relevant to the dominantly agricultural nature of the country and to an independent nation.

In recent years the whole concept of the role of education in the development of the nation has been examined. In 1967 the Arusha Declaration highlighted the national philosophy and emphasized *ujamaa* 'brotherhood' and self-reliance. This was followed by a unique contribution by President Nyerere in 'Education for self-reliance' providing a clear philosophical basis for the re-orientation of the educational system.

The emphasis at primary school will involve a much greater degree of training for life in the rural sector where a large percentage of young people will live. Besides the hierarchy of facilities described below there are other important educational channels. In agriculture there is a range of training levels upwards from local farmer-training centres.

National Service is a significant focus of training and education, and centres are located in various parts of the country.

Primary school education

In 1967, there were 3865 public primary schools in Tanzania and 758 unassisted schools (i.e. private schools not assisted by the government through grants or subventions). Enrolment totalled 823 024, 61·7 per cent of whom were boys. The teaching staff, which was almost entirely Tanzanian, numbered 16 514 so that the teacher-pupil ratio was approximately 1:50. The financing of primary schools is by government and local authorities: at present the government contributes approximately 55 per cent of the costs of rural schools and 80 per cent of urban schools, but this pattern will be changed with the abolition of district taxes.

Primary schooling is co-educational and consists of a seven-year course, although many schools as yet have only a four-year course. Of the 121 386 enrolled in Standard I in 1961, 42·4 per cent reached Standard VII. Approximately 10 per cent of Standard VII proceed to secondary school as a result of a selection examination.

Most children in urban areas attend primary schools and about half in rural areas have received some primary schooling. Kiswahili is now the teaching medium with English taught as a second language throughout the schools.

Regional variation in primary school enrolment, shown on the map, does not necessarily reflect economic development. Parts of southern and central Tanzania which are less developed and where population density is often low are well provided with schools, reflecting mission influence. More developed areas along the Great North Road, Sukumaland and the coastal areas are poorly served.

Secondary and technical education

Great expansion has taken place in secondary education since 1964. In 1967 there were 70 public secondary schools and 34 unassisted private schools, with a total enrolment of 31 542 pupils of which 75·2 per cent were boys. Enrolment figures for 1967 were:

Form 1 – 9226
Form 2 – 8571
Form 3 – 6554
Form 4 – 5460
Form 5 – 913
Form 6 – 816

In addition, at Dar es Salaam Technical College there were 577 full-time and 1500 part-time students.

All regions, as the map shows, have one or more secondary schools, but there is a marked concentration around a few urban areas: Dar es Salaam (14 schools), Moshi (14), Bukoba (6), Mwanza (6), Tabora (5). Approximately two-thirds of the schools are boarding schools, only one of which is co-educational. The teaching medium in all secondary schools is English, and most have a four-year course leading to the School Certificate examination. In 1967, 22 of the schools had fifth and sixth forms, catering for 1709 students, an increase of over 300 per cent since 1961. Of these students 83 per cent were boys.

The staffing of secondary schools has been mainly expatriate. In 1967, 72 per cent of the 1514 teachers were expatriate; the teacher-pupil ratio was 1:19·6. To enable secondary schools to be staffed by graduate Tanzanians, approximately 60 per cent of the bursaries at the University in the Faculty of Arts and Social Science and 85 per cent in the Faculty of Science have been allocated to education students. By 1970 the numbers of expatriate teachers had been considerably reduced.

Higher education

The locations of the fifteen Teachers' Colleges are shown on the map. Teacher Training at these colleges lasts two years and total enrolment for 1967 was 2590.

The University of Dar es Salaam formerly University College – was one of the three colleges constituting the University of East Africa. Founded in 1961 with a Law Faculty of 12 students, by 1969 the College had added Faculties of Arts and Social Science, Science and Medicine and Agriculture with 1400 degree students. Students wishing to take other courses go to either Nairobi or Makerere Universities. Non-degree courses are offered in Agriculture, Public Administration, Education, Statistical Training and Fisheries.

The Institute of Education, founded in 1965, associates together with the Teachers' Colleges, the University and the Ministry of Education in the development of education in Tanzania. It is involved in educational research, production of experimental teaching materials, syllabus revision and inservice courses for teachers. There is also an Institute of Adult Education which runs courses both in Dar es Salaam and in country centres.

N.B. The scale of values for primary school attendance on the map (below) is discontinuous, reflecting the grouping of the values.

JOAN BATTERSBY

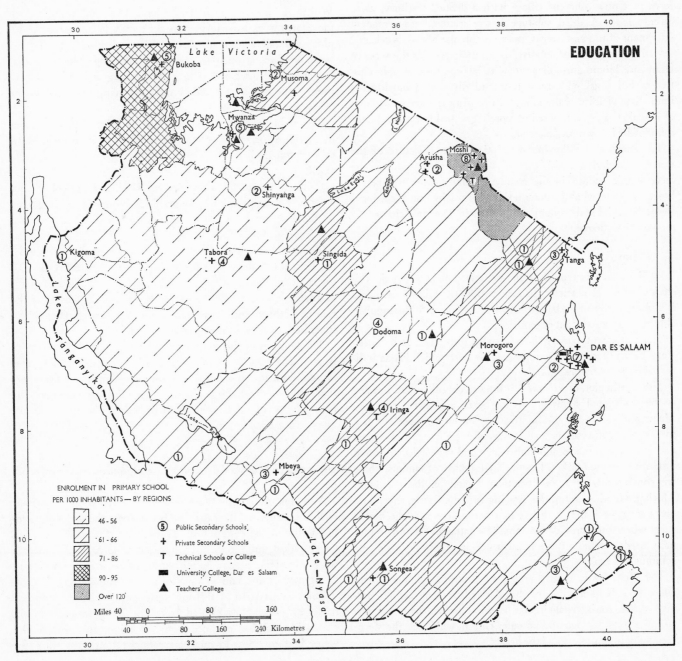

The form of traditional settlement is the most obvious manifestation of social and economic organization. In Tanzania the majority of the rural population lives in dispersed farmsteads and only in a few areas are more nucleated clusters to be found. However, the detailed distribution of houses in relation both to each other and to the land which the household farms varies considerably according to the nature of the social organization and to the form of economy.

In general five main types can be distinguished. Among dispersed settlement forms can be recognized those with complete individualization of homesteads, such as in the Meru and Kilimanjaro areas, and those where the dispersed homesteads form part of a coherent village with a defined territory, as in Sukumaland. A third sub-type is the scattered impermanent settlement of the pastoralists, most notably the Masai. Nucleated settlements can also be subdivided. In areas such as the western Usambara Mountains, villages tend to be comprised of tight clusters of buildings with most farmland distributed outside the immediate vicinity of the village. In contrast the age-set villages of Unyakyusa are composed of loosely grouped houses each surrounded by its own banana farm.

The maps and following descriptions give a picture of the range of variation which may be found between some of the large ethnic groups in the country. It must be remembered, however, that what is described is essentially the traditional form. As social and economic conditions in Tanzania change, so too do the settlements.

1. Umeru

The Meru area is typical of the densely populated fertile volcanic uplands of northern Tanzania. Like the Kilimanjaro area it is characterized by a banana-coffee economy but is distinguishable by its greater extent of pasture.

The settlement pattern is essentially dispersed, each homestead being sited on the family holding over which it has individual rights of tenure from the clan.

The family plot, or *kihamba*, is intensively cultivated. Banana is the traditional staple crop with beans and sweet potatoes. Maize and millet are the dominant grain crops. Since the late nineteenth century arabica coffee has been grown as a cash crop and is now dominant, although maize and vegetables are often produced for the market. Despite the intensity of land-use there are considerable areas of uncultivated land on the mountain which are used as communal grazing (*ngaro*). Cattle, sheep and goats are reared, the small livestock being kept near the homestead where they provide manure. The cattle are often communally herded, two or three farmers keeping their stock on one communal 'kraal'.

The Meru house is in characteristic 'cone-on-cylinder' form, although it is likely that this has derived from an earlier 'beehive' shape. An internal circular partition divides the house into an inner livestock pen and an outer ring in which are the sleeping and living quarters and the hearth.

2. Usukuma

The Wasukuma occupy part of the so-called cultivation steppe extending southwards from Lake Victoria. The region is the major source of cotton, Tanzania's leading export.

Although the pattern of settlement is dispersed in appearance it is tied to a clearly defined village organization. Each village, or *igunguli*, has a fixed boundary marked by streams or other natural features and so disposed as to comprise all of the soil categories of the local catena. This is an integral part of the village structure since each soil type has specific crop potentials. Where the village is large it may be divided into a number of sections (*vibanda*) each related to an age-set association of the young men of working age. These men carry out group work in farms and on house construction for individual families. The village is not, however, a lineage or clan unit, related families being dispersed among a number of widely scattered villages. Within the *kibanda* each family has a fixed holding in which most farm work is performed by the family labour force. Arable plots and fallows are intermixed but traditionally the fallow, *ikela* or *ilale*, is open to communal grazing. More recently, however, with pressure on land for grazing and for cash cropping, cattle owners are individually reserving grassland in the fallow for their own use.

The arable farming is characterized by ridging, in some areas by tie-ridges, on which most of the food crops are grown. However cotton, millet and tobacco are more commonly flat cultivated.

Cattle form an important part of Usukuma agriculture but are rarely integrated with the arable farming. They are grazed on the *idela* but if grass is scarce they may be sent away to better grazing elsewhere.

The Usukuma house compound (*kaya*) comprises a number of encircling hedges. The outer ring, up to fifty metres in diameter, is used as a garden for maize, potatoes or tobacco, or for pasturing calves. Inside the second hedge are the houses of the household head and of his wives, and a grain storehouse. An inner hedge encloses the *ngwalida*, or cattle pen.

The house is of the cone-on-cylinder type, about 8 m. (25 ft.) in diameter. An inner circular partition separates the outer *ibindo*, with storeroom and stall for calves, from the inner section which is divided into the *mbele*, the living section, and the *igalogalo*, which houses the small livestock. The roof space, or *kano*, is also used for storage.

3. Ugogo

Ugogo extends around Dodoma in a region of dry thorn-scrub plateau.

Although, unlike the Wamasai, the Wagogo are cultivators as well as pastoralists, the cattle herds dominate the social and economic life of the community. There is no distinct village as a geographical unit: rather the houses are spread thinly over a wide area. Houses may be moved at irregular intervals due to drought or famine, and old house sites form valuable farmland.

There is a system of shifting agriculture with cultivation of millet on large plots cleared from the scrub, usually within reasonable walking distance from the house and near to the valley bottoms. Smaller plots near to the house are tilled for groundnuts, maize and tobacco. Families have usufructuary rights on the land, deriving purely from membership of the village.

Each household has a herd of cattle which is usually pastured in common with those from four to six related households.

The squat, rectangular, flat-roofed houses are normally grouped around a square courtyard which acts as a cattle byre. The whole may or may not be surrounded by a thorn hedge.

The heavy outer posts support heavy rafters which are roofed by a mixture of dung and mud. The roof supports are set out from the walls proper which comprise closely spaced poles tied with laths and plastered with mud. Internally the house is divided into a number of rectangular rooms separating sleeping, living and cooking spaces. There is often a more open house facing the courtyard and occupied by young boys.

JOHN E MOORE

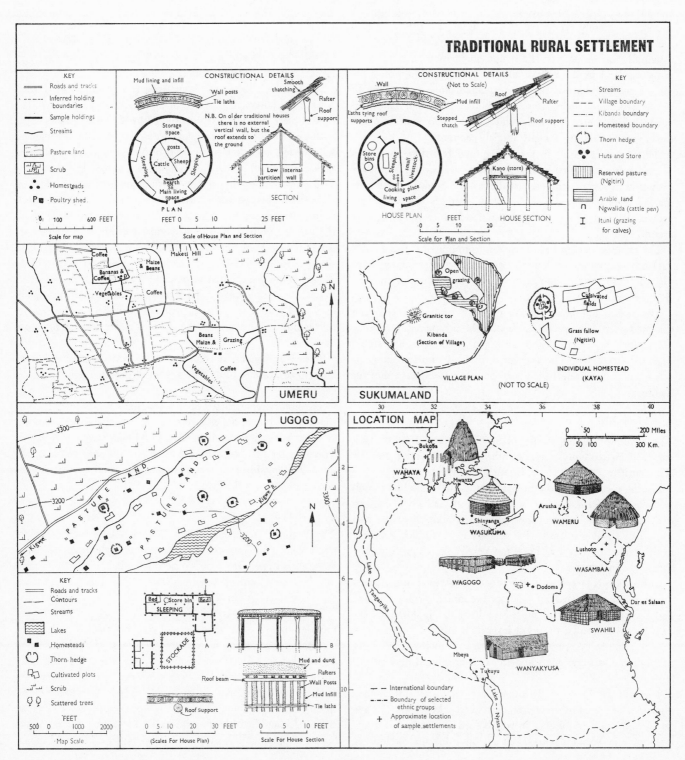

TRADITIONAL RURAL SETTLEMENT

UMERU

SUKUMALAND

UGOGO

LOCATION MAP

1. Usambaa

The western Usambara Mountains are one of the few areas of Tanzania where tightly clustered villages are found.

Most villages are sited on ridges or spurs. The number of houses varies from five or six to more than a hundred. Traditionally these settlements are lineage groupings and comprise a number of closely related families. Despite proximity of residence and relationship, however, the agricultural system is essentially individualistic. Each household owns a number of plots scattered in the valleys and on hillsides surrounding the village and are farmed by the household alone or, in case of need, with some help from neighbours. Although land was vested in the lineage it is now subject to *de facto* ownership and the buying and selling of rights is fairly common.

Bananas were formerly the staple food but they have now been largely superseded by maize and cassava. Coffee is a major cash crop in parts of the area, while around Soni, in particular, market vegetables are important. Black wattle is also extensively grown. Recently tea has become the major crop in the east around Balangai.

The farming system has developed from one of shifting cultivation, but pressure on land is now so great that fallows have virtually disappeared, and problems of soil exhaustion and erosion are serious.

The traditional house had a bee-hive form with a rough thatched roof to the ground. This has been replaced by a cone-on-cylinder type with mud plastered walls and a roughly thatched steep roof. The interior is divided into two more or less equal halves, one for living, the other for storage and for livestock.

2. Uswahili

The Swahili-speaking peoples occupy the coastal areas of Tanzania. Their economy combines fishing and cultivation and the characteristic settlement form is a nucleated village.

Fishing is carried out on the continental shelf from individually owned *ngalawa* (canoes, with a lanteen sail on a bamboo mainyard). A few dugout canoes and plank-built dhows are also used. Lines and drift and seine nets are used to catch a variety of fish including sardines, horse mackerel, sole, kingfish, tunny, barracuda and shark.

Cultivation is largely of a subsistence hoe-type, using a bush-fallow rotation. The main food crops are millet, sorghum, maize and cassava with rice and sugar-cane in wetter hollows. Where cash crops are grown the most important are coconut, mango, cashew and pawpaw. Few livestock are kept owing to tsetse-fly infestation, but some goats and chickens are found in most villages.

The village is normally a compact nucleation of houses aligned along a number of irregular streets. Most houses have an enclosed yard at the rear in which food preparation is done. The house is rectangular based on a central through-corridor. A covered porch, or *baraza*, occupies half of the frontage. The walls are of wattle-and-daub construction, and the overhanging four-sided ridged roof is loosely thatched.

3. Unyakyusa

Unyakyusa lies in southern Tanzania in the district of Rungwe.

The settlement form is a village based on a rigid social framework.

In an established village, at puberty the young men set up house apart from their parent homes and form a nucleus settlement from which they go to their parents' homes to work and eat. At the 'coming-out' of the principal heirs of the chief, the young men's settlement also 'comes out'. Land is allocated to it by the old chief and a new village is established for that age-group, their wives and families.

Within the village each homestead is a separate entity comprising the houses of the head of household and his wives. The central place, *ulubigilo*, is surrounded by the banana plots of the man and his wives. These plots are now generally interplanted with coffee. Here too are grown beans, groundnuts and vegetables. The main gardens, *imigunda*, are located in the pasture-land surrounding the village. Each household has a right to clear such plots, on which are cultivated millet, sweet potatoes, beans, groundnuts and vegetables. The uncultivated land, which is tilled in rotation, is used as communal pasture. The system is tending to change under conditions of cash cropping and land shortage so that there is often no land available for new villages. Hence many young men migrate to Dar es Salaam and other towns for employment. The cash crops vary according to locality. On the Lake Nyasa plains ox-ploughed paddy cultivation is important, while on the uplands coffee and tea predominate.

The village generally comprises a broad main street with the homesteads, often grouped by age-set of the men, aligned along each side.

The houses, constructed of bamboo, have two forms. That of the head of household is a rectangular long-house. The houses of senior wives are usually of cone-on-cylinder type similarly constructed from bamboo, with the internal walls plastered with red mud. The outside wall is unplastered, but the bamboo is often decorated with cut designs.

4. Uhaya

The Wahaya of northern West Lake Region live in compact stable village units in which the houses, as in the case of Unyakyusa, are set apart from each other. The village is not a lineage unit but most families forming a new village are friends and a close-knit social group often develops.

Each homestead forms a distinct and separate unit surrounded by the permanently cultivated *kibanja* land. Here bananas and coffee are interplanted and most of the basic foods such as beans, maize, sweet potatoes, sorghum and groundnuts are grown. Under more modern practices bananas and coffee may be grown separately and with officially recommended spacing. Surrounding the village is open grassland known as *rweya*. Although this serves primarily as pasture for the long-horned Ankole and short-horned Zebu cattle, with problems of land shortage, the *rweya* is being increasingly cropped on a land rotation system. Rights to use the *rweya* are free to all village members whereas *vibanja* land is normally individually owned.

The cultivated land on the *rweya, emisiri,* is used primarily for bambara nuts, groundnuts, beans, sweet potatoes, cassava, millet and maize.

Although livestock are important, by no means all families in a village own cattle. They are, however, an important part of the economy since one of their main functions is to provide manure.

The traditional house is of the bee-hive type with an extensive forecourt leading to the house porch. Low internal partitions divide the house into a number of sections for beds, for livestock and for cooking.

JOHN E MOORE

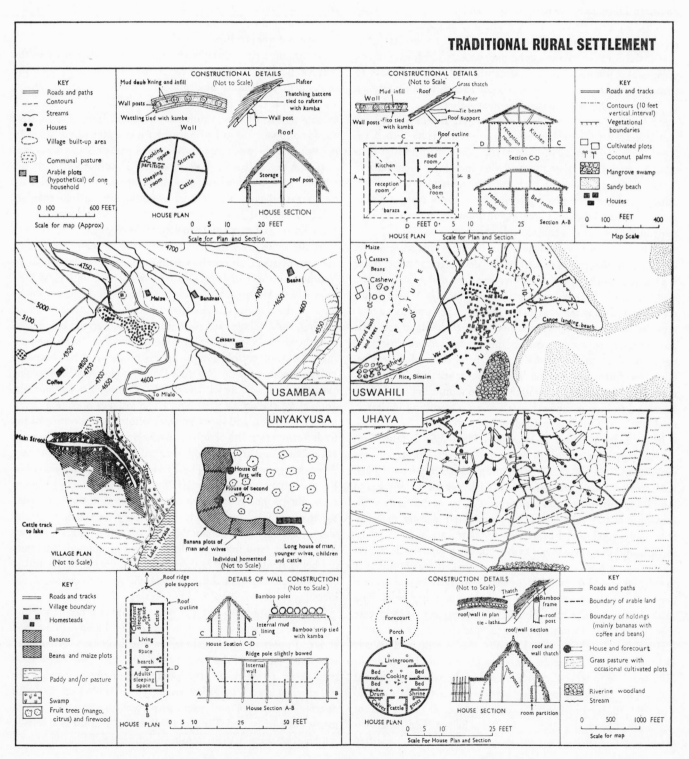

TRADITIONAL RURAL SETTLEMENT

The idea of establishing new agricultural villages has for some time been a cornerstone of Tanzania's development policy. Two basic considerations have always been part of the rationale for this approach. Firstly, there has been the desire to reduce population pressure in a number of high-density areas – notably in Kilimanjaro, the Pare and Usambara Mountains and part of the Southern Highlands – where there is land shortage. This could be achieved through the settling of the surplus population in less crowded, generally lowland, areas. Secondly, it has become clear that if the rural population could be concentrated into compact villages the provision of infrastructure and social services to them could be made much more simply and cheaply. Over most of Tanzania the traditional settlement pattern is one of scattered farmsteads and hamlets, and in 1962 President Nyerere noted that: 'Before we can bring any benefits of modern development to the farmers of Tanganyika, the very first step is to make it possible for them to start living in village communities.'

While these two considerations have remained important, other aims have been given prominence at various stages of the programme, and the form and organization of the proposed new settlements have shown considerable variation.

Even during the colonial period some new villages were set up, such as the compact settlements designed to make tsetse eradication more simple. However the first major programme resulted from the recommendations of the 1960 World Bank mission. A distinction was made between the 'transformation' and the 'improvement' approaches to rural development. The improvement approach involves the gradual improvement of agricultural methods through the existing extension service. The transformation approach, on the other hand, aims to achieve rapid progress through the concentration of investment and trained manpower in a few areas, resulting in drastic modifications of existing methods of production.

In the first Five Year Development Plan (1964–69) the Tanzanian Government clearly opted for the transformation approach, and proposed the setting up of seventy-four village settlements. These villages would each consist of some 250 families and involve a total investment of about 3 million shillings and would resettle farmers from high density areas in potentially good sites in less well-populated areas. Each settlement would grow one major cash crop, using new methods, fertilizers and a high degree of mechanization. It was hoped that the settlers would form a nucleus of modern farmers and act as a demonstration to farmers living in the surrounding areas. The Rural Settlement Commission had been set up in 1963 to initiate this programme, and in 1965 control was taken over by a new division in the Ministry of Lands, Settlement and Water Development. Considerable investment was to be made in infrastructure to serve these schemes, and the whole investment was to be recovered over a 20–25 year period. Supervision was also to be provided for each scheme, in the form of managers, technicians and clerks. The division also took over control of the settlements set up on the sites of the abortive

Groundnut Scheme, and the Israeli-sponsored Agridev Schemes in the Lake Victoria area. By the end of 1965 22 pilot settlement schemes had been established, consisting of a total of some 6000 hectares.

It soon became clear that the programme was running into severe difficulties. Most schemes had been overcapitalized, leaving the settlers with a heavy burden of debt. Many settlers were found to be unsuitable, and there were severe problems of discipline. Much of detailed planning had been poor, and there were problems of water-supply and general economic organization. The Government soon appreciated these problems and the whole programme was slowed down, and there were drastic cuts in cost wherever possible.

At the same time there were important developments in the political field, culminating in the Arusha Declaration. With the subsequent publication of President Nyerere's policy statement on 'Socialism and Rural Development' the whole approach to new settlement took a different direction. Instead of massive outside support, the importance of rural mobilization through ujamaa villages was stressed. The pilot village settlements had always suffered from a lack of settler identification with the scheme, so it was important to encourage farmers to build up their own villages. The aim of grouping people into compact villages remained, but the transformation approach was rejected as a solution to the national problem of development.

At the same time, there was a rejection of many features of the improvement approach. Communal work on land held in common by the village was to replace the previous pattern of improving existing smallholdings. The map opposite shows some of the ujamaa villages already established. At the time of writing, new villages are springing up all over the country so that there can be no claim of completeness for the map opposite. The most notable success in this programme has been the villages making up the Ruvuma Development Association. The most important of these, *Matetereka, Litowa, Liweta* and *Kakong'o* are shown on the map. These villages operate as communal, economic and social units, resembling the working of the traditional extended family. Another successful village is Mbambara, in Tanga Region, originally based on sisal but now diversifying its economy. The President has constantly stressed the need to persuade, rather than force, people to join together in such villages, and has pointed out the dangers of trying to build too many villages too quickly. An attempt was made to create, almost overnight, large numbers of ujamaa villages in Handeni District, and major problems were encountered. Attempts are being made to modify the village settlements set up in the earlier phase and to establish ujamaa villages to make use of the investments already made in these sites.

Mention should also be made of a number of other new settlement types, outside the main stream of developments described above. Important among these are the irrigation settlements, some of them established more than ten years ago. There have been some problems in developing the discipline needed for the efficient use of irrigation water, but it is obvious that such attempts to control and use water resources will be vital in many parts of central Tanzania. Moreover, it must not be forgotten that some settlements have been established with very little outside encouragement. The example of Changalikwa is shown. This is a village set up by farmers from the nearby Lushoto area, which has some problems of land shortage, and is in many ways an offshoot of the traditional farming system found there.

Thus the whole new settlement experienced has been extremely varied, and has met with mixed success. However, the success of many of the *ujamaa* villages already established gives real hope for the future.

JOHN McKAY

NEW RURAL SETTLEMENT

Former Agridev schemes
Village settlement schemes
State farms
Some early ujamaa villages
Irrigation settlements
Other selected new settlements

Although there is a tradition of urban life in Tanzania which goes back for nearly one thousand years, urban development has not been continuous, and many towns have remained small while some have degenerated and even disappeared as the basis of their livelihood changed or was destroyed. Such were the towns arising out of Portuguese trade or those associated with the slave trade. The distribution of the older towns was largely confined to the coastal areas (see Section 43, p. 102). The few towns in the interior which came to prominence mainly in the nineteenth century, notably Tabora, Mpwapwa and Ujiji, were partly a result of the westward penetration of Arab activity in East Africa. The major influence of the ancient towns was the evolution and dissemination of the Swahili language and, to a minor extent, the spread of Islam.

During the German period the establishment of an administrative structure, the evolution of a communication network, the establishment of social services, and the development of commerce and a monetary economy all contributed to the widespread distribution of incipient town forms. Since the establishment of the administration was often associated with pacification, in many of these places the *boma*, or office of the administration was the largest and most important physical structure. However, at Dar es Salaam and Tanga there was a formal attempt to define and to grant to the town a form of local government with the power to levy taxes and manage land.

A Township Ordinance was passed early in the British period. At the same time towns were officially gazetted on the suggestion of the administration and with the approval of the governor. Such townships had boundaries, could fix and levy rates and had a comprehensive set of laws pertaining to health and government. Starting with a few important centres like Dar es Salaam, Tanga, and Mwanza, nearly 50 townships were created. For only 34 of those townships was there any attempt made to keep up their status. Official concession of a township status, in fact, had little impact on its growth. After the late 1950s no other townships were created, and only 15 of the townships were granted urban local government. Dar es Salaam is a city, Tanga a municipality, while others have township authorities.

The collective growth of the thirty-four townships since 1948 is summarized in Table 54, p. 170.

These figures reflect the overwhelming rural component of the country's population. However, despite the small size of the urban population there have been some unfavourable developments. For instance, the urban population has more than trebled since 1948, but this has not been matched with comparable growth of amenities and services, thus leading to a breakdown in acceptable social conditions and response. As in most developing countries, there is the problem of the disproportionate growth of the capital city. In 1967 Dar es Salaam accounted for 40 per cent of the urban population. Factors leading to the concentration of development in Dar es Salaam have been described elsewhere. If the population of the nine other large towns were to be included, they would account for nearly 85 per cent of the urban

population, thus emphasizing the small size of the majority of towns in Tanzania. Singida, Shinyanga and Ruvuma Regions do not have any townships. The former townships and Bukoba all have fewer than 10 000 inhabitants. Table 55, p. 170, gives the percentage of people living in townships and former townships in the different regions.

Three major factors account for the varying growth of the urban areas in the different Regions. First, administrative decisions have played an important part. Thus the former provincial headquarters had a headstart and assured growth because the colonial administration was the main source of employment. Towns which grew from this impetus include Dar es Salaam, Morogoro, Dodoma, Tanga, Ujiji/Kigoma, Tabora, Mwanza, Lindi, Mtwara, and Mbeya. Among these towns only Lindi and Mbeya have populations below 20 000. The former was displaced by Mtwara which has taken over most of the functions once performed by Lindi. Since, with the exception of Lindi, all former provincial headquarters are capitals of Regions, sustained if modest growth for all these towns can be expected. However, the following must be added to the list: Bukoba, Musoma, Arusha, Shinyanga, Songea, Iringa, and Singida, all of which are new capitals. Secondly, the rate of the growth of the towns has been influenced by the productivity and development of the areas in which the towns are situated. In this respect Tanga (60 900), the second largest town in mainland Tanzania, is the centre for the sisal industry. Minor centres for the crop are Morogoro, Korogwe, Mtwara/Lindi and Kilosa. Mwanza (34 800), the third largest town in Tanzania, and Mtwara are centres of cotton and cashew-growing areas respectively. The production of yet another important crop, coffee, partly explains the growth of Bukoba, Moshi, Arusha, and Mbeya. There are only a few centres which have grown as a result of mineral exploitation. Mwadui, the diamond centre, has grown to an impressive town (though not gazetted) of 8000 inhabitants while Chunya, Mpanda and Uvinza had their heydays during the exploitation of gold, lead and salt respectively. Thirdly, transportation, especially where break of bulk occurs, is another important factor which influences urban growth. In an export-orientated economy the ocean terminals at Dar es Salaam, Tanga, Mtwara have benefited greatly. Similarly, but to a lesser degree, the lake ports of Mwanza, Musoma, Bukoba, and Kigoma have attracted population. Dodoma, Tabora, Arusha and Korogwe owe their importance to their position in the road-rail network.

Special mention must be made of Arusha which has risen from the tenth position in 1957 to become the fourth largest town in 1967, with a population of 32 300 inhabitants. Its position in relation to Kenya and Uganda made it the logical choice, in 1965, for the headquarters of the East Africa Community. In addition, the cultivation of cereals and coffee, and the development of pastoralism and dairying in the surrounding region help to emphasize its importance.

The second Five Year Development Plan proposes a re-orientation of urban growth and development. First, the growth of medium sized towns will be encouraged in order to provide facilities and stimulate economic growth of the surrounding regions. Secondly, attempts will be made to correct the excessive growth of Dar es Salaam by decentralization including the siting, wherever possible, of industries in other urban areas. Thirdly, urban areas showing a vigorous potential will be given a further boost during the plan as will areas which have hitherto suffered from neglect. In the former category will be Tanga, Moshi-Arusha, Mwanza; while in the latter will be towns in the areas to the south, especially Mtwara and Mbeya. Other towns selected for concentrated development are Morogoro, Dodoma and Tabora.

Service centres

With more pressing priorities in the nation, it is likely that the lapses and anomalies in the recognition and definition of towns will remain in Tanzania. Moreover, no attempt has ever been made to define towns on the basis of the threshold population, so that even as late as 1952, the smallest township of Kilwa Masoko had a population of only 175 inhabitants; at the other extreme, Dar es Salaam had a population of over 99 000 inhabitants. Yet there were numerous villages with populations several times larger than Kilwa Masoko which were not recognized as towns. These anomalies still remain so that Bukoba, capital of West Lake Region and with a population of 8300 is a township, but Singida, also a capital of a region and with a population exceeding 9000 is not. Since towns, whether they are recognized or not, come into being because of the services they provide for the rural areas, the lapses in recognition of towns give an inadequate picture of the service centres in the country. It is important that some attempt be made to bridge this gap especially

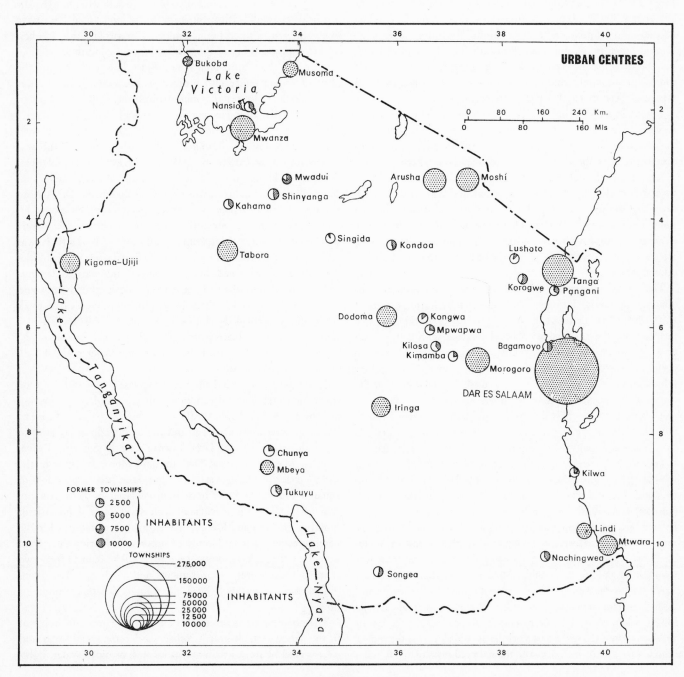

as in the future the quality of life and stimulation for the development of the rural areas will increasingly come from service centres.

Four very broad categories of services can be defined, namely, administration, communication, commerce and social services. Within each category are a variety of services. It will be noticed that some services are attracted because of location. For instance, junctions are considered as a service because these sites often attract amenities. Economics dictate that for most of the services there will be a hierarchy. Thus services at the lowest level will handle routine matters and those requiring only a small supporting population. For instance, the judiciary services have primary courts, district courts, resident magistrates' courts and at the apex there are the high courts with *puisne* judges. There are over 800 primary courts but high courts at only four places. High courts handle only major offences and appeals from the low courts. Table 58, p. 171, gives the variety of services and an allocation of points on a scale 'high', 'medium' and 'low'. Several other important variables could have been introduced, but the data for these could not be verified. Only centres with three or more points from two services have been considered. On this basis there are nearly two hundred centres.

The majority of people in Tanzania rely on these centres for services. This is indicated in their widespread distribution in the country (See map 58, p. 161). The clustering in the northern districts reflects the development that has gone ahead in these areas. Among the categories of services the administrative structure is best developed, while the social and commercial structures are the least developed. The majority of centres have a population in excess of 1000 inhabitants within a radius of 1½ kilometres. Improvements within these centres will therefore affect a larger percentage of the people than they will in the official 'towns'.

The major characteristics of Tanzanian towns can best be obtained by taking into consideration three background factors. First, the urban areas are largely a product of immigration of people from the rural areas. Natural increase within the urban areas is still insignificant. Secondly, during most of the colonial period the indigenous people were considered as temporary inhabitants of the towns to provide unskilled labour. Thirdly, towns were concentration areas for the non-African population.

Movement to towns is due to a combination of factors associated with the desire to experience a new way of life and earn a cash income. In contrast to immigration from selective regions to agricultural areas, movement to the towns is from diverse areas so that the composition of the urban population is very heterogeneous. For instance, even in a small township like Kahama (3400) it was found that nearly 70 tribes were represented. The pattern of immigration was for young able-bodied males to move into urban areas. However, owing to a number of factors, including low wages in the towns, the foothold in the rural areas was maintained as long as possible. More recently there has been a tendency for the young school-leavers to move to the towns and with this trend there has been a slight change in the male/female immigration ratio. However, despite improvements in recent years, the latest census shows a very large imbalance in the male : female ratio. Thus in contrast to the national ratio of 100 females

to 95 males, the average ratio for the towns was 100:117. The towns of Arusha, Moshi and Mtwara had unduly high figures of 132, 129 and 128 respectively. Only five small towns, viz. Nansio, Ujiji, Kahama, Kondoa and Tukuyu had ratios in which females exceeded males. Another demographic characteristic of the towns is that most of the population of the town is young.

Since most of the towns were a product of colonialism the non-African population tended to concentrate in the urban areas. This was specially marked in Dar es Salaam where since the 1930's nearly a third of the population consisted of non-Africans, though they constituted less than 5 per cent of the total population. Among the non-Africans the Asians are numerically more than the Europeans. The Asian population is nationally less diversified, over 50 per cent being from India, 25 per cent from the Arabian peninsula and about 6,000 are from Pakistan. The European population is nationally more diversified though the majority are still British. Superimposed along racial lines were wide differences in economic and social status and this was best reflected in the siting of the residential zones and their relationship to the other functional zones. Since independence and the shift of responsibility into indigenous hands the urban centres are gradually reflecting national involvement.

Functionally, all towns had three residential areas and a service zone consisting of government offices. The residential areas were designated as low, medium and high density zones and this was a euphemism for European, Asian and African residential areas. Since the colonial government in Tanzania absolved itself from any major municipality or township housing scheme, the African residential areas were a product of spontaneous development. The semi-permanent Swahili house-type constructed of wattle and mud became widespread in all towns. Basically it was designed as a six-roomed house which offered several possibilities for sub-dividing to accommodate single and married tenants. Where areas were planned, each block consisted of houses and compounds arranged back to back. Since the houses had weak foundations, vertical development was absent. All towns had a permanent market place which generally formed the core of the African residential areas. This was also the major node of long distance and countryside buses.

In the post-war period the rapid increase in migration to the towns accelerated the deterioration in the standard of housing and overcrowded, haphazardly built shelters began to appear. These squatter areas are large and frequently appear adjacent to the industrial zones of large towns: Dar es Salaam, Tanga, Arusha, Moshi, Mwanza, Dodoma and Morogoro. One of the major tasks of the government has been the demolition of squatter areas and these have been replaced by better quality cement houses with corrugated iron sheet roofs. The task of building medium and low cost housing has been allocated to the newly created National Housing Corporation. During the second Five Year Plan, 15,000 units of housing will be built in forty-two centres. To accelerate improvements and ameliorate living conditions most towns will have site and service preparation for housing tracts.

The non-African quarters of the town were generally adjacent to the service establishment, offices and commercial areas and were served by most urban amenities such as piped water, lighting and surfaced streets. In most towns the zone of government offices and services was distinctly set aside from other functional zones. Stretches of open spaces separated the different services. The bungalows of the senior administrative staff, mostly Europeans, were closest to government offices, and formed the second racial residential area. Finally, since commerce, both wholesale and retail, was entrenched in the hands of Asians, the commercial core formed the principal residential area for the Asian community. This aspect was more exclusive for the larger towns. In the small towns the commercial area was strung along the main road, while in the larger towns it consisted of several blocks with

storied buildings. Sports fields and major lines of communication separated various residential zones.

With independence the more obvious anomalies have begun to disappear. Although the low, medium and high density residential areas remain, there has been upward mobility based on economic rather than mainly along racial factors. This is especially true in the former low density residential areas. More attention is also being devoted to the high density residential areas. One must also anticipate other changes especially in the composition of the commercial structure of the towns.

ADOLFO MASCARENHAS

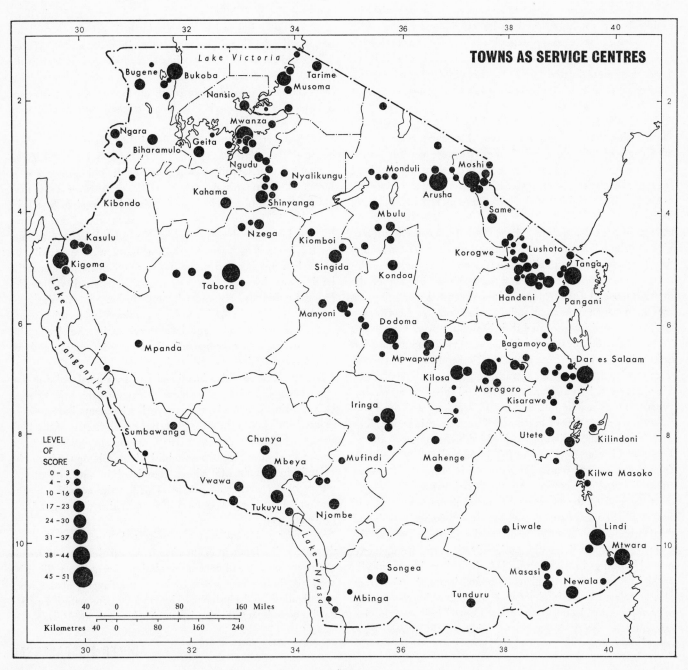

57 THE GROWTH AND FUNCTION OF DAR ES SALAAM

The area now covered by the city of Dar es Salaam had been the site of several villages, none of which were of any historical significance prior to the nineteenth century. Unlike the other coastal towns of Tanzania, the recorded history of Dar es Salaam is recent.

Therefore, the precursor of modern Dar es Salaam is often considered to be the settlement deliberately established in the 1860s by Sultan Majid of Zanzibar. A palace and several stone buildings were constructed mostly to the west of the present City Hall. By 1867, the settlement had nine hundred inhabitants. Following the death of the sultan in 1870, and in the absence of any active support to encourage its growth, the city rapidly began to decline and to lose in importance to older centres which were more natural centres of communication and which had stronger commercial links than Dar es Salaam.

German colonial activity in East Africa in the late nineteenth century resulted in a 'station' being established at Dar es Salaam in 1887 by the German East Africa Company (see Map 57a.). Although the Company appropriated land, its rule was of too short a duration to have any effect. However, some of the advantages of the site, especially the port, were not lost on the Germans. In January 1891 the German administration shifted the capital of their newly founded colony from Bagamoyo to Dar es Salaam. This decision revitalized the town and had a lasting influence. As a capital city, and the main link between the metropolitan power and the colony, there was a concentration of high-ranking civil servants and supporting staff. To accommodate them, impressive public and residential houses were built, most of them concentrated along the north-eastern side of the town. Imposing structures were also constructed along the present Independence Avenue and Azania Front by the German trading firms which relocated their businesses from Zanzibar to Dar es Salaam. However, without any good communication links with the interior, economic and other factors of growth were restricted. In 1905, the construction of the Central Railway Line was started from Dar es Salaam and this gave a new impetus to growth. The introduction of electricity and the establishment of a number of hotels also date from this period. The completion of the railway coincided with the outbreak of the First World War, so that the full impact of the railway was delayed for several years. After the British capture of Dar es Salaam in 1916, it became an important garrison town.

At the end of the German rule most of the town was still confined to the southern section, between Msimbazi Creek and the Harbour. However the basis for the future growth of the town was established. Firstly considerable investment in governmental buildings in the town made it difficult and economically prohibitive for any future plans for major decentralization from Dar es Salaam to be implemented. Secondly with the paucity of transportation in the country, the Central Railway Line became a major artery so that the town become the premier gateway of the country.

The third factor which had an important influence on the growth of the town, especially during the British period, was the socio-economic pattern of political development. In a situation in which colonial rule assured that comparatively well-paid and skilled jobs were the monopoly of aliens, the wages of the indigenous labour force were very low. The indivisibility factor, i.e. the interdependence of skilled and professionally qualified people also increased the number of aliens in Dar es Salaam. Thus, in 1913 18 per cent of all the Europeans and 11 per cent of all the Asians in the country were resident in Dar es Salaam. The corresponding figure in 1952 had increased to 30 per cent in both cases. It thus became viable for craftsmen and family enterprises to establish services and service industries. By the late 1940s some industrial establishments had become large enough to necessitate the creation of the Pugu Road Industrial Estate. For the reasons already mentioned and because of the availability of power, light, water and subsidiary services, other industries were established and Dar es Salaam became the leading industrial centre in the country. Wholesaling and import and export business made Dar es Salaam the leading commercial and financial centre of the country also. Developments were accelerated in all aspects during the post Second World War period, so that the population swelled from 69 000 in 1948 to 128 000 in 1957.

With the attainment of nationhood, in December 1961, there began a new phase in the growth of Dar es Salaam. As it was the capital of a sovereign state, many of the old functions were increased in magnitude. Thus, while there were only nine government ministries in 1955 they had increased to fifteen by 1963. In addition, new functions were taken on and two of these had an important bearing on the city growth. The nine consulates in Dar es Salaam prior to Independence rapidly increased in number and many were promoted to ambassadorial level. Thus there are now representatives from fifty countries living in the city. Secondly, because in 1961 it was the most southern country in Africa to have obtained Independence and because of Tanzania's stand in political affairs, the city has become an important centre for liberation movements and for Pan-African affairs.

Improved industrial, educational and vocational training and wage regulations have considerably increased the prosperity of Dar es Salaam. Already, three new developments have made a marked imprint on the city. First, the establishment of the University has almost created a large satellite town. Secondly, a new industrial estate was established at Ubungo where the Friendship Textile Mill alone, completed in 1967, offers employment for over 3000 people. Thirdly, the activities of the National Housing Corporation have opened new areas and improved others.

In 1967 a Canadian team presented a master plan for the future development of the city. If the existing growth trends continue the city will have a population of nearly 2 million by 1989. As the Government is aware of the dangers of the rapid urbanization of the principal city, more recent national policy has been to decentralize and plan development away from Dar es Salaam.

ADOLFO MASCARENHAS

134

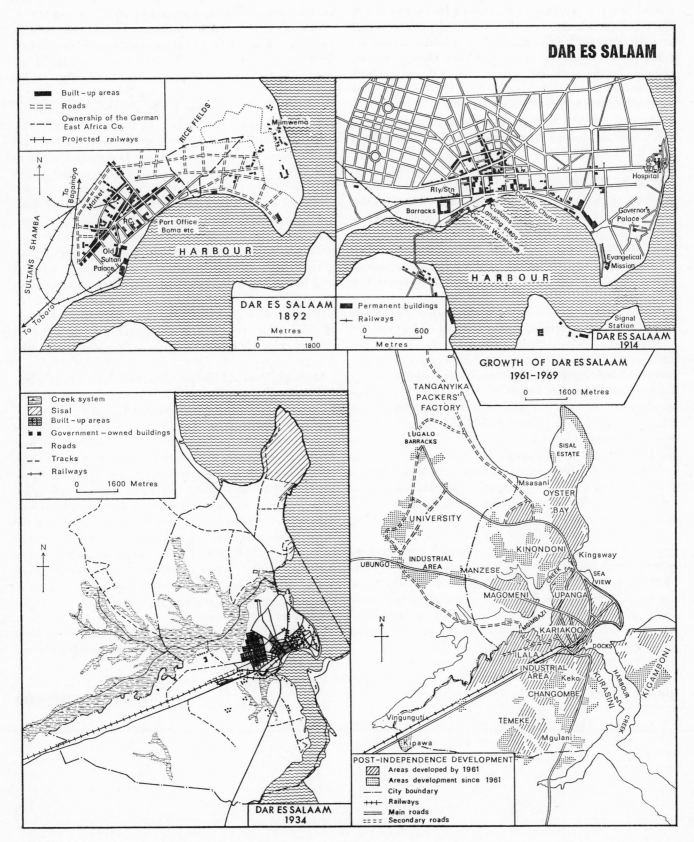

DAR ES SALAAM

Legend (top-left map):
- Built-up areas
- Roads
- Ownership of the German East Africa Co.
- Projected railways

RICE FIELDS

Mjimwema

N

To Bagamoyo

SULTAN'S SHAMBA

Market

To Tabora

R.C.

Old Sultan Palace

Port Office Boma etc

HARBOUR

DAR ES SALAAM 1892

Metres
0   1800

Legend (1914 map):
- Permanent buildings
- Railways

0   600
Metres

Rly/Stn

Barracks

Customs Landing steps
Central Warehouse

Catholic Church

Hospital

Governor's Palace

Evangelical Mission

HARBOUR

Signal Station

DAR ES SALAAM 1914

GROWTH OF DAR ES SALAAM 1961-1969

0   1600 Metres

TANGANYIKA PACKERS' FACTORY

LUGALO BARRACKS

SISAL ESTATE

Msasani

OYSTER BAY

UNIVERSITY

KINONDONI   Kingsway

UBUNGO   INDUSTRIAL AREA

MANZESE

MAGOMENI   UPANGA

SEA VIEW

CREEK

MSIMBAZI

KARIAKOO

DOCKS

ILALA

INDUSTRIAL AREA   Keko

CHANGOMBE

KURASINI

HARBOUR CREEK

KIGAMBONI

Vingunguti

Kipawa

TEMEKE

Mgulani

POST-INDEPENDENCE DEVELOPMENT
- Areas developed by 1961
- Areas development since 1961
- City boundary
- Railways
- Main roads
- Secondary roads

Legend (1934 map):
- Creek system
- Sisal
- Built-up areas
- Government-owned buildings
- Roads
- Tracks
- Railways

0   1600 Metres

N

DAR ES SALAAM 1934

Physical features and the effect of past social and economic conditions are very evident in the existing land use pattern of Dar es Salaam. The site of the city is contained within a lowland area. Development on the relatively even marine terrace has taken place without any major problems. Outside the city boundary to the north and west are low hills; to the north Observation Hill and to the west the Pugu Hills. In recent years the city has begun to encroach on to these hills.

The main physical features which have strongly influenced the spread and brought spatial discontinuity of the built-up areas have been the creek systems. For instance, the creek system centred around the harbour has restricted the southward expansion of the city. The city is further sub-divided into smaller segments by the minor east-to-west orientated Kurasini creek and the Mzinga creek and by the minor valleys which open into these creeks. The alignment of the other major creek, the Msimbazi, is also east to west. Tributary valleys, particularly north of the creek, once again break up the continuity of the built-up areas. Once the major creeks were crossed development was relatively simple.

Because land on the north-west of the harbour was already occupied before their arrival, the German East Africa Company and the German Administration focused attention on the north-eastern side of the harbour. Since the main function of the city was an administrative one, the Germans were quick to put up imposing administrative buildings along the sea front. Immediately to the north of the Government offices there was a large park which later became available for the extension of residential quarters for civil servants. The land use pattern in the north-west still retains its original function.

In the areas already occupied since the time of Majid, changes also took place. To keep down capital costs Asian businessmen reserved the section of the buildings closest to the lanes and streets for commerce, while the areas behind served as living quarters. Soon they consolidated their position and as business flourished the usual horizontal development of living quarters was restricted and the new buildings consisted of tall several-storeyed, multiple-dwelling units. By the 1930s the duality of commerce and residence in the same area was firmly established. New additions since Independence have increased vertical development in the central business area to ten or more storeys.

Little attention was given to the welfare of the masses of people during the colonial régime, although Kariakoo and parts of Ilala were planned. In these areas what emerged was the adaptability of the predominantly rural Swahili house to a high-density urban setting. Thus compared to the 87 persons per acre in the city centre the densities at Ilala and Kariakoo are 103 and 183 respectively. The large market places at Kariakoo and Ilala form the cores of their respective areas and Kariakoo is beginning to become a secondary central business area.

West of the port, land use is first dominated by the railways which branch out to the various industrial establishments along the Pugu Road. This industrial estate was started in the late 1940s. With the generally low wages, large influx of job seekers, and lack of accommodation, industrial activity triggered off slum development in the neighbouring district of Keko, and in parts of Yombo and Buguruni. In the early 1950s Msimbazi Creek was crossed by the Morogoro Road and the Magomeni residential area was rapidly developed and occupied. For the higher income bracket, low density housing, with all amenities and in close proximity to the sea was first opened at Sea View and in the 1940s at Oysterbay, Msasani and Kurasini. Later the high density areas of Msasani village and Kinondoni developed. Upanga and Changombe also developed as residential areas. Across Gerezani Creek development has generally been slower and since Independence more and more land is resorting to institutional use. With the increasing importance of the port, both sides of the southern creek are being developed, i.e. at Kurasini there is an important warehouse area and on the opposite shore at Kigamboni is located the oil refinery which will become the nucleus of yet another industrial estate.

Major additions and changes of emphasis have occurred since Independence. Expensive site development has taken place on Observation Hill and the high rise buildings at the University have created a satellite city. East of the University are the Lugalo barracks and beyond is the old meat-canning plant. To the west Ubungo is gradually being filled by squatters. Farther south along Morogoro Road Manzese is rapidly developing with densities higher than at Kariakoo and with even fewer amenities. These developments have been intensified by the creation of a large industrial estate. Apart from the extensive flat land the Ubungo industrial estate takes advantage of the major arterial roadway into the interior of the country and to Zambia. The National Housing Corporation has tried to forestall deteriorating living conditions. Slums at Keko, Buguruni, and parts of Magomeni have been replaced by better quality, multiple-dwelling residential houses.

The city propers covers only 82.59 square kilometres which is less than half of the statutory planning area and only 7 per cent of the Master Plan study area. The existing land use within the statutory planning area is summarized in Table 56, p. 170.

ADOLFO MASCARENHAS

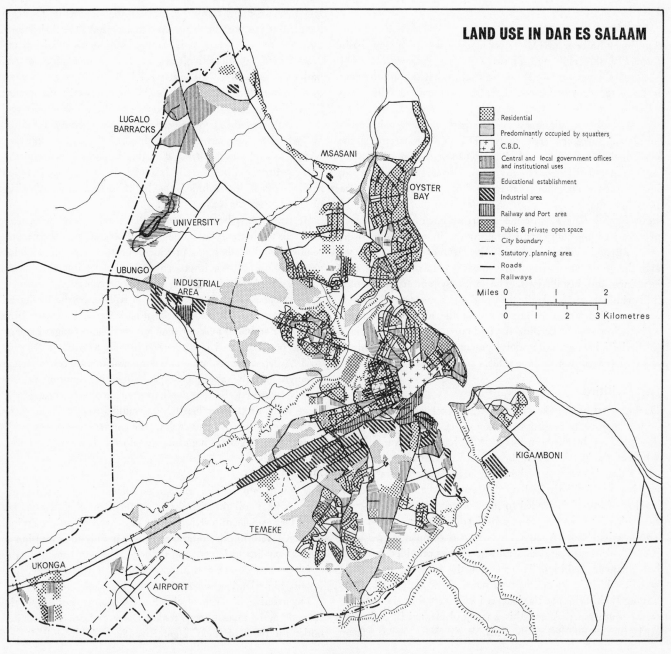

LAND USE IN DAR ES SALAAM

Residential
Predominantly occupied by squatters
C.B.D.
Central and local government offices
and institutional uses
Educational establishment
Industrial area
Railway and Port area
Public & private open space
City boundary
Statutory planning area
Roads
Railways

Miles 0   1   2

0   1   2   3 Kilometres

LUGALO
BARRACKS

MSASANI

OYSTER
BAY

UNIVERSITY

UBUNGO

INDUSTRIAL
AREA

KIGAMBONI

TEMEKE

UKONGA

AIRPORT

Though there was some Arab interest in the harbour of Dar es Salaam as early as the 1860s, the development of Dar es Salaam as a modern port dates from no further back than the German period. The imposition of effective European control over East Africa coincided with an era when steamships had already begun to dominate world ocean transport. The numerous calling stations for sailing vessels which were strung along the central and southern coast of East Africa and which had been used from time immemorial were generally unable to adjust to the new era and so they rapidly declined. In contrast, the site of Dar es Salaam lent itself to new developments, and once supporting overland lines of communication were established its position as the principal port was assured.

The site

The inner harbour of Dar es Salaam consists of a tidal basin formed by the coalescence of two drowned creek systems. The physical advantages of the site are considerable. In the first instance the drowned creeks have so far provided fairly deep water – certainly adequate for most ships on the East African run. Secondly the alignment and shape of the two main creeks supply safe, well-sheltered waters. Thirdly, the streams at the head of the creeks have a low incidence of sedimentation and so, to date, dredging has only been necessary to bring about improvements and not merely to keep the channel open. Fourthly, the infusion of fresh water and the two-way tidal scour forcing its way through a narrow opening have helped to form an important channel linking the inner harbour to the ocean beyond. Fifthly, although the terraces between the sea and the shore are narrow they have provided sites for port buildings and installations. The creek system has prevented indiscriminate use of land, thus making development possible as the need arose. The importance of the natural advantages and the low cost of keeping the harbour operational, especially in the initial stages, when developments leading to the growth of the port were not so discernible, cannot be over stressed.

Port facilities

During most of the German period the port was not modified by any major engineering operation. Since the early town had developed on the northern shores of the harbour, advantage was taken of the north-western beach-head at Kurasini creek. For over a decade cargo was laboriously man-handled from lighters and boats and then rolled up the beach. To facilitate the unloading of materials needed for the construction of the railway, a wooden jetty and a crane capable of lifting two tons were completed in 1905. A quay on piles was completed two years later. Sheds, four cranes and railway sidings provided primitive but adequate facilities. To cater for the growing number of vessels, which included coasters, naval ships and vessels functioning within the port, a dockyard was started at the entrance to the southern creek and this was supplemented by a floating dock. By the outbreak of the First World War, Dar es Salaam handled nearly 50 per cent of the country's imports but only 16 per cent of its exports.

The basic German plan for the port was retained by the British. To handle the increasing volume of trade, a lighterage wharf was added in 1929 and reclamation work towards the south-west made it possible to extend the wharf for another 245 metres. In addition a passenger pier was built, sheds were extended and a tug was ordered. The tonnage handled rose from 56 000 harbour tons in 1923 to 273 000 tons in 1930–31. The depression and the Second World War put an end to any further developments.

Postwar improvements to the port were mainly put in hand because of congestion in the port and because of the needs of the ill-fated Overseas Food Corporation. Tonnages handled at the port increased from 269 900 in 1945 to 504 000 in 1948. Although discussions regarding the proposed deep-water berths were started around this period, work did not begin until 1953 and they were not completed until 1956. Meanwhile tonnages handled at the port in the intervening period exceeded 970 000 tons. It was only the spatial reorganization of activities, improved land transportation, and an increase in equipment and harbour vessels which made it possible to handle the enormous increase in traffic. To make it possible for the maximum amount of cargo to be handled, the schooner and dhow anchorages and the petroleum landing sites were shifted away from the lighterage wharf to the southern creek. In the late 1950s an oil jetty with a T-head was constructed so that large tankers could discharge directly into the oil installations at Gerezani. Other specialist facilities included the bulk loading and unloading of cement from the coaster wharf.

At the time when the deep-water berths were being constructed, the harbour was dredged and several large shoals were removed and anchorages provided for ten large ocean-going vessels. With all these improvements it was envisaged that port facilities would be adequate for several years to come.

All calculations were thrown out of balance by the Unilateral Declaration of Independence by Rhodesia, and the resulting need for Zambia to look for new outlets. The tonnages handled by the port increased from 905 000 in 1965 to over 2 128 000 in 1968. A depot to regulate goods for Zambia was constructed at Ubungo and the amount of cargo-handling equipment was greatly increased. In 1967 work started on the construction of three other deep-water berths, thus adding another 600 metres of quayage. Current plans include the construction of two additional berths capable of handling containerized cargo.

Hinterland

The immediate vicinity of Dar es Salaam is not particularly productive. Until the completion of the Central Railway Line from Dar es Salaam to Kigoma the port handled only a limited tonnage. With improved transportation, mainly the extension of the railway line to Mwanza in the 1920s, the port benefited from developments covering nearly two-thirds of the country. The import hinterland now covers nearly the whole country.

The relative distance of the Eastern Congo from both the Atlantic and Indian Oceans makes Dar es Salaam a convenient outlet for parts of the Congo, Rwanda and Burundi. By an agreement signed in 1921 Britain granted enclaves to Belgium at Dar es Salaam and Kigoma at nominal rents. By the 1930s nearly forty per cent of all the exports passing through Dar es Salaam consisted of copper from the Congo. The sudden termination of this traffic during the depression brought a great loss of revenue to both the Central Line and the port. At the time of the construction of the deep-water berths, Belgium made a request for improved facilities and agreed to pay the construction costs for one berth. A new agreement was signed in 1963, between Tanzania, the Congo, Burundi and Rwanda.

Since 1965 the port has become an important outlet for Zambian traffic. Specially significant, in this respect, has been the completion of the refinery at Dar es Salaam and the construction of the pipeline to supply Zambia's petroleum needs. Since petroleum demands will increase, plans are under way to construct an ocean terminal away from the harbour, thus permitting very large tankers to discharge safely and economically.

In recent years the tonnage of imports handled through Dar es Salaam has been nearly twice that of exports. Petroleum in bulk is the principal import. A wide variety of goods, ranging from piece-goods and vehicles to chemicals and food items constitute the main imports. The major exports consist of sisal, cotton, coffee, cashew nuts, various grains and oil seeds. Since 1965 copper from both Zambia and the Congo have been displacing the traditional exports.

ADOLFO MASCARENHAS

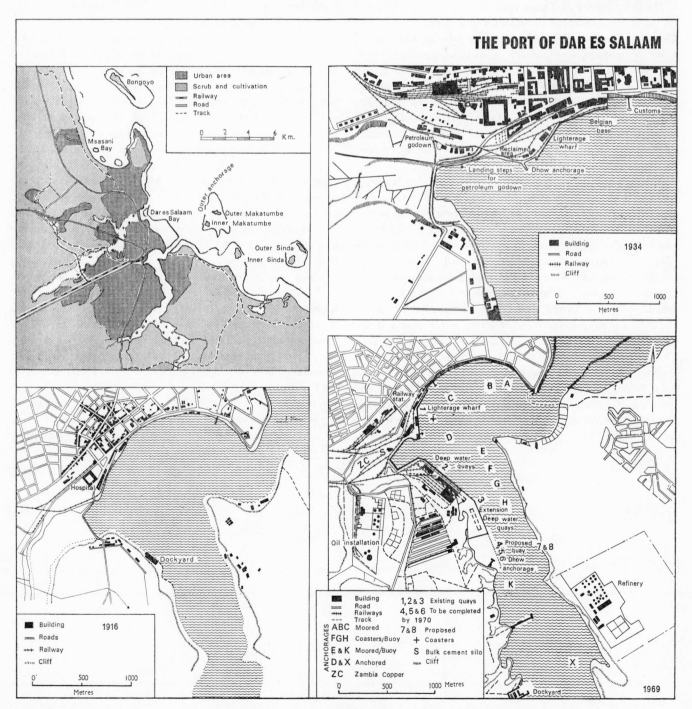

THE PORT OF DAR ES SALAAM

60 MTWARA AND TANGA

Apart from Dar es Salaam, Tanzania has two important ocean ports, Tanga and Mtwara. The two ports, situated at the extreme ends of the 800 km. (500 mile) long coastline of Tanzania, contrast with each other in many respects.

Tanga, lying in the north, was the first of the modern seaports to be developed in East Africa. The modern development of Mtwara dates only from 1954. However, Mtwara, despite its late start, was the first Tanzanian port to have deep-water quays, while Tanga is still a lighterage port. The first impetus to the development of Tanga came in 1893 largely because of the need for unloading facilities for the construction of the Usambara Railway line. Although the railway took several years to complete, it stimulated agricultural development. In spite of the interior communications from Tanga being well developed, there being good roads in addition to the railway, they are effective for the port only over a limited area. The development of Tanga with its 384 m. (420 yd) of lighterage wharf is almost entirely because of sisal. The major drawback of the port is its close proximity to the two well-developed ports of Mombasa and Dar es Salaam.

Although the site of Mtwara was long known to seafarers, its came into use only after 1920 when a small private jetty was built to carry sisal from an adjacent estate to Mikindani. The whole of the southern region of Tanzania was served by the nearby port of Lindi. Mtwara came into being because of the plans of the Overseas Food Corporation which earmarked large sections of southern Tanzania for one of the most ambitious schemes in tropical Africa. Lindi and Kilwa were examined as possible port sites for the 'Groundnut Scheme', but because of the difficulty of constructing deep-water port facilities, it was recommended that Mtwara be developed as the groundnut port. Despite the failure of the groundnut scheme, two deep-water quays, each measuring 284 m. (320 yd), were completed in 1954. To remedy the situation the newly constructed railway was extended to Masasi, some 408 km. (234 miles) from Mtwara. Even this measure did not revitalize agriculture and so the line was uprooted. The existence of Tanga and Mtwara can be explained largely by the past importance of sisal and the recent expansion of cashews as a Tanzanian export. Cashews are a very seasonal export so that from December to March the port facilities are worked to capacity.

The nine lighterage points of Tanga and the two deep-water berths of Mtwara give a capacity of 320 000 tons and 400 000 tons respectively. Despite this capacity the volume of traffic handled at Tanga has not exceeded 220 000 per annum and at Mtwara the maximum handled per annum now hovers around 155 000 tons. The implications of this excess capacity at the two ports is that Tanga could, as it has done at times since 1954, handle overflow traffic from Mombasa. Similarly, the Mtwara capacity assures that at least the port facilities will not be a bottleneck to proposed developments in the southern part of the country or even for Zambia.

The figures shown in Table 57, p. 170, are a good reflection of recent trends of the trade handled through Mtwara. As usual exports are roughly twice as much as imports. Groundnuts, for which the port was specifically developed, hardly account for 1 per cent though tonnages can increase erratically. The mainstay of the port is the cashew trade. With the move to processing the nuts before they are exported, tonnages, though not the value, will fall. The present hinterland of Mtwara is confined to a narrow belt of about 400 km. (250 miles). With improved communications an increase in tobacco and coffee exports can be expected. Copper exports from Zambia will also increase, for the 1966–67 tonnage only represents the return cargo of aircraft which took petroleum products to Zambia. Inward cargo generally consists of bulky development items such as cement, bulk oil and foodstuffs. With the anticipated changes in the southern part of the country this trend is likely to continue.

The predominance of sisal in Table 59, p. 172, reflects the importance of the crop to Tanga. The coffee exported through Tanga represents only a small proportion of northern Tanzania's production. The rest of the coffee is diverted through Mombasa. The other products are typical of the Usambara Mountains, thus once again emphasizing the restricted hinterland of Tanga. The imports are mainly reciprocal to the sisal industry and this is attested by the considerable imports of fertilizers, vehicles and bulk oil.

ADOLFO MASCARENHAS

MTWARA AND TANGA

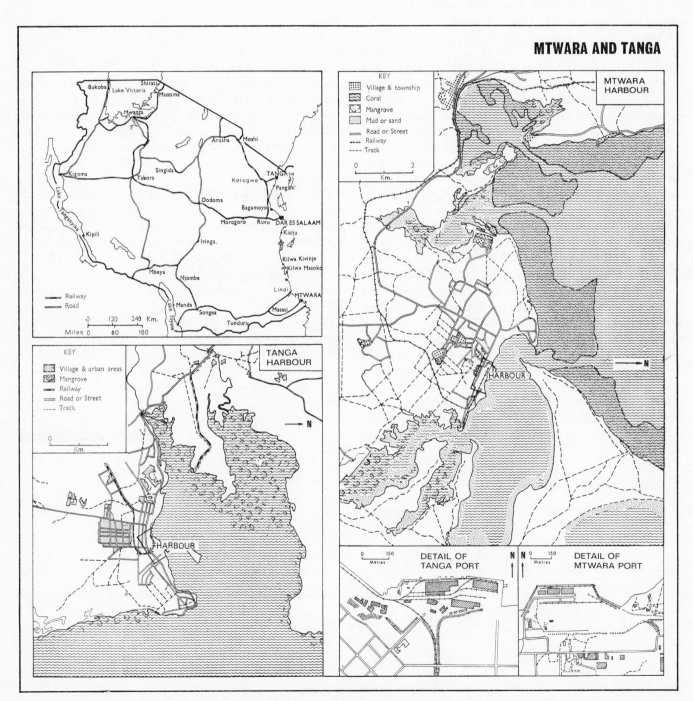

KEY
- ▦ Village & township
- ▨ Coral
- ▧ Mangrove
- ▦ Mud or sand
- ─ Road or Street
- +++ Railway
- --- Track

0 — 2 Km.

MTWARA HARBOUR

HARBOUR

N →

KEY
- ▨ Village & urban areas
- ▧ Mangrove
- ╫ Railway
- ═ Road or Street
- --- Track

0 Km.

TANGA HARBOUR

N →

HARBOUR

Bukoba · Lake Victoria · Shirati · Musoma · Mwanza · Arusha · Moshi · Kigoma · Singida · Tabora · Korogwe · TANGA · Pangani · Dodoma · Bagamoyo · Morogoro · Ruvu · DAR ES SALAAM · Kisiju · Iringa · Kilwa Kivinje · Kilwa Masoko · Mbeya · Njombe · Lindi · MTWARA · Manda · Songea · Masasi · Tunduru

- ─ Railway
- ═ Road

0 — 120 — 240 Km.
Miles 0 — 80 — 160

0 — 150 Metres — DETAIL OF TANGA PORT   N ↑   ↑ N   0 — 150 Metres — DETAIL OF MTWARA PORT

61 EXTERNAL TRADE

Between 1947 and 1957 the volume of Tanzania's trade increased over threefold and in the current decade (1960) has nearly doubled. The *per capita* trade during these same years increased from Shs. 62 to Shs. 194 and now stands at Shs. 276. Fortunately too, Tanzania has a favourable overall balance of trade (see Table 60, p. 172).

Tanzania exhibits the trade pattern typical of most developing countries, in that the chief imports are manufactured goods and the country depends on primary agricultural and mining production for most of its exports. Although this pattern will remain for the foreseeable future, structural changes have in fact taken place. For instance, there is a break from the dependence on one crop, and sisal, which in 1947 accounted for 52 per cent of the country's exports, had by 1967 been relegated to fourth place. Cotton, diamonds, coffee and sisal together now account for over half of the exports (see Table 61, p. 172).

Agricultural products rank high among the items of Tanzania's trade, but unfortunately the general decline of world prices in these products makes long-range dependence on them unsatisfactory. However, declining prices, especially in sisal, have been offset by diversification and increased output, often through increased acreage. Weather also is an important factor in annual production and export totals. The drop in export of coffee in 1967 is an example of such effects. The Commonwealth is the main partner in trade, and in 1967 accounted for 58 per cent of exports. Britain is the largest customer and, although Zambia has moved to second place, the traditional importers of Tanzania products are India, Hong Kong and Canada. The USA, Italy, West Germany, Japan and France are all important buyers of Tanzania's products. The distribution of products is wide, but certain items have very specific markets, for example, diamonds are exclusively sent to the UK, and cloves mainly to Indonesia and Singapore. New outlets and more favourable terms of trade are constantly being sought after. Since Independence, for instance, trade with socialist countries had increased from 11 million shillings in 1961 to 232 million in 1967.

Imports to Tanzania have hitherto consisted largely of consumer goods led by textiles. Since 1966 there has been a sharp fall in the imports of consumer goods, notably imports of cement and textiles, which are now largely substituted by local production. With the policy of national self-reliance, the value of imported capital goods and transport equipment is on the increase. The Commonwealth is again the chief supplier, Britain leading the way by providing 28 per cent of the imports. The USA and Iran (petroleum products), West Germany, Italy, the People's Republic of China, France and others are among the leading suppliers of Tanzania's needs.

The value of trade cannot be over-estimated. Nearly a third of the nation's revenue comes directly from import and export duties. Development in many cases will only be possible through imports, especially imports of equipment. Invisible returns are obtained mainly from the successful East Africa Airways. Investments have been made on ocean-going vessels operated by the East African National Shipping line and another shipping line owned jointly with China.

A very remarkable feature of the trade of Tanzania is the inter-territorial transaction with Kenya and Uganda. In contrast with the overseas trade, Tanzania has a heavy deficit in the local trade. In 1966 imports from Kenya alone were nearly four times the value of exports. The signing of the Treaty of East African co-operation in June 1967 paved the way for some degree of equity.

Tanzania and other developing countries face long-term trade problems which need tackling on an international basis. World commodity prices of agricultural export crops show a tendency to fall and there is overproduction in some fields. On the other hand, freight rates and prices of imported goods show a consistently rising trend. These price differences counterbalance much of the very considerable increases in production which have been achieved.

It is important in the long run that international agreements are made on a wide range of crops so that the developing countries can be guaranteed a fair and stable price for their products. Such agreements are in some ways more important than aid, and would greatly help the struggle for national progress and self-reliance.

ADOLFO MASCARENHAS

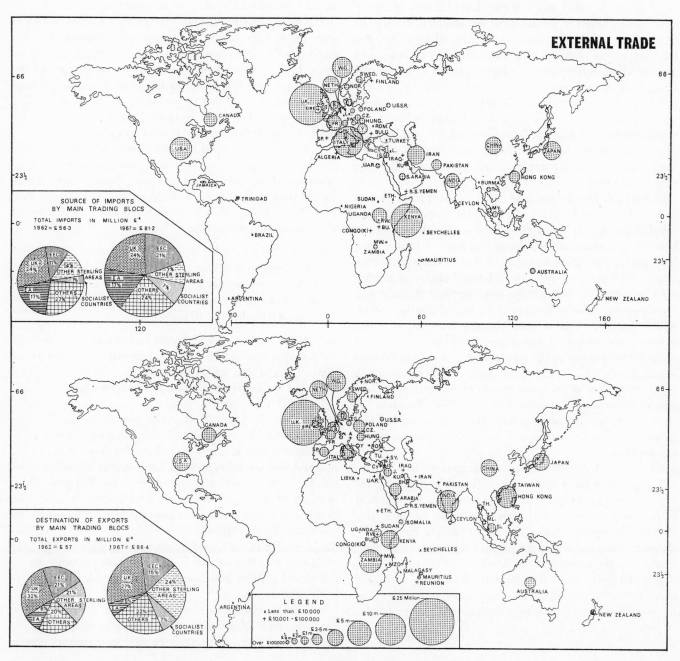

EXTERNAL TRADE

SOURCE OF IMPORTS BY MAIN TRADING BLOCS

TOTAL IMPORTS IN MILLION £'s
1962 = £ 56·3   1967 = £ 81·2

1962
EEC 11%
UK 24%
14% OTHER STERLING AREAS
1%
E.A. 17%
OTHERS 27%
SOCIALIST COUNTRIES

1967
UK 24%
EEC 21%
7%
OTHER STERLING AREAS
1%
E.A. 17%
OTHERS 24%
SOCIALIST COUNTRIES

DESTINATION OF EXPORTS BY MAIN TRADING BLOCS

TOTAL EXPORTS IN MILLION £'s
1962 = £ 57   1967 = £ 86·4

1962
EEC 21%
UK 32%
21% OTHER STERLING AREAS
6%
E.A.
OTHERS 20%
SOCIALIST COUNTRIES

1967
EEC 15%
UK 27%
24% OTHER STERLING AREAS
5%
E.A.
OTHERS 22%
7%
SOCIALIST COUNTRIES

LEGEND
x Less than £10 000
+ £10,001 - £100 000

Over £100 000   £¼m £½m £1m £2·5m £5m £10m £25 Million

143

CONCLUSION

The maps, statistics and text of this book show Tanzania as a developing country, not only in the euphemistic sense but also in the sense of a country undergoing change, sometimes radical change.

References to standard economic texts on underdevelopment and to Ginsberg's *Atlas of Economic Development* [1] would suggest that Tanzania has many features in common with other African, Asian and Latin American countries: low *per capita* income, the dominance of agriculture in the national economy, the dual nature of the economy with 'modern' and traditional sectors, and so on. It is clear that there are such common denominators, and there may even be some common approaches to the problems raised, but it is also clear that there are many other factors, historical, spatial, social and economic which must be assessed in problems of underdevelopment. Many of these factors may also be common to a whole range of countries, but some of which in their particular expression and in their spatial arrangement are unique.

Tanzania's *per capita* income is still low; cotton, sisal, coffee and diamonds are her main sources of foreign exchange, the communication net is as yet incomplete and does not reach all parts of the country; industry, though growing fast, is still on a small scale as befits the rather limited markets and the early stage of industrial growth.

However, despite the low level of development at the time of Independence in 1961 and despite inevitable mistakes and miscalculations, there is a real atmosphere of growth and nationhood in the country, and the preceeding pages show that there is considerable promise for the future. Tanzania has so far been able to avoid the worst problems of internal dissension and has been fortunate in having wise and clear-sighted leadership. Future growth will partly depend on the continuation of internal effort, the spread of monetary agriculture and continued industrial growth but, as with many developing countries, part of the future depends on the pattern of growth of external markets. It is to be hoped that a realistic international agreement on prices may be one of the forms of help to the developing countries in the future. In the first Five Year Plan, Tanzania has increased the production of a wide range of her agricultural products only to see the effects of this partly negated by falls in export prices.

Early in the Independence period Tanzania made a decision to concentrate a large part of her initial effort in solving the high-level manpower problem. In some ways she is in the lead of African countries in the systematic way she has attempted to assess the problem and deal with it. Already the policy is showing results and within a short time the supply of graduate teachers for the secondary schools will have resulted in a high degree of localization in this important field. Now, at the end of the first Five Year Plan Tanzania is quite well advanced in her aim of self-sufficiency by 1980, though there has been a short-

[1] Ginsberg, *Atlas of Economic Development, 1961*, Chicago University Press.

fall in science graduates. In the field of education also, Tanzania has been prominent in her attempts to reorientate the primary school syllabus and outlook to the training of people for life in the rural sector.

In her political development since Independence, Tanzania has chosen a one-party state and a socialist ideology. The one-party system is unique in that, while providing a genuine unity in terms of national ideals and goals, it allows a democratic choice of candidates at the constituency level. The government has, through the Arusha Declaration and the subsequent nationalization of the banks and the 'commanding heights of the economy', taken firm control of the destiny of the country. The early experiments of rather heavily capitalized village settlements have been replaced by a rural-based policy of *ujamaa*, co-operation at village level and the coming together of people in villages for co-operative endeavour. This policy is linked with the establishment of state farms in many areas.

The co-operative marketing system, which has been strong in some parts of the country (particularly the cotton and coffee-growing areas) but stagnant and inefficient in others, has recently been overhauled and forms an important part of the official marketing system. In the industrial sector the National Development Corporation (a para-state body) has controlling shares in many industrial enterprises, and has performed efficiently and profitably in its first years of operation.

As Jensen (p. 46) points out, the activity and growth of the past few years has to a considerable extent directly profited the urban sector, particularly Dar es Salaam, though there are substantial indirect benefits to the rural sector. In the second Five Year Plan 1969–74, the Government sets out to redress some of this imbalance, stating that

'Policy will be extended beyond a general emphasis on rural programmes to a specific strategy for regional development, which incorporates not only a specifically rural element, but which also incorporates an urban development programme consistent with the regional objectives.'

Volume III of the plan analyses the regional effects of the plan and lays down policies for increasing growth rates in the poorer areas. There is thus an important need to develop a regional analysis of the country in relation to growth potentials.

Tanzania is at present poor, but given continued stable government, the prospects of steady growth are good. Long-term prospects in terms of hydro-electric power and the development of river basins are excellent. The development of the coal and iron ore reserves of the south-west is beginning to be possible with the spread of communications. The possibilities in terms of forest products and animal husbandry are in the long run favourable, though to some extent offset by the uncertainties with other agricultural products. The prospects of continued growth in the tourist industry are very promising. Tanzania may even become a net exporter of some consumer goods, though competition from home industries in other countries is likely to be strong.

Such transformation is, however, long term, partly because of the long period of gestation of river basin or mineral deposit development programmes, partly because such schemes need a highly developed infrastructure which is only gradually being built up in the country, and partly because such innovations need experience and education at all levels: the farmer the manager and the engineer. Such education and experience can only come from the current programme of training in primary schools, in agricultural colleges and farmers' training centres, in the University and in the smaller agricultural schemes currently being developed. Many traditional attitudes and barriers still need to be overcome, and education is probably the only real answer, long term though it may be.

To readers outside Africa it is difficult to convey the immensity of the task when *per capita* income is only Shs. 450 per annum, and when doubling this would still produce a figure which is less than the *monthly* wage of a vast majority of the workers in developed countries. It is equally difficult to describe the firmness and resolution of Tanzania in tackling her problems and her development.

LEN BERRY

GENERAL BIBLIOGRAPHY

ANDERSON, B 'Soils of Tanganyika', Ministry of Agriculture, Bulletin No. 16, Dar es Salaam, 1963

BLIJ, de H J *Dar es Salaam, a Study in Urban Geography*, Northwestern University Press, 1963

BUREAU OF RESOURCE ASSESSMENT AND LAND USE PLANNING University of Dar es Salaam, *Research Notes* and *Research Papers*

CLIFFE, L(ed.) *One Party Democracy*, East African Publishing House, Nairobi, 1967

DRYDEN, S *Local Administration in Tanzania*, East African Publishing House, Nairobi, 1968

INTERNATIONAL BANK FOR RECONSTRUCTION AND DEVELOPMENT *The Economic Development of Tanganyika*, Johns Hopkins University Press, 1960

—— *Prospects for Economic Development in East Africa*, Vol. III, Tanzania, 1967

JOURNAL OF THE GEOGRAPHICAL ASSOCIATION OF TANZANIA

KIMAMBO, I N and TEMU, A J (eds.) *From Stone Age to the Arusha Declaration: A History of Tanzania*, East African Publishing House, Nairobi, 1969

LESLIE, J A K *A Survey of Dar es Salaam*, Oxford University Press, London, 1963

LISTOWEL, J *The Making of Tanganyika*, Chatto and Windus, London, 1965

MOFFETT, J P (ed.) *Tanganyika, a Review of its Resources and their Development*, Government of Tanganyika, 1955

MORGAN, W T W (ed.) *East Africa: its Peoples and Resources*, Oxford University Press, Nairobi, 1969.

NYERERE, PRESIDENT J K *Freedom and Unity*, Oxford University Press, Dar es Salaam, 1967

—— *Freedom and Socialism*, Oxford University Press, Dar es Salaam, 1968

QUENNELL, A M, McKINLAY, A C M and AITKENS, W G *Summary of the Geology of Tanganyika* Part I, 1956, Part II, 1960. Government Printer, Dar es Salaam

RUTHENBERG, H *Agricultural Development in Tanganyika*, IFO-Institut, Afrika Studien Nr. 2, Weltforum Verlag, Munchen, 1964

—— (ed) *Smallholder Farming and smallholder development in Tanzania*, IFO-Institut, Afrika Studien Nr. 24, Weltforum Verlag, Munchen, 1968

SMITH, H E (ed.) *Agricultural Development in Tanzania*, Institute of Public Administration and Oxford University Press, Dar es Salaam, 1965

—— *Readings on Economic Development and Administration in Tanzania*, Institute of Public Administration and Oxford University Press, Dar es Salaam, 1966

STOCKLEY, G M 'The Geology and Mineral Resources of Tanganyika Territory', *Geological Survey Department, Bulletin No. 20*, 1948

SVENDSEN, K E *An Introduction to the Economic Problems of Tanzania*, East African Publishing House, Nairobi, 1970

TANGANYIKA AFRICAN NATIONAL UNION *The Arusha Declaration and TANU'S Policy on Socialism and Self-Reliance*, Government Printer, Dar es Salaam, 1967

TANGANYIKA *Five Year Plan for Economic and Social Development 1946–69*, Government Printer, Dar es Salaam

TANZANIA *Second Five Year Plan for Economic and Social Development 1969–74*, Government Printer, Dar es Salaam

TANZANIA, CENTRAL STATISTICAL BUREAU *Background to the Budget: An Economic Survey*, Government Printer, Dar es Salaam (annual)

—— *Census of Large Scale Commercial Farming*, Government Printer, Dar es Salaam (annual)

—— *Employment and Earnings in Tanzania*, Government Printer, Dar es Salaam (annual)

—— *Preliminary Results of the Population Census 1967*, Government Printer, 1968

—— *Recorded Population Changes 1948–67, Tanzania*, Government Printer, 1968

—— *Statistical Abstract*, Government Printer (annual)

—— *Survey of Industrial Production*, Government Printer (annual)

TANZANIA, MINISTRY OF LANDS, SETTLEMENT AND WATER DEVELOPMENT *Atlas of Tanzania*, 1967

TANZANIA NOTES AND RECORDS

TORDOFF, W *Government and Politics in Tanzania*, East African Publishing House, Nairobi, 1967

SELECT BIBLIOGRAPHY AND SOURCES BY CHAPTERS

Abbreviations:

BRALUP Bureau of Resource Assessment and Land Use Planning (University of Dar es Salaam)
CSB Central Statistical Bureau (Dar es Salaam)
EAAFJ *East African Agricultural and Forestry Journal*
EAAJ *East African Agricultural Journal*
GP Government Printer (Dar es Salaam)
JE *Journal of Ecology*
JGAT *Journal of the Geographical Association of Tanzania*

1. Tanzania in Africa

GINSBERG, N *Atlas of Economic Development,* University of Chicago Press, 1964
HANCE, W A *A geography of Africa,* University of Chicago Press, 1961
KIMAMBO, I N and TEMU, A J *A History of Tanzania,* Dar es Salaam, 1969
NYERERE, PRESIDENT J K *The Arusha Declaration,* GP, 1967

2. Tanzania and her neighbours

GRIFFITHS, I L 'Zambia's links with East Africa', EAGR, April 1968
NYERERE, PRESIDENT J K *Freedom and Socialism,* especially East African Treaty, Zambia and Tanzania, Policy on Foreign Affairs, Dar es Salaam, 1968

3. Administrative areas, 1967

DRYDEN, S 'Local administration in Tanzania', *EAPH Political Studies 5,* East African Publishing House, Nairobi, 1968
THOMAS, I D 'Population Density: Tanzania, 1967, *BRALUP Research Notes No. 5b,* revised and reprinted as Appendix to *Tanzania Census Report,* Vol. I: 'Enumeration' Area Statistics, pp. 262–342

4. Political geography

BIENEN, H *Tanzania—Party Transformation and Economic Development,* Princeton, 1967
CLIFFE, L (ed.) *One Party Democracy,* Nairobi, 1967
CLIFFE, L and SAUL, J S 'The District Development front in Tanzania', *Rural Development Paper No. 1,* 1970
DRYDEN, S *Local Government in Tanzania,* Nairobi, 1967
PENNER, R 'Local Government Finance in Tanzania', *Economic Research Bureau Paper,* (forthcoming)
TORDOFF, W *Government and Politics in Tanzania,* Nairobi, 1967

5 and 6. Population, 1967; population change, 1957–67

Demographic Yearbook, 1967, UN, New York, 1968
Tanganyika African Census Report, 1957, GP, 1963
Tanganyika Report on the Census of the Non-African population, 1967, GP, 1958
Tanzania 1967 Population Census, Vol. I, 'Enumeration' Area Statistics, CSB, 1969
Tanzania Provisional Estimates of Fertility, Mortality and Population Growth for Tanzania, CSB, 1968
Tanzania Recorded population changes, 1948–67 Tanzania, CSB, 1968
THOMAS, I D 'A Survey of Administrative Boundary Changes in Tanganyika/Tanzania, 1957–67, for use in intercensal comparisons', *Research Notes No. 3, BRALUP,* 1967

7 and 8. Relief and physical features

Atlas of Tanzania, 1st ed., Dar es Salaam, 1968
AITKEN, W G 'Geomorphology of parts of the Kondoa District', *Tanganyika Notes and Records,* No. 29, pp. 55–8, 1950

DIXEY, F 'Erosion and Tectonics in the East African Rift Systems', *Quarterly Journal of the Geological Society of London,* Vol. 102, pp. 339–88, 1946
DOWNIE, C 'Special Sheet (Geol.) Kilimanjaro—Moshi 1 : 125 000 with explanatory notes, *Map of the Geological Survey, Tanzania, 1805,* 1965
HALDIMANN, E G 'Note on structural features and erosion in eastern and southern Tanganyika', *East-central regional Commission Geology,* Dar es Salaam, pp. 99–105, 1956
HANDLY, J R F 'Geomorphology of the Nzega area of Tanganyika with special reference to the formation of granite tors', *XIXth International Geological Congress,* Algiers, 1952, Vol. 21, pp. 201–10, 1954
HARPUM, J R 'Evolution of granite scenery in Tanganyika', *Records of the Geological Survey, Tanganyika,* Vol. 10, pp. 39–46, 1963
MORGAN, W T W op cit, p. 144
QUENNELL, A M; McKINLEY, A C M and AITKEN, E G *Summary of the geology of Tanganyika,* Part 1, 1956, Part 2, 1960
RUSSELL, E W *Natural Resources of East Africa,* Nairobi, 1962
TEALE, E O 'River Systems in Tanganyika in relation to tectonic movement', *XVIth International Geological Congress,* Lisbon, 1949, Vol. 2, pp. 233–41, 1950

9. Soils

ANDERSON, B 'Soils of Tanganyika', *Ministry of Agriculture Bulletin No. 16,* 1963
CALTON, W E 'An experimental pedological map of Tanganyika', *Proceedings of the 2nd Inter-African Soils Conference,* Leopoldville, 1954, doc. No. 11, pp. 237–40
—— 'Generalisations on some Tanganyika soil data', *Journal of Soil Science,* 10, 1959, pp. 169–76
CALTON, W E, TIDBURY, G E and WALKER, G F 'A Study of the more important soils of Zanzibar Protectorate'. *EAAJ 21,* 1955, pp. 53–60
DAMES, T W G *The soils of the Pangani valley,* Dar es Salaam, 1956
GIBB, SIR A and Partners and Overseas Consultants, Inc. *Report on Central African Rail Link Development Survey,* London, 1952
MALCOLM, D W *Sulumaland,* London, 1953
MILNE, G A with BECKLEY, V A, GETHIN JONES, G H, MARTIN, W S, GRIFFITH, G and RAYMOND, L W 'A provisional soil map of East Africa', *East African Agricultural Research Station Memoirs,* Amani, 1936
—— 'Soils reconnaissance journey through parts of Tanganyika Territory', *JE,* 35, 1947, pp. 192–265
SCOTT, R M 'The soils of East Africa', pp. 67–76 in E W Russell, *op cit.,* 1962
SPURR, A M M 'The soils of Mbozi', *Geological Survey, Bulletin 24,* Dar es Salaam, 1955
—— 'The soils of South Uwemba', *Geological Survey of Tanganyika, Report AMMS/33,* Dar es Salaam, 1955
—— 'Note on black cotton soils', *Geological Survey of Tanganyika, Report AMMS/25,* Dar es Salaam, no date
UNFAO *The Rufiji Basin, Tanganyika,* Vol. VII, Parts 1 and 2, Rome, 1961

10. Vegetation associations

BURTT, B D 'Some East African vegetation communities', *JE, 30,* 1942, pp. 65–146
EVANS, I B P 'Roadside observations on the vegetation of East and Central Africa', Union of South Africa, *Botanical Survey Memoir 22,* Pretoria, 1948
GIBB, SIR H *et al* op cit., 1952
GILLMAN, C 'A vegetation-types map of Tanganyika Territory', *Geographical Review, 39,* 1949, pp. 7–37
GRANTHAM, D R and PILSON, R D 'The geology and ecology of the Nachingwea region', *Geological Survey Department, Bulletin 26,* Dar es Salaam, 1955
GREENWAY, P J 'The vegetation of Mpwapwa, Tanganyika Territory', *JE, 21,* 1933, pp. 28–43
—— *A Swahili-botanical-English dictionary of plant names,* Dar es Salaam, 1940
—— 'Second draft report on vegetation classification for the approval of the Vegetation Committee, *Pasture Research Conference',* mimeo, 1943

GROOME, J S 'Muninga (Pterocarpus angolensis, D C) in the Western Province of Tanganyika', *EAAFJ, 21,* 1955, pp. 130–7, 189–200 and 248–54

HUBBARD, C E and MILNE-REDHEAD, E (eds.), *Flora of tropical East Africa,* Secretariat for Technical Co-operation, London

MICHELMORE, A P G 'Observations on tropical African grasslands', *JE, 27,* 1939, pp. 282–312

NAPPER, D M 'Gasses of Tanganyika', Ministry of Agriculture, Forests and Wildlife, Bulletin No. 18, Dar es Salaam, 1965

PRATT, D J, GREENWAY, P J and GWYNNE, M D A 'Classification of East African Rangeland', *Journal of Applied Ecology 3/2 1966,* pp. 369–82

PHILLIPS, J F V 'Some important vegetation communities in the Central Province of Tanganyika Territory: a preliminary account', *JE, 18,* 1930, pp. 193–234

PIELOU, E C 'Notes on the vegetation of Rukwa rift valley', *Tanganyika Journal of Ecology,* 40, 1952, p. 383 ff.

PITT-SCHENKEL, C J 'Some important communities of warm temperate rainforest at Magamba, west Usambara, Tanganyika Territory', *JE, 26,* 1938, pp. 50–81

REA, R J A 'The forest types of vegetation in Tanganyika Territory', *Empire Forestry Journal, 14,* 1935, pp. 202–08

SALT, G 'A contribution to the ecology of upper Kilimanjaro, *JE, 42,* 1954, pp. 375 ff.

STEINER, H W and STEINER, M translation of Jaenecke, M C *The ecology of East African mangroves,* Dar es Salaam, 1968

11.   Hydrology of major rivers

CHABLANI, M 'An outline plan for the development of the Ruvu Basin', *Rome, FAO, EPTA, Report 1316,* 1961

DOLFI, D 'The Nyumba ya Mungu storage scheme on the Pangani River', *FAO Report, 1365,* Rome, 1961

—— 'Report on Water Resources Potential of the Wami Basin, *FAO Rome Report on the Rufiji Basin,* Vol. 1–7, 1963

FAWLEY, H *Notes on Pangani Water Development,* 1951

GILLMAN, C *A reconnaissance survey of the hydrology of Tanzania. Tanganyika Territory in its geographic setting,* 1944

SPOONER, R J, and SOGREAH, N *The Development of the Lower Mgeta River Area,* Land Resources Division, Directorate of Overseas Surveys, Tolworth, England, 1965

—— *Report of the French Technical Mission for the Development of the Ruvu Basin,* Paris, 1962

TANZANIA, MINISTRY OF AGRICULTURE *Hydrological Year Book, 1950–9,* 1963

TANZANIA, MINISTRY OF LANDS SETTLEMENT AND WATER DEVELOPMENT *Hydrological Year Book 1960–5,* 1968

12–15.   Atmospheric pressure and winds; Rainfall; Evaporation; Other climatic elements

Atlas of Tanzania, 'Climate', pp. 6–7, 1967

GRIFFITHS, J F 'The Climate of East Africa' in *The Natural Resources of East Africa,* Nairobi, pp. 77–87, 1962

JOHNSON, D H and MORTH, H T 'Forecasting Research in East Africa' in *Tropical Meteorology in Africa,* WMO and Munitalp Foundation (Nairobi), p. 56, 1960.

JOHNSON, D H 'Rain in East Africa', *Quarterly Journal of the Royal Meteorological Society* 88, p. 19, 1962

KENWORTHY, J M 'Rainfall and Water Resources of East Africa', in *Geographers and the Tropics,* STEEL, R W and PROTHERO, R M (eds) Longmans, pp. 111–37, 1964

THOMPSON, B W 'Some Reflections on Equatorial and Tropical Forecasting', *East African Meteorological Department Technical Memoirs No. 7,* 1957

—— *The Climate of Africa,* Oxford University Press, 1965

TREWARTHA, G T *The Earth's Problem Climates,* Methuen, Chapter 9, p. 121, 1961

16.   Geology

ASGA/UNESCO, Geological map of Africa, 1:5 000 000; Sheets 5 and 6, Paris, 1963

Bibliography of the geology and mineral resources of Tanzania to December 1967. Compiled by staff of Mineral Resources Division, Dodoma, published *BRALUP Research Notes 5c,* 1969

CAHEN, L and SNELLING, N J *The geochronology of Equatorial Africa,* N Holland, Amsterdam, 1966

PALLISTER, J W 'Explanatory note on the tectonic map of eastern Africa', Comm. Sci. Carte 1963, *Géologie du Monde,* 75–8

QUENNELL, A M, McKINLAY, A C M and AITKEN, W G *Summary of the geology of Tanganyika: Part 1 Introduction and Stratigraphy,* 1956: *Part 2 Geological map,* 1960 (part 1 includes a full bibliography of work done before 1956)

17.   Faults

DUNDAS, D L *Review of Rift Faulting in Tanzania,* in *Report on Field Explorations in 1968, Soviet Geological and Geophysical Expedition to East Africa,* pp. 95–100, 1965

GORYACHEV, A V 'Tectonics of the southern part of the Gregory rift and adjacent areas', in *Report on Field Explorations in 1968, Soviet Geological and Geophysical Expedition to East Africa,* pp. 22–7, 1969

JAMES, T C 'The nature of rift faulting in Tanganyika', *Comm. Tech. in Africa,* East-Central Regional Committee for Geology, Leopoldville, pp. 81–94, 1956

KENNERLEY, J B *Bibliography of the Rift System in Tanzania,* in *East African Rift System Report of UMC/UNESCO Seminar,* pp. 101–02, 1965

McCONNELL, R B 'The East African Rift System', *Nature, 215, 5101,* pp. 578–81, 1967

MILANOVSKY, E E *Geomorphology and Neotectonics and the correlation between Volcanism and Tectonics,* in *Report on Field Explorations in 1968, Soviet Geological and Geophysical Expedition to East Africa,* pp. 28–54, 1969.

PALLISTER, J W 'The rift system in Tanzania', in *East African Rift System Report of UMC/UNESCO Seminar,* pp. 86–91, Nairobi, 1965

18.   Gross domestic product in 1967

CSB *Basic material on employment and earnings,* 1967

—— *District figures from Punch Card Print on employment and earnings,* 1967

—— *National average prices for 1967*

MINISTRY OF AGRICULTURE 1968 *Files in the Livestock, Fishery and Forestry Division*

—— *Livestock Marketing Report,* 1967

MINISTRY OF ECONOMIC AFFAIRS AND DEVELOPMENT PLANNING AND MINISTRY OF FINANCE *Background to the Budget 1968–9,* GP, 1968

MKAMA, J and JENSEN, S 'District Data', 1967, *Ministry of Economic Affairs and Development Planning,* Dar es Salaam, 1968

REGIONAL AND DISTRICT AGRICULTURAL OFFICES *Final estimates 1967*

19.   Types of rural economy

BERRY, L and BERRY, E 'A preliminary subdivision of Districts into Rural Economic Zones', *BRALUP, Research Notes, No. 4,* March, 1968

MKAMA, J and JENSEN, S 'District Data, 1967', *Ministry of Economic Affairs and Development Planning,* Dar es Salaam, 1968

20.   Sisal

LOCK, G W *Sisal,* London, 1962

GUILLEBAUD, C W *An Economic Survey of the Sisal Industry in Tanganyika,* Welwyn, England, 1966

MASCARENHAS, A C 'Resistance and Change in the Sisal Plantation System of Tanzania', Ph.D. Dissertation, University of California, 1970, pp. 275

WALLER, C M 'A case study of a Sisal Estate: Kinglowira and Pangani Sisal Estates, Morogoro, Tanzania', *Journal of Geographical Association, Tanzania, 3,* pp. 5–24, 1968

21.   Coffee, tea, sugar

Background to the Budget, 1968–9, GP, 1969

BECK, R S 'An economic study of coffee, banana farms in the Central Machame Area, mimeo, 1963

Census of Large Scale Commercial Farming, 1964, CSB
DAYA, M F 'A Micro-study of a banana-coffee farm at Tengeru, Arusha', *JGAT* 2, pp. 39–49, 1968
RALD, J 'Land Use in a Buhaya Village. A case study from Bukoba District, West Lake Region', *BRALUP Research Papers No, 5*, 1969
RUTHENBERG, H *Smallholder farming and smallholder development in Tanzania: Ten case studies*, Berlin, 1968
'The Kilombero Valley Development Plan, 1965–9', mimeo, Dar es Salaam, 1964

22. Cotton

Background to the Budget, 1968–9, 1969–70, GP
COLLINSON, M P *Farm Management Survey Reports*, Western Research Centre, Ministry of Agriculture, Tanzania, 1962–3
DE WILDE *et al Agricultural development in Tropical Africa*, esp. Vol. II 'Sukumaland section', Johns Hopkins Press, Baltimore, 1967

23. Maize, wheat and other grains

BERRY, L and BERRY, E 'Land use in Tanzania by Districts', *BRALUP Research Notes No. 6*, 1969
FUGGLES-COUCHMAN, N R 'Agricultural Change in Tanganyika 1945–60', Stanford, California, *Food Research Institute*, 1964
JENSEN, S and MKAMA, J 'District Data, 1967', *Ministry of Economic Affairs and Development Planning*, Dar es Salaam, 1968

24. Tobacco, cashew, pyrethrum

Background to the Budget, 1968–9, 1969–70, GP
RUTHERNBERG, H *Smallholder farming and smallholder development in Tanzania: Ten case studies*, Berlin, 1968
Agricultural Development in Tanzania, Berlin, 1964
WESTERGARD, P 'Farm surveys of cashew producers in Mtwara Region', preliminary results. *ERB Paper 68/3*

25. Cattle

DESCHLER, W 'Cattle in Africa', *Geographical Review* 53, 1963, p. 52.
EPSTEIN, H 'The Sanga cattle of East Africa', *EAAFJ* 22, 1957, pp. 149–64
FALLON, L E *Development of the range resources, Republic of Tanzania*, Dar es Salaam, 1963
HEADY, H F *Range Management in East Africa*, Nairobi, 1960
JOSHI, N R, McLAUGHLIN, E A and PHILLIPS, R W 'Types and breeds of African cattle.' *FAO Rome*, 1957
MASON, I L and MAULE, J P *The indigenous livestock of eastern and southern Africa*, London, 1960
TANZANIA, MINISTRY OF AGRICULTURE AND CO-OPERATIVES; AGRICULTURAL DIVISION. *Annual Report*, 1966, Dar es Salaam
TANZANIA, MINISTRY OF AGRICULTURE AND CO-OPERATIVES; PLANNING UNIT *Livestock Marketing Reports*, 1967, Dar es Salaam
UNFAO *East African Livestock Survey*, 2 Vols, Rome, 1967
WILLIAMSON, G and PAYNE, W J A *An introduction to animal husbandry in the tropics*. London, 1959
Information supplied by The Ministry of Agriculture, Food and Co-operatives, Dar es Salaam

26. Animal diseases

HAGAN, W A and BRUNER, D W *The infectious diseases of domestic animals*, Ithaca, New York, 1961
HORNBY, H E *Animal trypanosomiasis in East Africa*, London, 1952
SWYNNERTON, C F M 'The tsetse flies of East Africa.' *Transactions of Royal Entomological Society of London, 84*, 1936
TANZANIA, MINISTRY OF AGRICULTURE AND CO-OPERATIVES; VETERINARY DIVISION. *Annual Reports*, Dar es Salaam
—— *Statistical summaries of diseases*, 1967
WILLIAMSON, G and PAYNE, W J A *op cit.* 1959

YEOMAN, G H *The occurrence of East Coast Fever in Tanganyika and its large-scale control by dipping*, Dar es Salaam, 1956
YEOMAN, G H and WALKER, J B *The ixodid ticks af Tanzania*, London, 1967

Map sources:
Tsetse-fly distribution: *Atlas of Tanzania*; 'Surveys and Mapping' Division, Ministry of Lands, Settlement and Water-development, Dar es Salaam, 1967 and information supplied by Veterinary Division, Ministry of Agriculture and Co-operatives, Dar es Salaam
All other map information supplied by The Veterinary Division, Ministry of Agriculture and Co-operatives, Dar es Salaam

27. Fisheries

Atlas of Tanzania Fisheries, p. 11, 1967
BAILEY, R G 'The Dam Fisheries of Tanzania.' *EAAFJ, July*, pp. 1–14, 1966
Tanzania *Second Five Year Plan*, Vol. I, pp 53–4, Vol. II, pp. 47–8, 1969
BELL, B E 'History of the activities of the East African Marine Fisheries Research Organisation.' *FAO Indian Ocean Fishery Commission, Rome*, September 1968
MINISTRY OF AGRICULTURE AND CO-OPERATIVES 'Report on the progress of the Fisheries Division of the Ministry of Agriculture and Co-operatives' (cyclostyled) 1968

28 and 29. Forestry and forest products

Atlas of Tanzania Surveys and Mapping Division Ministry of Lands Settlement and Water Development, Dar es Salaam
BRYCE, J M 'The commercial timbers of Tanzania', Forest Division Utilisation Section, Moshi, 1967
GREENWAY, P J 'Mahogany in East Africa', *EAAJ 13*, 1967, pp. 8–14
MALCOLM, D W *Report on gum and gum arabic*, Dar es Salaam, 1936
PARRY, M S *Recent Progress in the development of miombo woodland in Tanganyika*, Forest Division, Dar es Salaam, 1962
PRIDHAM, F H 'Shume forest: a guide to Shume-Magamba forest reserve, Lushoto District, Tanganyika', *Forest Division*, Dar es Salaam
SANGSTER, R G 'Forestry in East Africa: Tanganyika', pp. 122–5 in RUSSELL, E W *The natural resources of East Africa*, Nairobi, 1962
SMITH, F G *Beeswax*, Beekeeping Division, Forest Department, Dar es Salaam, 1955
Information supplied by The Forest Division, Ministry of Agriculture, Food and Co-operatives, Dar es Salaam
TANGANYIKA, MINISTRY OF LANDS, FOREST AND WILDLIFE, FOREST DIVISION, *Annual Report*, 1963, Dar es Salaam
TANZANIA, MINISTRY OF AGRICULTURE AND CO-OPERATIVES, FOREST DIVISION, *Monthly Area Returns*, 1967, Dar es Salaam
WILLAN, R L 'Natural regeneration of high forest in Tanganyika', British Commonwealth Forestry Conference, 1962, Dar es Salaam, 1961
WOOD, P J *Teak planting in Tanzania*, Forest Division, *Sylviculture, Research Section*, Dar es Salaam, 1967

30. Co-operative marketing

Background to the Budget, 1968–9, GP
LAMADE, W 'The role of the marketing boards in Tanzania'. *Economic Research Bureau Paper*, University College, Dar es Salaam, 1967

31. Utilization of water resources

COSTER, F M 'Underground water in Tanganyika'. Department of Water Development and Irrigation, Dar es Salaam, 1960
FOWLEY, A P 'Water resources of Dodoma and vicinity', *Records of the Geological Survey of Tanganyika* Vol. 6, pp. 56–63, 1956

GILLAM, C 'Reconnaissance survey of the hydrology of Tanganyika Territory in its geographical setting'. *Water consultants report No. 6*, Dar es Salaam, 1943

HEIJNEN, J 'Water. Guide to Basic Data on Resource Assessment and Land Use Planning'. *BRALUP Research Notes 5e*, Dar es Salaam, 1969

National Atlas of Tanzania, Vol. I, 1968

32. Density of road networks

HAZLEWOOD, A *Rail and Road in East Africa*, Oxford, 1964

MKAMA, J 'Transport Planning in Tanzania: An Assessment', *BRALUP Research Papers No. 8*, mimeo, 1969

33. Railways

EAST AFRICAN RAILWAYS AND HARBOURS, *Annual Reports*

GILLMAN, C 'A short history of the Tanganyika railways', *Tanganyika Notes and Records*, 1942

HAZLEWOOD, A *Rail and Road in East Africa*, Oxford, 1964

HILL, M F *Permanent Way*, Vol. II, The story of the Tanganyika Railways, *East African Railways and Harbours*, 1947

O'CONNOR, A M 'Railway construction and the pattern of economic development in East Africa', *Transactions of the Institute of British Geographers*, 36, 1965

34. Shipping trade

EAST AFRICAN COMMUNITY, EAST AFRICAN CUSTOMS AND EXCISE, *Annual Report (Trade)*, 1968

EAST AFRICAN RAILWAYS AND HARBOURS, *Annual Reports*, 1958–68

National Capital Master Plan, Dar es Salaam, June 1968

35. Air transport

Air Navigation Direction, *GP*, 1931

Data from airlines and travel offices, Dar es Salaam

36 and 37. Industrial production

Background to the Budget 1968–9, *GP*

JENSEN, S 'Regional Economic Atlas of Tanzania', *BRALUP Research Papers No. 1*, Dar es Salaam, 1969

JENSEN, S and MKAMA, J 'District Data, 1967', *Ministry of Economic Affairs and Development Planning*, 1968

38. Mineral occurrences

MINERAL RESOURCES DIVISION, MINERAL OCCURRENCES (map and text) ATLAS OF TANZANIA, GP, 1969

EDWARDS, C B and HAWKINS, J B 'Kimberlites in Tanganyika with special reference to the Mwadui occurrence', *Economic Geology, 61*, pp. 537–554

HARRIS, J F 'Summary of the geology of Tanganyika': Part 4. *Economic Geology*, 1961 (comprehensive pre-1961) GP

39. Mining

HARRIS, J F 'Summary of the geology of Tanganyika', *Economic Geology*, 61 (comprehensive pre-1961) *GP*

HMSO *Statistical Summary of the mineral industry; world production, exports and imports, 1961–6*, London, 1968

Tanzania Second Five Year Plan for economic and social development, Vol. 1, pp. 82–93 (general analysis), GP, 1969

40. The tourist industry

CSB *Some Statistics on tourism in Tanzania*, 1967, 1968

GRZIMEK, B and GRZIMEK, M *Serengeti Shall Not Die*, London, 1960

41. Energy supplies

HARKIN, D A 'The Mabamba bay coalfield, Tanganyika Territory'. *The Mining Magazine*, 1948

—— 'The geology of the Mhukuru coalfield', *Geological Survey Department, Short paper No. 28*, 1953

—— 'The geology of the Songwe-Kiwira coalfield, Rungwe District', *Geological Survey Department, Bullet 27*, 1955

McCONNELL, R B 'The geology of the Namwele-Mkomolo coalfield'. *Geological Division, Short paper No. 27*, Dar es Salaam, 1947

McKINLAY, A C M 'Coal in Tanganyika'. *Geological Survey Department, Report ACMMCK/28*, 1956

—— 'The coalfields and the coal resources of Tanzania'. *Geological Survey of Tanzania, Bulletin 38*, 1965

Management of the Agip. Caltex, Esso, Shell and Total Companies Ltd. *Depot Area Sales, 1967* (personal communication)

MINISTRY OF AGRICULTURE AND CO-OPERATIVES, FOREST DIVISION *Monthly Area Returns*, 1967

MINISTRY OF COMMERCE AND INDUSTRIES *Annual Report of the Mineral Resources Division*, 1967

SANGSTER, R G *op cit* 1962

SPENCE, J 'The geology of the Galula coalfield, Mbeya'. *Geological Survey Department, Bulletin 25*, 1954

STOCKLEY, G M 'New coal discoveries in Tanganyika'. *The Mining Magazine*, 1947

STOCKLEY, G M and OATES, F 'Report on the Geology of the Ruhuhu coal fields'. *Geological Survey Department, Bulletin 2*, 1931

TANZANIA ELECTRICITY SUPPLY COMPANY *Directors report and accounts*, 1968

UN *Statistical Yearbook*, 1968

42. Archaeology

COLE, S *The Prehistory of East Africa* (2nd edn.) New York, 1963; London, 1964

KIMAMBO, I N and TEMU, A J (eds.) *Zamani: a survey of East African History*, Chaps 3–6, London and Nairobi, 1968

OGOT, B A and KIERAN, J A (eds.) *A History of Tanzania*, Chaps 1–4, Nairobi, 1968

SHINNIE, P L (ed.) *The Iron Age in Africa*, Oxford, 1970

SUTTON, J E G 'The East African Coast: A Historical and Archaeological Review', *Historical Association of Tanzania, Paper No. 1*, 1966

43. Patterns of ports and trade-routes in different periods

FREEMAN-GRENVILLE, G S P *The East African Coast: Select Documents from the First to the Earlier Nineteenth Century*, Oxford, 1962

HOYLE, B S 'Early Port Development in East Africa: an illustration of the concept of changing port hierarchies', *Tijdscrift voor Economische en Sociale Geografie*, LVIII, 1967, pp. 94–102

KIMAMBO, I N and TEMU, A J (eds) *History of Tanzania*, Nairobi, 1969

KIRKMAN, J S *Men and Monuments on the East African Coast*, London, 1964

McMASTER, D N 'The Ocean-going Dhow Trade to East Africa', *The East African Geographical Review, No. 4*, 1966, pp. 13–24

OGOT, B A and KIERNAN, J A (eds.) *Zamani: a survey of East African History*, Nairobi, 1968

OLIVER, R and MATHEW G (eds.) *History of East Africa*, Vol. I, Oxford, 1963

PRINS, A H J *The Swahili-speaking peoples of Zanzibar and the East African Coast*, Ethnographic Surveys of Africa, London, 2nd edn, 1967, esp. pp. 38–49

SUTTON, J E G 'The East African Coast: an Historical and Archaeological Review', *Historical Association of Tanzania Paper No. 1*, Nairobi, 1966

44. The German administration

ADMIRALTY AND WAR OFFICE *1916 Handbook of German East Africa*, London, 1916

CALVERT, A F *German East Africa*, London, 1917

EBERLIE, R 'German achievement in East Africa', *Tanganyika Notes and Records*, 55, September 1960, pp. 181–214

ILIFFE, J *Tanganyika under German rule 1905-12*, Cambridge, 1969

45. Evolution of the administrative framework 1919–61: the British administration

MOFFETT, J P (ed.) *Handbook of Tanganyika*, 2nd edn., GP, 1958
Reports on Tanganyika 1922–38 to League of Nations. 1947–60 to United Nations

46. Languages and peopling

GREENBERG, J H *Languages of Africa*, Indiana, 1963
KIMAMBO, I N and TEMU, A J (eds.) *A History of Tanzania*, Chap. I, Nairobi, 1969
OGOT, B A and KIERAN, J A (eds.) *Zamani: a survey of East African History*, Chap. 4, Nairobi, 1968

47. Tribes

FORDE, D (ed.) 'Ethnographic Survey of Africa', *International African Institute*, London

East Central Africa:—

ABRAHAMS, R G Part XVII 'The peoples of greater Unyamwezi, Tanzania', 1967
BEIDELMAN, T O Part XVI 'The matrilineal peoples of eastern Tanzania', 1967
PRINS, A H J Part XII 'The Swahili-speaking peoples of Zanzibar and the East African Coast', 1967
TEW, M Part I 'Peoples of the Lake Nyasa region' 1950
WILLIS, R G Part XV 'The Fipa and related peoples of south-west Tanzania and north-east Zambia', 1907
GULLIVER, P H 'A Tribal map of Tanganyika', *Tanganyika Notes and Records, Vol. 52*, pp. 61–74, 1959
MOFFETT, J P (ed.) *Handbook of Tanganyika*, 2nd edn, GP, 1598
Tanganyika Population Census 1957, 'General African Census'. Tribal analysis' Parts 1 and 2. *East Africa Statistical Department*, Dar es Salaam, 1957

48. Population density, 1967

GILLMAN, C '1936 A population map of Tanganyika Territory'. GP 1936. Also in *Geographical Review, 26, 3* (1936) pp. 353–75
TANZANIA; *Population census*, Vol. I 'Enumeration' Area Statistics, CSM, 1969
THOMAS, I D 'The density and distribution of population in the Southern Highlands of Tanganyika', unpublished MA thesis, University of Wales, 1966
'Population density in Tanzania, 1967', *BRALUP Research Notes 5b*, UCD, Dar es Salaam, 1968

49. Population characteristics

African Census Report, GP, 1957
CSB *Provisional estimates of fertility, mortality and population growth.* 1968

50 and 51. Health services and the incidence of disease

General:

CLYDE, D F History of the medical services of Tanganyika, GP, 1964
Tanzania, Five Year Plan for Economic and Social Development, GP, 1964

Malaria:

CLYDE, D Malaria in Tanzania, Oxford University Press, 1967
East African Institute for malaria and vector-borne diseases, *Report on the Pare-Taveta Malaria Scheme*, 1954–7, GP
Annual Reports (particularly sections by Clyde, Lane, Lelijveld, Mzoo, Otieno, Pringle, Smith, White)
PROTHERO, R M *Migrants and malaria*, Longmans, London, 1965
WHO *Quarterly Field Reports*, Malaria Eradication Project, Zanzibar

Schistosomiasis:

East African Institute for malaria and vector-borne diseases, *Annual Reports* (particularly sections by Otieno)
East African Institute for medical research, *Annual Reports* (particularly sections by Forsyth, Jordan, Purnell, Sturrock, Webbe)

McCULLOUGH, F S, EYAKUZE, V M, MSINDE, J and NDITI, H 'Water resources and bilharziasis transmission in the Misungwi area, Mwanza District, North-West Tanzania', *East African Medical Journal, 45*, pp. 295–308, 1968
WEBBE, G 'Population studies of intermediate hosts in relation to transmission of bilharziasis in East Africa', *CIBA Symposium on bilharziasis*, Churchill, London

Filariasis:

East African Filariasis Research Unit, *Annual Reports*
East African Institute for medical research, *Annual Reports* (particularly sections by Jordan)
JORDAN, P 'Epidemiology and control of Bancroftian filariasis in Africa with particular reference to Tanganyika', *Proceedings of the Sixth International Congress on Tropical Medicine and Malaria*, 1958

Onchocerciasis:

East African Institute for malaria and vector-borne diseases, *Annual Reports* (particularly sections by Choyce, Laing, Pringle, Raybould, Sprengle, Wegesa, Woodruff, Yagunga)
FREEMAN, P and DE MEILLON, B *Simulidae of the Ethiopian Region*, London, 1953
GABTHULER, M J and GABATHULER, A W 'Onchocerciasis in the Ulanga District', *East African Medical Journal, 25*, pp. 188–95
HAUSERMANN, W 'Preliminary notes on a Simulium survey in the onchocerciasis infested Ulanga District, Tanzania', *Acta Tropica, 23, pp. 365–73, 1966*
WOODRUFF, A W 'Distribution of onchocerciasis in Tanzania', WHO Onch/32.65
WOODRUFF, A W, CHOYCE, D P, PRINGLE, G, LAING, A B G, HILLS, M and WEGESA, P 'Onchocerciasis in the Usambara Mountains: the disease, its epidemiology and its relationship to ocular complications', *Transactions of the Royal Society for Tropical Medicine and Hygiene, 600*, pp. 695–706, 1966

Trypanosomaisis:

EAST AFRICAN TSETSE RESEARCH ORGANISATION, *Annual Reports*
TANGANYIKA, MINISTRY OF AGRICULTURE, *Tsetse control reports*
TANGANYIKA, MINISTRY OF HEALTH AND HOUSING, *Sleeping-sickness reports*

52. Education

JENSEN, S 'Regional Economic Atlas Mainland Tanzania', *BRALUP, Research Paper No. 1*
MINISTRY OF EDUCATION, *Annual Report*, 1967
NYERERE, PRESIDENT, J K *The Arusha Declaration*, February, 1967
Education and Self-Reliance, 1968

53 and 54. Traditional rural settlement

ATTEMS, M *Permanent cropping in the Usambara mountains*, pp. 137–74
in Ruthenburg, H *op. cit.*
GEORGULAS, N *Settlement patterns and rural development in Tanganyika*, pp. 24, 121, 180–92, 1967
GULLIVER, P H 'Land tenure and social change among the Nyakysa', *East African Institute of Social Research*, East African Studies, No. 11, 1968
MALCOLM, D W *Sukumaland: An African people and their country*, London, 1953
MILNE, G 'African village layout', *Tanganyika Notes and Records*, 13, 1942, pp. 3–5
MTENGA, P and LADAK, N F 'Student field reports on peasant agriculture in the Meru area', Department of Geography, University College, Dar es Salaam, 1966
NATIONAL MUSEUM OF TANZANIA, *Guide to Village Museum*, Dar es Salaam, 1966
PRINS, A H J *The Swahili-speaking peoples of Zanzibar and the East African Coast*, London, 1961

RALD, J 'Land-use in a Buhaya village', *BRALUP Research paper No. 5*, Dar es Salaam, 1969

REHSE, H KIZIBA *Land und Leute*, Stuttgart, 1910

REINING, P C 'Land resources of the Haya', pp. 217–44 in Brokensha, D (ed.) *Ecology and Economic Development in Tropical Africa, Berkeley*, 1965

RIGBY, O H A 'Aspects of residence and co-operation in a Gogo Village', *East African Institute of Social Research Conference Papers*, January, 1962

ROTENHAM, VON D 'Cotton farming in Sukumaland', pp. 51–86 in Ruthenburg, H *op. cit.*

ROUNCE, N V *et al The Agriculture of the cultivation steppe*, Cape Town, 1949

RUTHENBURG, H (ed.) *Smallholder farming and smallholder development in Tanzania*, London, 1968

SENIOR, H S 'The Sukuma homestead', *Tanganyika Notes and Records*, 9, 1940, pp. 42–4

TANZANIA, MINISTRY OF LANDS, HOUSING AND URBAN DEVELOPMENT, SURVEY DIVISION. Air photographs

WILSON, G 'The land rights of individuals among the Nyakusa', *Rhodes-Livingstone Papers, No. 1*, 1938

WILSON, M Good Company. *A study of Nyakyusa-age villages*, London, 1951

VINANS, E V *Shambala: the constitution of a traditional state*, London, 1962

Map data from :

Umeru

MTENGA, P and LADAK, N F 'Student fields reports on peasant agriculture in the Meru area', Department of Geography, Univesity College, Dar es Salaam, 1966
Directorate of Overseas Survey, Tolworth, UK, Air photographs, 60 TN 5 Nos. 19 and 20

Usukuma

MALCOLM, D W *Sukumaland: An African people and their country*, London, 1953, pp. 35, 74

Ugogo

SURVEY MAPPING DIVISION, MINISTRY OF LANDS, HOUSING AND URBAN DEVELOPMENT, Dar es Salaam, Topographic map 1 : 50 000 sheet 162/1, Dodoma West

Usambaa

DIRECTORATE OF OVERSEAS SURVEY, Tolworth, UK, Air photographs of Tanganyika 29, Nos. 102 and 103

Uswahili

DIRECTORATE OF OVERSEAS SURVEY, Tolworth, UK, Air photographs HAS/TK/G3/PR/11 Nos. 4504 and 4505

Unyakyusa

GULLIVER, P H 'Land tenure and social change among the Nyakyusa', *East African Institute of Social Research, East African Studies*, No. 11, 1958, p. 29

WILSON, G 'The land rights of individuals among the Nyakyusa', *Rhodes-Livingstone Papers No. 1*, 1938, p. 17

Uhaya

REINING, R C 'Land resources of the Haya', pp. 217–44 in Brokensha, D (ed.) *Ecology and Economic Develoment in Tropical Africa, Berkeley*, 1965, p. 225

House types :

NATIONAL MUSEUM OF TANZANIA, *Village Museum*

SENIOR, H S *op. cit.*

REHSE, H KIZIBA *Land und Leute*, Stuttgart, 1910

55. New rural settlement

INTERNATIONAL BANK FOR RECONSTRUCTION AND DEVELOPMENT, *The Economic Development of Tanganyika*, Dar es Salaam, 1960

NYERERE, PRESIDENT, J K *Socialism and Rural Development*, Dar es Salaam, 1967
Speech to the National Assembly, 10 December, 1962

56. Major urban centres

MASCARENHAS, A M, and JENSEN, S 'Service Centres in Tanzania', *BRALUP Research Papers No. 11* (forthcoming)

MOFFETT, J P *Handbook of Tanganyika*, 2nd edn, GP, 1958

TANZANIA, Second Five Year Plan, Vol. 1, 'General analysis', GP 1969

TANZANIA *Laws of Tanganyika*, Title XIV, Chap. 101, (Township Ordinances)

TANZANIA SURVEYS *District Map Series*. Scales 1 : 100 000 to 1 : 500 000, Dar es Salaam (various dates)

TANZANIA *Population Census, 1967*, Vol. 1. 'Enumeration' Area Statistics, CSB, 1969

57–59. The growth and function of Dar es Salaam; The port of Dar es Salaam; Land use in Dar es Salaam

DE BLIJ, H J *Dar es Salaam: a study in urban geography*, Northwestern University Press, 1963

GILMAN, C 'Dar es Salaam 1860–1940' *Tanganyika Notes and Records* 20, pp. 1–23, 1945

GREY, J M 'Dar es Salaam under the Sultan of Zanzibar', *Tanganyika Notes and Records 31*, pp. 1–21, 1952

HANCE, W A and DONGEN, VON I S 'Dar es Salaam: the port and its tributary area', *Annals of the Association of American Geographers, Vol. 48*, pp. 419–35, 1958

HOYLE, B S 'Expansion of facilities at East African sea ports', *EAGR No. 5*, 1967

LESLIE, J A K *A survey of Dar es Salaam*, Oxford University Press, London, 1963

MASCARENHAS, A C 'The impact of nationhood on Dar es Salaam', *EAGR No. 5*, 1967

MASCARENHAS, A C 'Urban Development in Dar es Salaam', M.A. Thesis, University of California, Los Angeles, 1965

PIORO, Z *et al* 'Dar es Salaam City and Region', Ministry of Housing, Dar es Salaam

'Dar es Salaam, City, Port and Region', *Tanzania Notes and Records*, Dar es Salaam, 1970

60. Mtwara and Tanga

HOYLE, B S *The seaports of East Africa*, East African Publishing House, Nairobi, 1967

—— 'Expansion of facilities at East African seaports', *EAGR No. 5*, 1967

EAST AFRICAN RAILWAYS AND HARBOURS, *Annual Reports*, 1967, 1968

Appendix 1

O'CONNOR, A M 'East African Topographic Mapping', *EAGR, Vol. 4*, 1966

TANZANIA, *Catalogue of Maps*, Survey Department 3rd edn, January, 1969

TEMPLE, P H 'Geological Mapping in East Africa', *EAGR, Vol. 3*, 1965

APPENDIX I

POPULATION DATA

District	Population	Area in square km.	Population density
ARUSHA	610 474	82 098	7·4
Arusha	181 764	2 978	61·0
Masai	106 892	63 063	1·7
Mbulu	289 366	16 057	18·0
Arusha Town	32 452		
COAST	511 506	33 719	15·2
Bagamoyo	117 547	9 842	11·9
Kisarawe	180 536	8 936	20·2
Mafia	16 748	518	32·2
Mzizima	75 651	1 084	69·8
Rufiji	121 024	13 339	9·1
DODOMA	709 380	41 311	17·2
Dodoma	297 440	16 576	17·9
Kondoa	212 195	13 208	16·1
Mpwapwa	176 186	11 526	15·3
Dodoma Town	23 559		
IRINGA	689 905	56 845	12·1
Iringa	230 881	28 619	8·1
Mufindi	118 467	7 117	16·6
Njombe	318 811	21 109	15·1
Iringa Town	21 746		
KIGOMA	473 443	37 039	12·8
Kasulu	207 611	9 324	22·3
Kibondo	136 918	16 058	8·5
Kigoma	107 545	11 657	9·2
Kigoma-Ujiji Town	21 369		
KILIMANJARO	652 722	13 209	49·4
Kilimanjaro	476 223	5 310	89·7
Same/Pare	149 635	7 900	18·9
Moshi Town	26 864		
MARA	544 125	21 797	25·0
Musoma	340 177	17 871	19·0
North Mara	188 536	3 885	48·5
Musoma Town	15 412		
MBEYA	969 053	83 139	11·7
Chunya	53 618	27 066	2·0
Mbeya	180 208	18 519	9·9
Mobzi	147 489	9 583	15·4
Rungwe	359 971	5 180	69·5
Sumbawanga	215 288	22 792	9·4
Mbeya Town	12 479		
MOROGORO	685 104	73 038	9·4
Kilosa	193 810	14 245	13·6
Morogoro	291 110	19 296	15·1
Ulanga	174 922	39 498	4·4
Morogoro Town	25 262		
MTWARA	1 041 146	82 751	12·6
Kilwa	97 957	13 852	7·1
Lindi	228 062	9 454	24·1
Masasi	213 683	8 936	23·9
Mtwara	114 345	3 756	30·4
Nachingwea	80 482	42 735	1·9
Newala	272 852	4 015	68·0
Mtwara Town	20 396		
Lindi Town	13 352		
MWANZA	1 055 141	19 684	53·6
Geita	371 407	9 065	41·0
Malya/Kwimba	305 516	6 087	50·2
Mwanza	234 080	3 885	60·3
Ukerewe	109 277	640	170·7
Mwanza Town	34 861		
RUVUMA	393 043	61 254	6·4
Mbinga	144 098	8 418	17·1
Songea	151 390	34 059	4·4
Tunduru	97 555	18 778	5·2
SHINYANGA	899 468	50 764	17·7
Kahama	147 628	19 943	7·4
Maswa	430 916	21 368	20·2
Shinyanga	320 924	9 450	34·0
SINGIDA	457 938	49 340	9·3
Iramba	183 962	7 900	23·3
Manyoni	80 157	28 620	2·8
Singida	193 819	12 821	15·1
TABORA	562 853	121 989	4·6
Mpanda	60 803	45 843	1·3
Nzega	302 017	13 727	22·0
Tabora	179 039	62 419	2·9
Tabora Town	21 012		
TANGA	771 060	26 807	28·8
Handeni	133 235	13 209	10·1
Korogwe	140 306	3 756	37·4
Lushoto	210 484	3 497	60·2
Pangani	28 426	1 425	19·9
Tanga	197 551	4 921	40·1
Tanga Municipality	61 058		
WEST LAKE	658 712	28 749	22·9
Biharamulo	81 854	10 878	7·5
Bukoba	374 988	8 029	46·7
Karagwe	97 407	6 700	14·5
Ngara	96 322	2 849	33·8
Bukoba Town	8 141		
DAR ES SALAAM	272 821	88	3 100·2
ZANZIBAR AND PEMBA	354 815	2 644	134·2
Zanzibar	190 494	1 660	114·2
Pemba	164 321	984·2	167·0
Zanzibar Town	68 490	6·5	1 053·7

APPENDIX II
MAPS AND AIR PHOTOGRAPHS OF TANZANIA

This appendix briefly reviews the available map and air photographs of Tanzania and provides some suggestions for detailed study. The larger-scale maps currently available include topographical maps in scales of 1 : 2 000 000 for the whole country, 1 : 1 000 000 covering the whole country in six sheets, 1 : 250 000 and 1 : 50 000. There are also maps in the scales of 1 : 10 000, 1 : 5000 and 1 : 2500 of the major townships of Tanzania, and special maps at various scales – ranging from 1 : 100 000 to 1 : 125 000. These are of tourist or technical significance.

Geological maps are available in scales of 1 : 125 000 and 1 : 2 000 000 (coloured). There are a few other maps available especially in the *National Atlas* where the basic map is in a scale of 1 : 3 000 000. Air photographs are available for certain areas at scales of 1 : 120 000 and 1 : 50 000; but the whole of Tanzania has been completely covered by aerial photography of varying age and at different scales. Generally the photography used for small-scale mapping is about 1 : 30 000 – 1 : 40 000 and a print of each photograph is filed in the Air Photograph Library in Dar es Salaam, where it is available for inspection.[1]

Topographic maps

Several editions of a 1 : 2 000 000 map covering the mainland of Tanzania (Tanganyika) have been produced and there is now a first edition (1965) for the whole of Tanzania at this scale. This map depicts physical features, roads, railways and administrative boundaries. The sheet is in several colours, and layered or contoured versions are available.

There should be six sheets in a scale of the international 1 : 1 000 000 covering the whole of Tanzania, but only four sheets are available at present. These are the Lindi sheet (SC 37), Dar es Salaam sheet (SB 37), Tabora sheet (SB 36) and Mwanza sheet (SA 36). Sheets SA 37 and SC 36 are in preparation. The available sheets are extremely well produced. (See Map 2 for coverage.)

The 1 : 250 000 maps (Series Y 503) show clearly major relief features with contours or form lines at 200 ft. intervals up to 5000 ft. above sea-level and at 500 ft. intervals above this height and with layer colours at each 1000 ft. They also provide some indication of vegetation, of the extent of rural settlement and of the nature of the land surface in areas with little vegetation or settlement. Adjacent sheets may be joined together for a very effective display of a large tract of country. The country, however, has a very incomplete coverage with only 24 sheets published and 10 sheets being mapped. (See Map 2.) Some parts of the country, such as the central part, are covered by old maps which are out of date and cartographically poor.

The whole of the Tanzanian mainland is to be covered at 1 : 50 000 in 1250 sheets of which only about half have yet been published in any form. (See Map 3 for coverage.) These sheets are compiled from aerial photographs and ground control. The quality varies, however, from single colour planimetric sheets to good quality five-colour contoured maps. High-standard maps in this series number about 180 and are largely confined to the Coast, Tanga, Kilimanjaro and Dodoma Regions. Parts of the Southern Highlands are represented on satisfactory contoured sheets dating from 1960, but generally the sheets in the west and south-west are of poorer quality than the remainder and were published on a provisional basis. The sheets of the Biharamulo area in the north-west are noteworthy for their portrayal of the remarkable ridge and valley country there. A small group of useful maps covers Mara Region, but the country south of Lake Victoria is only now being mapped at this scale. Physically the Rift Valley features are well portrayed by the Ngorongoro sheet 53/1, Mto wa Mbu sheet 53/4, Oldonyo Lengai sheet 39/4, and Kwa Kuchinja sheet 69/2; the coastal features by Tanganyika sheet 186/IV, Tanz, Mafia (N) 223 and sheets in group 222. In this category of maps is a special map for Mt Kilimanjaro with contours with a 100 ft. vertical interval, hill-shading and excellent representations of the fringing zone of settlement.

Mention should be made of the Zanzibar and Pemba maps. They differ from the mainland cartographically as they are mapped at a scale of 1 : 63 360, two sheets covering each island. The Zanzibar sheets were last revised in 1964, but those of Pemba have not been revised since 1942. These four are among the most interesting of East African topographical maps, showing a wealth of detail on both physical and human phenomena.

There are fifteen township maps covering the legally defined townships in Tanzania. Each township is, or will be, covered by a composite sheet (C) and also by an individual series of large scale maps at 1 : 2500 or 1 : 5000. The maps are based on aerial photography and show contours and plot boundaries. (See table below.) As well as township maps, there are 30 maps covering the developed extent of certain urban areas in Tanzania. The majority of these sheets are based on aerial photography and show contours and plot boundaries. (See list below.)

National Atlas

The first edition of the *Atlas of Tanzania* 1968 is a bound volume 22 in. × 18 in. containing 28 sheets with facing descriptive information and a gazetteer. The basic map is 1 : 3 000 000 and the *Atlas* is divided into the following sections:

Physical Geography
Climatic
Flora and fauna
Human geography
Medical
Resources
Statistics

Geological mapping

The country is covered by a 1 : 2 000 000 sheet published as Part 2 of Memoir I, *Summary of the Geology of Tanganyika*, 1960. This map is accompanied by a comprehensive and scholarly

---

[1] No stock is held in respect of photographs, print laydowns or mosaics and copies are prepared in accordance with individual orders, which should be placed well in advance of requirement. (See Map 1 for coverage.)

account (Quennell, McKinlay and Aitken, 1956). About 418 984 sq. km. (188 400 sq. miles) of Tanzania are covered by basic maps on the scale of 1:125 000; of these, several sheets represent the plateau areas that form most of the country. The eastern zone is well illustrated by the Morogoro area sheets depicting a well-defined meridional structural trend, extensive erosion surfaces, inselbergs and old faults. The Geita sheet represents the pediment and aspect of the eroded granites of Sukumaland. The Mahenge sheet shows the well-defined faulted junction of the pre-Cambrian rocks with a weaker continental basin of Karroo sediments. The Lushoto and Lake Jipe sheets also portray clearly the fault structures where these are well defined in relation to the block mountains. The Manda area sheet shows the Karroo sediments which have Tanzania's most important coalfields. The Kilwa sheet indicates the breakdown from the plateau to the coast. The Tukuyu, the Angata Salei and the Kilimanjaro sheets exemplify the later volcanic history of the eastern rift. (See Map 4 for coverage.)

JOSEPHINE KADUMA

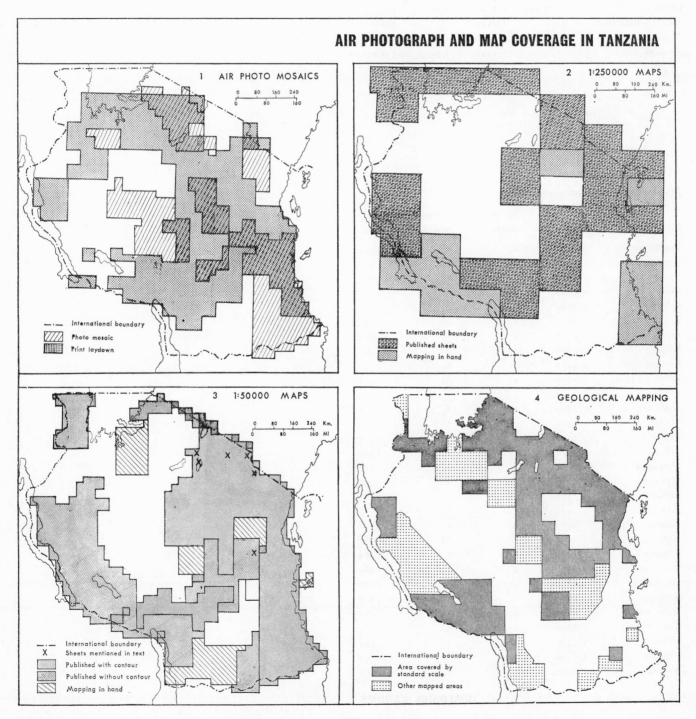

Maps of towns in Tanzania

	Composite		Sheets	
Arusha	1/10 000	1/2500	1/5	1966
Bukoba	1/5000	1/2500	1/5	1962
Dar es Salaam	1/25 000	1/5000	1/11	1957/59
		1/2500	1/6	1957/59
Dodoma		1/2500	1/16	1962/63
Iringa		1/2500	1/6	1957
Kigoma-Ujiji		1/2500	1/4	1964
		1/2500	1/4	1961
Lindi		1/2500	1/3	1960
Mbeya	1/5000	1/2500	1/4	1965
Morogoro	1/10 000	1/2500	1/6	1963
Moshi	1/10 000	1/2500	1/10	1962
Mtwara-Mikindani		1/2500	1/10	1964
Musoma		1/2500	1/5	1960
Mwanza		1/2500	1/9	1963
Tabora	1/10 000	1/2500	1/7	1957/65
Tanga	1/10 000	1/2500	1/17	1958/59

Maps of other urban areas

Urban Area	Scale	No. of sheets	Coloured or monochrome	Year
Bagamoyo	1/5000	1	M	1953
Bagamoyo	1/2500	1	C	1968
Biharamulo	1/2500	2	C	1962
Geita	1/5000	1	C	1966
Ifakara	1/5000	1	M	1961
Kilosa	1/2500	1	M	1958
Kilwa Kivinje	1/2500	1	C	1963
Kissessa	1/1000	1	M	1961
Kondoa	1/5000	1	C	1957
Korogwe (old)	1/2500	1	M	1951
Kyela	1/2500	2	C	1965
Lushoto	1/2500	3	C	1963
Malya	1/2500	1	C	1967
Manyoni	1/2500	1	C	1967
Mbulu	1/5000	1	C	1966
Misungwi	1/2500	1	M	1957
Mpwapwa	1/2500	4	C	1964
Mufindi	1/2500	1	C	1964
Nansio	1/2500	1	C	1962
Njombe	1/2500	2	C	1962
Nyakata	1/1000	1	M	1960
Pangani	1/2500	1	C	1965
Shinyanga	1/2500	4	C	1961
Singida	1/2500	4	C	1962
Songea	1/5000	1	C	1963
Sumbawanga	1/2500	2	C	1967
Tarime	1/2500	1	C	1965
Tukuyu	1/2500	2	C	1963
Usagara	1/2500	1	M	1957
Vwawa	1/2500	1	C	1967

JOSEPHINE KADUMA

TABLES

TABLE 1 Administrative structure, 1967

Region	Regional Headquarters	District	District Headquarters
Arusha	Arusha	Arusha	*Arusha*
		Masai	Monduli
		Mbulu	Mbulu
Coast	Dar es Salaam	Bagamoyo	Bagamoyo
		Kisarawe	Kisarawe
		Mafia	Kilindoni
		Mzizima	*Dar es Salaam*
		Rufiji	Utete
Dodoma	Dodoma	Dodoma	*Dodoma*
		Kondoa	Kondoa
		Mpwapwa	Mpwapwa
Iringa	Iringa	Iringa	*Iringa*
		Mufindi	Kibau
		Njombe	Njombe
Kigoma	Kigoma/Ujiji	Kasulu	Kasulu
		Kibondo	Kibondo
		Kigoma	*Kigoma/Ujiji*
Kilimanjaro	Moshi	Kilimanjaro	*Moshi*
		Same/Pare	Same
Mara	Musoma	Musoma	*Musoma*
		North Mara	Tarime
Mbeya	Mbeya	Chunya	Chunya
		Mbeya	*Mbeya*
		Mbozi	Vwawa
		Rungwe	Tukuyu
		Sumbawanga	Sumbawanga
Morogoro	Morogoro	Kilosa	Kilosa
		Morogoro	*Morogoro*
		Ulanga	Mahenge
Mtwara	Mtwara/Mikindani	Kilwa	Kilwa
		Lindi	*Lindi*
		Masasi	Masasi
		Mtwara	*Mtwara/Mikindani*
		Nachingwea	Nachingwea
		Newala	Newala
Mwanza	Mwanza	Geita	Geita
		Malya/Kwimba	Malya
		Mwanza	*Mwanza*
		Ukerewe	Nansio
Ruvuma	Songea	Mbinga	Mbinga
		Songea	*Songea*
		Tunduru	Tunduru
Shinyanga	Shinyanga	Kahama	Kahama
		Maswa	Nyalikungu
		Shinyanga	*Shinyanga*
Singida	Singida	Iramba	Kiomboi
		Manyoni	Manyoni
		Singida	Singida
Tabora	Tabora	Mpanda	Mpanda
		Nzega	Nzega
		Tabora	*Tabora*
Tanga	Tanga	Handeni	Handeni
		Korogwe	Korogwe
		Lushoto	Lushoto
		Pangani	Pangani
		Tanga	*Tanga*
West Lake	Bukoba	Biharamulo	Biharamulo
		Bukoba	*Bukoba*
		Karagwe	Bugene
		Ngara	Ngara
Zanzibar	Zanzibar	Pemba	Chake Chake
		Zanzibar	*Zanzibar*

TABLE 2 Size of administrative units, 1967: Area and population

Admin. units/size	Region	District	Division	Subdivision
No. of Units	18	62	360	1 290
a AREA				
Average size (km.²)	49 232	14 293	2 462	687
Largest (km.²)	121 989	63 063	23 986	10 233
Smallest (km.²)	13 209*	518	75	1
b POPULATION				
Average size (km.²)	684 081	198 604	34 204	9 545
Largest (km.²)	1 055 141	476 223	177 666	54 623
Smallest (km.²)	393 043*	16 748	2 269	221

Source: Thomas, *Tanzania 1967 Population Census Report*, Vol. 1, Appendix, pp. 262-342

* Zanzibar Region has 354 815 people and is only 2644 sq. km.

TABLE 3 Areas, population and population density of selected countries of Africa*

Country	Population 1967 (thous.)	Area sq. km. (thous.)	Population density (p.s.k.)
Tanzania	12 313	886	14
Kenya	9 948	583	17
Uganda	7 934	236	34
Malawi	4 130	118	35
Burundi	3 340	28	120
Rwanda	3 306	26	126
Zambia	3 947	753	5
Congo (K)	16 353	2 345	7
Algeria	12 540	2 382	5
Morocco	14 140	445	32
Nigeria	61 450	924	67
			—
AFRICA	328 000	30 313	11
			—

* *Demographic Yearbook 1967*, UN, New York, 1968; *Tanzania 1967 Population Census*, Vol. 1, Dar es Salaam, 1969

TABLE 4 Area, population and population density by Regions, 1967*

Region	Area sq. km. (thous.)	Percentage of total	Population (thous.)	Percentage of total	Population density p.s.k
Arusha	82	9·3	610	5·0	7·4
Coast (incl. DSM)	34	3·8	784	6·4	23·3
Dodoma	41	4·7	709	5·8	17·2
Iringa	57	6·4	690	5·6	12·1
Kigoma	37	4·2	473	3·8	12·8
Kilimanjaro	13	1·5	653	5·3	49·4
Mara	22	2·5	544	4·4	25·0
Mbeya	83	9·4	969	7·9	11·7
Morogoro	73	8·2	685	5·6	9·4
Mtwara	83	8·4	1041	8·5	12·6
Mwanza	19·5	2·2	1056	8·6	53·6
Ruvuma	61	6·9	393	3·2	6·4
Shinyanga	51	5·7	899	7·3	17·7
Singida	49	5·6	458	3·7	9·3
Tabora	122	13·8	563	4·6	4·6
Tanga	27	6.2	771	6·3	28·8
West Lake	29	3·2	659	5·3	22·9
Zanzibar	2·5	0·3	355	2·9	134·2
TOTAL	886·0	100·0	12 313	100·0	13·9

* *Tanzania 1967 Population Census*, Vol. 1, Dar es Salaam, 1969

TABLE 5 Population, 1967: density classes by District*

Density class p.s.k.	No. of Districts	Pop. total in class (thous.)	Percentage of total pop.	Total area in class (thous. sq. km.)	Percentage of total area
0– 4·9	8	908	7·4	343	38·7
5–14·9	14	2014	16·4	219	24·7
15–29·9	20	4532	36·8	243	27·4
30–49·9	8	1652	13·4	41	4·7
50–99·9	8	2394	19·4	36	4·0
100 and over	4	812	6·6	4	0·5
TOTAL	62	12 312	100·0	886	100·0

* *Tanzania 1967 Census Report*, Vol. 1, Appendix, Dar es Salaam, 1969

TABLE 6 Percentage of urban population for selected countries of Africa*

Country	Total population (thous.)	Urban population (thous.)	Urban percentage
Tanzania	12 313	831	6·7
Kenya	8 636	671	7·8
Zambia	3 490	738	21·1
Burundi	3 210	71	2·2
Chad	2 524	173	6·9
Congo (B)	582	68	11·6
Nigeria	55 670	8971	16·1
Congo (K)	12 734	2795	21·9
Ghana	6 727	1551	23·1
Morocco	11 626	3412	29·3

* *Demographic Yearbook 1967*, U.N., New York, 1968
  Tanzania 1967 Population Census, Vol. 1, Dar es Salaam, 1969

TABLE 7   Racial composition of the population of Tanganyika (1957) and Zanzibar (1958)*

Racial/ethnic group	Tanganyika (thous.)	Zanzibar (thous.)	Total (thous.)
African and indigenous	8665	275	8940
Arabs	19	5	24
Asians other than Arabs	77	18	95
Europeans	21	0·5	21
Somalis and others	7	0·3	7
TOTAL	8789	299	9087

* Tanganyika Census of the non-African population, 1957, Dar es Salaam, 1958;
Zanzibar Report of the Census, 1958, Zanzibar, 1960

TABLE 8   Population recorded in censuses 1913-67 (thous.)*

Census year	Tanganyika Afr. pop.	Non-Afr. pop.	Total	Zanzibar	Total Tanganyika & Zanzibar
1913	4145	21	4166	—	—
1921	4107	17	4124	217	—
1928	4741			—	—
1931	5023	41	5064	235	5299
1948	7410	70	7480	264	7745
1952		95		—	—
1957/58	8665	123	8788	299	9088
1967	—	—	11959	355	12314

* Tanzania 1967 Population Census, Vol. 5, Ch. 1, Dar es Salaam (forthcoming)

TABLE 9   Birth and death rates, natural increase and expectation of life for selected countries of Africa[1]

Country (and reference date)	Birth rate per thousand	Death rate per thousand	Infant mortality rate per thousand	Natural increase	Expectation of life[2] M. combined F.
Tanganyika (1957)	46	24–25	190	21–22	35–40
Zanzibar (1958)	30	21	157	9	43
Tanzania (1967)	47	22	160/165	25	40–41
Uganda (1959)	42	20	160	22	—
Kenya (1962)	50	20	—	30	40–45
Zambia (1963)	51	20	259	31·8	40
Burundi (1965)	46	26	150	20·5	35–39
Madagascar (1966)	46	25	102	21	38–38
Chad (1963/4)	45	31	160	14	39–35
Gambia (1963)	39	21	—	17·7	43
AFRICA (1960–67)	46	22	—	24	—

[1] Demographic Year Book, 1967, U.N., New York, 1968, Tanzania, 1968
[2] Expectation of life at birth for Males and Females separately, or for total population (as single figure, or an estimated range)

Table 10   Absolute increment and percentage change in population, 1957-67, for selected Districts*

District	1957 Pop. ('000)	1967 Pop. ('000)	Population change Absolute ('000)	1957-67 Percentage
Biharamulo	41	80	39	95
Nachingwea	56	81	25	45
Rungwe	271	359	88	33
Geita	270	371	101	37
Kilimanjaro	351	476	125	36

* Tanzania: Recorded Population Changes, 1948-67, Central Statistical Bureau,
Dar es Salaam, 1968

TABLE 11   Run-off data for selected rivers

	Av annual discharge m of cubic metres	Run-off in cubic metres per square kilometre
Pangani	968 000	19 400
Wami	2 030 000	43 650
Ruvu	2 960 000	116 000
Rufiji	33 500 000	196 000

TABLE 12   Evaporation rates and rainfall at various stations (mm.)

	J	F	M	A	M	J	J	A	S	O	N	D	Year
DAR ES SALAAM													
Evaporation	208	203	188	151	172	155	160	179	195	209	207	210	2237
Rainfall	60	74	122	264	228	34	22	25	27	48	63	74	1041
TABORA													
Evaporation	167	129	142	169	202	211	239	271	311	314	209	164	2528
Rainfall	136	125	161	140	33	3	0	1	4	14	81	184	882
MOSHI													
Evaporation	281	270	259	193	143	136	125	182	251	319	334	345	2838
Rainfall	44	45	110	306	187	29	11	14	14	29	36	49	874

TABLE 13   Dew point temperatures (°C) and relative humidities (%)

	Time (GMT)	J	F	M	A	M	J	J	A	S	O	N	D	Year
DAR ES SALAAM														
D.P.	0600	23·4	23·7	24·4	23·8	22·5	21·2	20·3	20·4	20·9	21·8	23·0	23·6	22·4
	1200	23·1	23·2	23·6	23·6	21·7	19·7	18·8	18·1	19·0	20·6	22·2	23·1	21·4
R.H.	0300	94	95	96	97	96	97	97	96	96	97	97	95	96
	1200	65	65	68	74	67	60	59	54	55	58	64	66	63
MWANZA														
D.P.	0600	17·6	17·6	18·0	18·2	17·4	14·6	13·2	13·6	14·8	16·4	17·0	17·8	16·3
	1200	18·0	18·2	18·6	19·2	18·5	16·3	14·9	15·4	16·1	16·9	17·6	17·7	17·3
R.H.	0300	88	89	90	90	88	81	77	77	78	85	87	89	85
	1200	63	62	63	67	62	53	48	51	52	56	59	63	58
IRINGA														
D.P.	0600	15·6	15 6	15·6	14·7	12·8	10·2	9·0	9·2	10·2	11·0	12·3	14·6	12·5
	1200	15·6	15·7	16·2	15·6	13·3	10·6	9·1	9·0	9·6	10·2	11·4	14·3	12·6
R.H.	0300	94	89	93	95	84	89	79	89	80	80	89	91	88
	1200	65	64	67	64	56	48	45	43	40	38	40	57	52

TABLE 14   Gross Domestic Product at current factor cost (mill. shs.)

Industry	1962	1965	1967	Annual growth rate 1962–67	Annual growth rate per inhabitant	Relative composition
Agriculture	993	1298	1368	7%	4%	24·0
Mining	103	121	154	8%	5%	2·7
Manufacturing	154	234	314	15%	12%	5·5
Construction	122	151	215	12%	9%	3·8
Public utilities	30	37	51	11%	8%	0·9
Commerce	484	658	781	10%	7%	13·7
Transport	188	216	280	8%	5%	4·9
Other services	448	580	649	8%	5%	11·4
Rent	175	246	304	12%	9%	5·3
MONETARY TOTAL	2697	3541	4116	9%	6%	72·2
Subsistence	1492	1953	1576	1%	−2%	27·8
TOTAL	4189	5494	5692	6%	3%	100·0
TOTAL IN CONTRACT PRICES	3796	4271	4731	4%	1%	—

TABLE 15 Marketed production of major agricultural crops, 1962-67 (tons)

	1962-64	1965	1967
Cotton	46 000	67 000	69 700
Coffee	31 000	44 000	50 000
Sisal	219 000	214 000	216 000
Sugar	50 000	66 000	70 600
Cashew	62 000	73 000	75 300
Tea	4 600	5 600	7 000
Tobacco	2 000	5 200	7 700
Pyrethrum	2 100	3 600	6 600
Maize	100 000	83 000	104 100
Cassava	71 000	106 000	—
Bananas	106 000	96 000	124 000

TABLE 16 Gross Domestic Product, 1967, by Districts

District	Marketed crop	Wage bill	GDP	GDP per in. shs.	District	Marketed Crop	Wage bill	GDP	GDP per in. shs.
Arusha d.	57·6	50·6	194·3	934	Kilwa d.	3·3	2·2	22·5	228
Masai d.	7·2	2·1	29·1	279	Lindi d.	17·4	12·6	78·7	332
Mbulu d.	28·0	14·8	97·9	339	Masasi d.	11·4	8·0	29·0	258
Arusha R.	92·5	67·4	321·1	534	Mtwara d.	11·4	16·3	68·9	512
Bagamoye d.	13·1	5·9	39·3	338	Nachingwea	4·0	3·1	19·9	247
Kisarawe d.	14·8	35·6	110·4	617	Newala	22·0	1·6	63·1	236
Mafia d.	2·8	1·1	7·3	437	Mtwara R.	70·0	43·8	308·7	299
Mzizima d.	4·7	10·3	32·9	437	Geita d.	43·0	12·0	123·3	332
Rufiji d.	5·8	3·0	27·2	224	Kwimba d.	26·3	7·0	85·2	279
Coast R.	41·6	55·9	217·4	427	Mwanza d.	24·8	39·6	182·6	673
Dar es Salaam	—	400·3	1131·5	4152	Ukerewe d.	8·4	3·8	38·1	349
Dodoma d.	2·7	21·6	112·2	350	Mwanza R.	102·6	62·4	429·1	406
Kondoa d.	2·8	3·5	42·7	201	Mbinga d.	12·8	2·6	38·5	267
Mpwapwa	5·8	5·0	41·6	237	Songea d.	5·7	8·4	44·6	294
Dodoma R.	11·5	30·1	196·6	278	Tunduma d.	3·8	1·6	20·1	207
Iringa }d. Mufindi	39·8	23·2 7·5	148·4	404	Ruvuma R.	22·2	12·6	53·5	262
Njombe d.	29·4	11·2	88·9	282	Kahama d.	5·8	3·0	32·1	235
Iringa R.	69·2	41·9	227·3	347	Maswa d.	42·9	6·9	124 3	289
Kasulu d.	5·5	1·6	36·7	177	Shinyanga	31·2	34·0	218·4	680
Kibondo	1·5	2·7	24·6	184	Shinyanga R.	80·0	43·9	374·8	422
Kigoma d.	9·3	9·9	64·5	495	Iramba d.	2·2	1·0	37·3	205
Kigoma R.	16·3	14·2	125·7	267	Manyoni d.	1·0	2·2	17·2	214
Kilimanjaro	168·1	72·8	373·8	746	Singida d.	2·7	6·7	48·8	254
Pare d.	11·5	14·1	55·2	369	Singida R.	5·8	9·9	103·2	227
Kilimanjaro R.	179·8	86·9	429·2	660	Mpanda d.	2·3	2·1	16·8	274
Musoma d.	19·5	18·0	138·6	395	Nzega d.	15·7	5·0	76·9	258
Northmara d.	7·1	2·7	45·4	246	Tabora d.	23·1	29·2	118·2	613
Mara R.	26·7	20·7	184·0	343	Tabora R.	41·1	36·3	212·0	384
Chunya d.	2·0	4·0	17·1	317	Handeni d.	2·0	3·9	26·1	197
Mbeya d.	14·1	13·8	75·9	397	Korogwe d.	46·3	37·6	88·4	630
Mbozi d.	9·2	1·8	33·0	227	Lushoto d.	16·7	10·6	62·9	300
Rungwe d.	24·2	15·3	96·6	269	Pangani d.	12·8	8·0	21·7	767
Sumbawanga	4·7	2·4	40·9	199	Tanga d.	83·7	104·8	306·3	1186
Mbeya R.	54·2	34·7	263·4	276	Tanga R.	161·4	164·9	505·4	657
Kilosa d.	32·5	27·3	82·7	428	Biharamulo	3·8	2·3	20·3	252
Morogoro	32·6	47·3	152·6	485	Bukoba d.	37·0	26·4	154·5	403
Ulanga d.	139·0	19·1	379·7	425	Karagwe d.	3·7	2·5	25·7	259
Morogoro R.	105·0	89·7	309·0	452	Ngara d.	3·1	1·5	19·1	201
					West Lake R.	48·0	32·7	219·6	334
					TANZANIA	1130·0	1260·0	5680·0	478

TABLE 17 Production and export of coffee, tea and sugar, 1962-67

PRODUCTION

Marketed quantities (000 tons)

	Av. 1960/1962	1964	1965	1966	1967
Coffee	34	52·4	66·0	77·6	69·0
Tea	4·1	4·7	5·6	6·7	7·0
Sugar	32·2	60·5	66·3	69·9	70·6

Value (million shillings)

Coffee	109·3	164·2	209·7	261·6	246·6
Tea	30·7	30·5	36·9	43·8	46·0
Sugar	29·0	55·6	61·0	64·3	65·0

EXPORTS

Volume (000 tons)

Coffee	25·7	32·7	27·8	49·8	43·7
Tea	3·9	4·4	4·2	6·2	6·0

Value (million shillings)

Coffee	132	221	172	301	237
Tea	32	31	29	45	43

TABLE 18 Production and export of tobacco, cashew, pyrethrum, 1962-67

PRODUCTION

Marketed quantities (000 tons)

	Av. 1960-62	1964	1965	1966	1967
Tobacco	2·2	2·1	5·1	5·2	7·7
Cashew	45·8	72·9	73·1	81·2	85·9
Pyrethrum	1·7	2·3	3·6	4·4	6·6

Value (million shillings)

Tobacco	10·6	12·2	27·8	18·9	28·4
Cashew	26·5	46·6	62·6	79·6	69·5
Pyrethrum	7·9	12·2	20·0	23·9	34·0

EXPORTS

Volume

	Av. 1960-62	1964	1965	1966	1967
Tobacco (000 lb.)	905	385	3674	5232	9032
Cashew (000 tons)	59	55·8	63·6	71·1	69·8

Value (million shillings)

Tobacco	2	1	10	16	34
Cashew	47	66	83	100	92

TABLE 19 Estimates of grain crops marketed, by Region, 1967*

Region	Maize tons	Maize % of total	Paddy tons	Paddy % of total	Millet & Sorghum tons	Millet & Sorghum % of total	Wheat tons	Wheat % of total
Arusha	2 200	17·7	400	1·2	2 300	6·2	19 400	64·7
Coast	200	0·2	4 000	12·1	100	0·3	—	—
Dodoma	16 000	12·9	—	—	1 200	3·2	—	—
Iringa	30 600	24·7	400	1·2	300	0·9	100	0·3
Kigoma	2 400	1·9	200	0·6	400	1·1	—	—
Kilimanjaro	14 300	11·5	300	1·0	4 000	10·8	9 200	30·7
Mara	6 000	4·8	1 000	3·0	7 500	20·4	—	—
Mbeya	1 700	1·4	11 800	35·6	5 800	15·8	1 100	3·6
Morogoro	5 100	4·1	4 100	12·1	7 800	21·2	—	—
Mtwara	200	0·2	300	1·0	1 500	4·1	—	—
Mwanza	3 700	3·0	1 000	3·0	100	0·3	—	—
Ruvuma	1 600	1·3	—	—	100	0·3	200	0·7
Shinyanga	600	0·6	2 400	8·0	700	1·9	—	—
Singida	2 500	2·0	—	—	3 500	9·5	—	—
Tabora	6 000	4·8	6 500	19·0	1 300	3·5	—	—
Tanga	10 700	8·6	700	2·2	—	—	—	—
West Lake	300	0·3	—	—	200	0·5	—	—
TOTAL	104 100	100·0	33 100	100·0	36 800	100·0	30 000	100·0

* Regional Agricultural Officers' estimates

TABLE 20 Livestock population, 1965*

Region	Cattle	Sheep	Goats	Pigs
Arusha	1 880 000	706 000	843 000	3 381
Coast	67 794	7 402	19 487	305
Dodoma	1 143 348	469 212	803 019	550
Iringa	617 865	97 237	141 135	1 526
Kigoma	50 645	23 327	86 059	—
Kilimanjaro	213 554	77 495	141 524	1 160
Mara	726 000	214 000	160 400	—
Mbeya	579 711	28 330	60 360	4 959
Morogoro	80 674	29 059	68 880	1 650
Mtwara	12 298	5 370	52 632	1 093
Mwanza	622 439	208 051	316 722	40
Ruvuma	7 284	2 474	24 118	1 035
Shinyanga	2 681 597	543 062	762 378	132
Singida	620 777	180 153	279 474	—
Tabora	637 322	123 541	158 195	9
Tanga	259 000	103 500	200 500	150
West Lake	99 609	28 000	124 000	45
Zanzibar/Pemba	46 748	144	14 197	—
TOTAL	10 346 665	2 846 267	4 266 080	16 035

It was also estimated that there were 210 horses, 172 000 donkeys and 15 million poultry.

* United Nations F.A.O. *Census of livestock, 1965*

TABLE 21 National ranches in Tanzania, 1965

Ranch	Total stock	Bulls	Steers	Cows	Heifers
Kongwa	14 240	496	5 424	4 458	3 763
Mkata	9 863	208	2 611	2 897	2 437
Nachingwea	3 207	71	1 578	1 102	456
W. Kilimanjaro	5 157	138	1 303	1 534	1 258
Ruvu	8 960	NO DATA			
Kitengule	1 551	93	554	185	704

TABLE 22 Net output of private agriculture at current prices*

	1964	1965	1966	1967
Livestock—subsistence	271	277	311	371
—commercial	114	122	142	130
All agriculture	2745	2592	2844	2879

* Background to the Budget, 1968–9

TABLE 23 Cattle sales, 1961 and 1967 (Primary markets only)*

	Slaughter stock	Immature stock	Heifers	Goats	Sheep
1961	234 000	42 000		87 000	16 147
1967	251 215	32 727	22 149	96 935	55 569

In addition 55 497 slaughter stock were sold on secondary markets.

* United Republic of Tanzania, Ministry of Agriculture and Co-operative Planning Unit, *Livestock Marketing Reports*

TABLE 24 Exports of hides and skins, 1966 and 1967*

	1966		1967	
	Pieces	Value (million shillings)	Pieces	Value (million shillings)
Hides	987 790	22·1	868 075	21·6
Hides (wet salted)	106 021	4·6	78 753	4·1
Goatskins	1 387 665	11·6	919 600	6·8
Sheepskins	686 650	4·0	662 224	4·3

* United Republic of Tanzania, Ministry of Agriculture and Co-operatives, Planning Unit, *Livestock Marketing Reports*

TABLE 25 Annual production of fish (*All figures are estimates)

	1962		1963		1964	
	Weight (1000's tons)	Value (m. shs.)	Weight (1000's tons)	Value (m. shs.)	Weight (1000's tons)	Value (m. shs.)
FRESHWATER						
L. Victoria	18·8	15·0	42·5	30·4	49·4	33·6
L. Tanganyika	12·0	2·6	15·1	3·3	16·2	3·6
L. Rukwa	3·0	1·4	11·3	5·0	10·0	4·4
L. Kitangiri*	3·0	0·6	2·5	0·5	7·8	1·5
Minor waters*	9·0	5·2	4·0	—	4·0	—
MARINE*						
Fish	9·0	9·0	9·0	10·0	10·0	12·0
Crustacea	—	—	—	—	—	—
TOTAL	54·8	33·8	84·4	49·2	97·4	55·1

Table 25 (continued)

	1965 Weight (1000's tons)	1965 Value (m. shs.)	1966 Weight (1000's tons)	1966 Value (m. shs.)	1967 Weight (1000's tons)	1967 Value (m. shs.)
FRESHWATER						
L. Victoria	46·9	30·6	41·2	27·2	38·7	33·3
L. Tanganyika	15·8	3·4	15·0	3·3	22·5	12·9
L. Rukwa	7·0	3·1	19·3	5·8	22·0	6·6
L. Kitangiri*	7·0	1·6	4·0	1·6	5·5	2·2
Minor waters*	5·0	1·6	5·5	3·7	5·5	3·7
MARINE*						
Fish	12·0	16·8	19·0	26·6	19·0	26·6
Crustacea	0·3	1·3	0·4	2·8	0·4	3·2
TOTAL	94·0	58·4	104·4	71·0	113·6	88·5

TABLE 26   Types of forest reserve

Closed high forest	9 196 sq. km.	3 592 sq. miles
Woodland (mostly miombo)	115 673 sq. km.	45 185 sq. miles
Mangrove swamp	791 sq. km.	309 sq. miles
Open grassland	3 520 sq. km.	1 375 sq. miles
TOTAL	129 180 sq. km.	50 461 sq. miles

TABLE 27   Softwood projects

Project	Area, 1967 acres	Area, 1967 approx. hectares	Development Plan, 1965-69, annual targets approx. acres	Development Plan, 1965-69, annual targets approx. hectares
Burhindi	100	40	300	120
Kawetire ⎫ Kiwira ⎬	8 000	3 200	—	—
Matogoro	500	200	100	40
N. Kilimanjaro ⎫ W. Kilimanjaro ⎬	8 500	3 400	{ 670 , 400	268 , 160
Rondo	300	120	200-250	80-100
Rubya	2 500	1 000	500	200
Sao Hill	14 000	5 600	2 000	800
Magamba ⎫ Shagayu ⎬ Shume ⎭	8 000	3 200	{ 50 , 150 , 300-400	20 , 60 , 120-160
Olmotonyi ⎫ South Meru ⎬	5 500	2 200	{ 350 , 325	140 , 130
Ukaguru	3 500	1 400	600	240
Rubare	500	200	No data	
Bana	500	200	No data	

TABLE 28   Timber production by circles (in cu. m. and cu. ft)*

Circles	Non-coniferous cu. m.	Non-coniferous cu. ft	Coniferous cu. m.	Coniferous cu. ft	Poles cu. m.	Poles cu. ft	Fuel wood cu. m.	Fuel wood cu. ft
Arusha	1 989	71 042	6 923	247 255	913	32 596	28 847	1 030 236
East and Coast	16 520	589 995	44	1 602	8 448	301 713	158 119	5 671 853
Kilimanjaro	4 758	169 920	6 915	246 980	808	28 864	21 994	785 483
Mtwara/Ruvuma	13 897	496 306	—	—	2 288	81 716	13 675	488 387
Mwanza	2 573	91 894	9 970	356 067	216	7 717	16 331	583 250
S. Highlands	5 169	184 616	4 305	153 767	1 085	38 766	39 224	1 400 857
Tabora	16 683	595 814	—	—	1 334	47 659	123 002	4 392 940
Tanga	31 987	1 142 402	9 052	323 295	1 039	37 090	16 063	573 697
TOTAL	93 576	3 341 989	37 209	1 328 966	16 131	576 121	417 255	14 926 703

* Monthly Area Returns, Forestry Division, 1967

TABLE 29 Log production, 1966

		cu. m.	cu. ft.
Forest Reserves	Coniferous	31 588	1 128 128
	Non-coniferous	30 322	1 082 936
Unreserved land	Coniferous	176	6 279
	Non-coniferous	78 268	2 795 290

TABLE 30 Exports of major forest produce

	Overseas	East Africa	Total
Logs and lumber	11 032 360	1 833 800	12 866 160
Plywood	31 200	2 565 940	2 597 140
Wood carvings	1 296 420	1 039 380	2 335 800
Minor forest produce	17 082 260	1 197 760	18 280 020
TOTAL	29 442 240	6 636 880	36 079 120

TABLE 31 Log removals, 1966

Species	Reserved cu. m.	cu. ft	Unreserved cu. m.	cu. ft	Total cu. m.	cu. ft
Pterocarpus angolensis	7 921	282 888	22 160	791 441	30 081	1 074 329
Brachylaena hutchinsii	—	—	24 684	881 583	24 684	881 583
Podocarpus spp.	22 122	790 085	24	859	22 146	790 944
Brachystegia spiciformis	2 457	87 758	12 275	438 406	14 732	526 164
Cupressus spp.	8 061	287 879	292	1 042	8 353	288 921
Ocotea usambarensis	7 651	273 234	148	5 272	7 799	278 506
Cephalosphaera. us.	4 822	172 216	13	448	4 835	172 664
Khaya nyasica	123	4 407	4 555	162 687	4 678	167 094
Chlorophora excelsa	259	9 262	2 936	104 857	3 195	114 119
TOTAL					120 503	4 294 324

These nine species account for 85·7 per cent of all log production

TABLE 32 Exports of minor forest products, 1966

	Shillings
Honey	1 224 380
Palm nuts	1 475 180
Gum arabic	1 087 180
Beeswax	4 099 760
Wattle extract	9 589 660
TOTAL	17 476 160

TABLE 33 Growth of tonnage, ton/miles and average length of haul, 1963-67*

	Tonnage (thous.)	Ton/miles (millions)	Average haul (miles)
1963	1215	417	212
1964	1281	408	205
1965	1335	470	215
1966	1488	565	229
1967	1495	574	n.a.

* East African Railways and Harbours Statistics

TABLE 34 The balance of trade between Europe and the Far East and Tanzania (in £ mill.)

Europe Favourable		Unfavourable		Far East Favourable		Unfavourable	
Belgium	0·7	U.K.	3·7	Hong Kong	3·6	China	1·0
Sweden	0·5	Italy	3·3	Indonesia	1·0	Japan	0·5
Spain	0·5	France	2·4	Siam	1·0	Malaysia	0·1
Eire	0·4	W. Germany	1·4	Singapore	0·8		
Denmark	0·2	Netherlands	0·4				
USSR	0·2	Norway	0·4				
Yugoslavia	0·2	Switzerland	0·3				
		Czecho-slovakia	0·3				
		Hungary	0·2				
		E. Germany	0·1				
TOTALS	2·7		12·5		6·4		1·6

TABLE 35 Main origins of major shipped imports in 1968 (in £ million) (only values of over £0·5 m. included)

	UK	W. Germany	Netherlands	Norway	Italy	France	Iran	S. Arabia	India	Pakistan	USA	Hong Kong	China	Japan	Total value of products from countries cited	Total value of products from world
1 Machinery and transport equipment	8·4	2·1	1·0		3·2	2·4					1·9			1·8	20·8	26·3
2 Manufactured goods (including tyres, paper, textiles, metal tubes and fittings)	3·2	1·3	0·8	0·5	0·8				1·7	1·0		0·8	1·9	3·2	15·2	19·7
3 Petrol & petroleum products							4·9	0·8							5·7	7·2
4 Chemicals (including paints, medicines, fertilizers)	2·0	1·1													3·1	4·2
5 Miscellaneous manufactured articles (mainly clothing)												1·3	0·8	0·7	2·8	2·8
6 Food and live animals	1·1												0·7		1·8	2·8
Total value of major imports from each country	14·7	4·5	1·8	0·5	4·0	2·4	4·9	0·8	1·7	1·0	1·9	2·1	3·4	5·7		
Grand total of all imports from each country	16·3	5·0	3·5	0·5	5·0	3·3	4·9	0·8	2·4	1·2	3·3	2·2	3·7	6·0		

TABLE 36 Main destinations of major shipped exports in 1968 (in £ million) (only values of over £0·5 m. included)

	UK	W. Germany	Netherlands	Belgium	Sweden	Italy	Bahrein	S. Arabia	India	USA	Australia	China	Japan	Siam	Singapore	Indonesia	Canada	Hong Kong	Total value of products for countries cited	Total value of products for world
Cotton	0·5	0·8										2·0	3·6					5·9	13·8	14·1
Coffee	1·3	1·2	0·7		0·7	0·8	0·7	0·5		2·5			0·6	1·0			0·6		10·6	13·3
Sisal & sisal rope	1·5	0·8	0·9	0·7						1·0	0·6						0·5		6·0	9·0
Cashew nuts									5·1										5·1	5·6
Cloves															0·9	1·1			2·0	3·0
Meat & meat preparations	2·0																		2·0	2·4
Oil seeds, nuts & kernels					All under £0·5 m., but mainly to Europe & Far East															2·2
Tea	1·8																		1·8	2·2
Tobacco	1·8																		1·8	1·9
Hides & skins	0·5					0·5													1·0	1·6
Animal foodstuffs	1·2																		1·2	1·2
Pyrethrum	0·5																		0·5	1·0
Total value of major exports to each country	11·1	2·8	1·6	0·7	0·7	1·3	0·7	0·5	5·1	3·5	0·6	2·0	4·2	1·0	0·9	1·1	1·1	5·9		
Grand total of all exports to each country	12·5	3·7	3·1	1·4	1·0	1·7	0·7	0·6	5·7	4·7	0·8	2·7	5·5	1·0	1·0	1·1	1·2	6·3		

TABLE 37 East African ports: total tonnage handled

	1958	1968	per cent change
Mtwara	68 072	173 475	150
Tanga	184 226	245 695	30
Dar es Salaam	705 326	2 127 734	200
Mombasa	2 529 730	5 407 837	110
TOTAL	3 487 354	7 954 741	130

TABLE 38 Categories of industrial establishments and industrial workers, 1967*

Category	No. of firms	No. of employees	Percentage of total employees
Beverage and tobacco	16	1 665	2·6
Chemical and oil	27	1 510	2·4
Electricity and water	20	1 765	2·9
Food	145	9 425	15·4
Footwear	36	2 880	4·6
Leather and rubber	15	435	0·7
Metal and machinery	41	3 970	6·4
Paper and printing	27	1 685	2·7
Stone and lime	12	780	1·3
Textile (inc. processing)	190	25 470	41·1
Transport	111	6 100	9·9
Wood and furniture	125	5 565	9·0
Miscellaneous	14	615	1·0
TOTAL	779	61 865	100·0

* Central Statistical Bureau

TABLE 39 Production of selected industries, 1963 and 1967*

Industry	Unit	1963	1967
Beer	'ooo gallons	1 962	5 102
Cement	tons	Nil	146 000
Cigarettes	millions	1 144	2 044
Oil refining	metric tons	Nil	660 000
Paints	gallons	95 357	274 623
Plywood	'ooo sq. ft	2 004	8 808
Pyrethrum extract	tons	99	238
Saw milling	'ooo cu. ft	3 676	4 585
Sisal twine	tons	Nil	14 887
Wheat flour	tons	28 378	41 159

* Central Statistical Bureau

TABLE 40 Mainland Tanzania: imports 1962 and 1967 by items (value in million shillings)

Class of item	1962	1967
Consumer goods	493	536
Intermediate	149	293
Transport equipment	93	212
Capital goods	269	507
Miscellaneous	26	30
TOTAL	1030	1578

TABLE 41 Gross mineral sales, 1966-68

		Value: Millions of Shs.			Percentage		
		1966	1967	1968	1966	1967	1968
1	Diamonds	180·0	222·9	135·4	83·3	89·8	82·8
2	Gold	14·1	4·7	4·8	6·5	1·9	2·9
3	Tin concentrates	8·8	6·2	6·9	4·1	2·5	4·2
4	Salt	6·2	7·2	9·6	2·9	2·9	5·9
5	Gemstones	2·2	2·9	2·8	1·0	1·2	1·7
6	Mica	1·8	1·7	1·3	0·8	0·7	0·8
7	Others	3·0	2·6	2·7	1·4	1·0	1·7
	TOTAL	216·1	248·2	163·5	100·0	100·0	100·0

TABLE 42 Fuel sales (revenues), 1967 (in shs)

Circle	Charcoal	Bush fuel	Plantation fuel	Total
Arusha	9 290	21 639	5 886	36 815
Kilimanjaro	5 745	17 383	3 954	27 082
East & Coast	144 991	36 753	11 640	193 384
Tanga	9 658	19 038	5 974	34 670
Tabora	69 811	183 520	—	253 331
Mwanza	11 567	10 923	8	22 498
S. Highlands	4 176	54 039	49 433	107 648
Mtwara/Ruvuma	2 361	14 755	4 021	21 137
TOTAL	257 599	358 050	80 916	696 565

TABLE 43 Petroleum product sales, 1967

Product	Sales (million gallons)	(million litres)
Illuminating kerosene	11·7	53·18
Motor fuels	45·5	206·84
Industrial fuels	40·9	185·98
TOTAL	98·1	446·00

TABLE 44 Coal reserves

Field	Reserves (million tons) Proved	Indicated
Ruhuhu fields		
Mbalawala	97·7	—
Ngaka	—	15·0
Mchuchuma	186·6	12·0
Kiwira-Songwe field	20·0	—
Galula field	negligible	—
Ufipa fields		
Mkomolo	—	2·5
Namwele	—	5·0
Muze	—	3·5
Mhukuru field	—	7·8
Mbamba Bay field	negligible	—
Njuga field	negligible	—

TABLE 46 Estimated value of produce, 1903 and 1911 (in rupees)

1903		1911	
Rubber	52 400	Rubber	239 050
Ivory	44 900	Sisal	226 600
Copra	27 870	Hides	151 750
Livestock	14 130	Copra	92 250
Sesame	13 960	Cotton	66 600
Coffee	12 850	Coffee	63 300
Hides	6 520	Wax	40 850
Grain	3 900	Groundnuts	24 500
		Ivory	24 300
		Timber	24 000
		Sesame	20 200
		Samli (Native butter)	9 350
		Rice	6 000
		Copal	5 035
		Capok	1 150

TABLE 45 Key to tribal reference on Map 47

1	Luo	39	Matumbi	75	Haya
2	Kuria	40	Mwera	75A	Nyambo
3	Suba	41	Machinga	76	Ruanda
4	Kwaya	42	Ngindo	77	Hangaza
5	Jita	43	Makonde	78	Subi
6	Kerewe	43A	Mawia	79	Rundi
7	Kara	44	Matambwe	80	Ha
8	Shashi	45	Makua	81	Jiji/Rundi
9	Zanaki	46	Yao		and Ha mix
10	Ikizu	47	Ndendeuli	82	Vinza
11	Ikoma	48	Ngoni	83	Tongwe
12	Nguruimi	49	Matengo	84	Holoholo
13	Sonjo	50	Nyasa	85	Bende
14	Masai	51	Pangwa	86	Konongo
15	Arusha	52	Bena	87	Pimbwe
16	Meru	53	Ngoni of Mpepo	88	Rungwa
17	Chagga	54	Pogoro	89	Fipa
18	Kahe	55	Ndamba	90	Rungu
19	Arusha Chini (Kuma)	56	Mbunga	91	Kimbu
20	Pare	57	Hehe	92	Nyika
21	Sambaa (Shambala)	58	Gogo	93	Wanda
		59	Turu	94	Mambwe
		60	Sandawe	95	Nyamwanga
22	Mbugu	61	Burungi	96	Nyiha
23	Digo	62	Rangi (and Wasi)	97	Wungu
24	Segeju	63	Barabaig	98	Safwa
25	Bondei	64	Iraqw	99	Sangu
26	Zigua	65	Gorowa	100	Wanji
27	Kwavi	66	Mbugwe	101	Kinga
28	Ngulu	67	Hadzapi (Kindiga or Tindiga)	102	Nyakyusa
29	Kaguru			103	Kisi
30	Doe	68	Isanzu	104	Ndali
31	Kwere	69	Iambi	105	Malila
32	Zaramo	70	Iramba	106	Lambia
33	Luguru	71	Sukuma	107	Pemba
34	Sagara	72	Nyamwezi	108	Tumbatu
35	Ndengereko	73	Sumbwa	109	Hadimu
36	Rufiji	74	Zinza	110	Swahili/ Shirazi of Mafia
37	Kutu				
38	Vidunda				

TABLE 47 Results of administrative reorganization

Year	Provinces	Districts	Year	Provinces	Districts
1924	nil	22	1947	8	45
1925	11	22	1948	8	49
1926	11	37	1950	8	54
1927	11	39	1954	8	56
1928	11	42	1958	8	58
1931	11	44	1959	9	57
1932	8	43	1961	9	57
1938	8	41			

TABLE 48 Main tribes of Tanganyika, 1957

	thous.	%		thous.	%
Sukuma	1094	12·6	Gogo	299	3·5
Nyamwezi	364	4·2	Ha	290	3·3
Makonde	334	3·9	Hehe	252	2·9
Haya	326	3·8	Nyakyusa	220	2·5
Chagga	318	3·7	Luguru	202	2·3

Source: *Tanganyika Census, 1957—Tribal analysis*, Dar es Salaam, 1958

TABLE 49 Main tribes of Uganda (1959) and Kenya (1962)

Kenya	thous.	%	Uganda	thous.	%
Kikuyu	1642	19·8	Baganda	1048	16·3
Luo	1148	13·8	Iteso	525	8·1
Luhya	1086	13·1	Banyankore	519	8·1
Kamba	933	11·3	Basoga	502	7·8
Kisii	538	6·5	Bakiga	460	7·1

Sources: *Uganda Census, 1959; Kenya Census, 1962*

TABLE 50 Tanzania: Population and area by landform category (grouped by divisions)

Category	Population thous.	% of total	Area thous. sq. km.	% of total	Average population density (p.s.k.)
1 MOUNTAINS					
A. Volcanic	832	6·8	28	3·1	29·9
B. Non-volcanic	1363	11·1	45	5·1	30·1
Mountain & plain mixed	291	2·4	24	2·7	12·3
TOTAL	2486	20·3	97	10·9	25·7
2 HILL COUNTRY					
A. High altitude (1000 m.+)	3050	24·8	281	31·7	10·9
B. Low altitude (1000 m.—)	536	4·4	45	5·1	11·8
TOTAL	3586	29·2	326	36·8	11·0
3 FLAT					
A. Upland lakeshore	1233	10·0	29	3·2	43·1
B. Upland plateau	2039	16·6	251	28·3	8·1
C. Lowland plateau	1503	12·2	164	18·5	9·1
D. Coastal	688	5·6	20	2·2	34·9
TOTAL	5463	44·4	464	52·3	11·8
Urban population	778	6·3	—	—	—
TANZANIA TOTAL	12 313	100·0	887	100·0	13·9

Note: Small discrepancies in the total of percentages are the results of rounding off individual figures

TABLE 51 Age and sex composition of the population of Tanzania, 1967

Age group	Males (thous.)	Females (thous.)	Male sex ratio	Total population (thous.)	Per cent of total
0– 4	1090	1097	99·3	2188	18
5–14	1607	1628	98·7	3234	26
15–44	2566	2714	94·6	5279	43
45–64	599	663	90·4	1263	10
65 & over	144	205	70·2	349	3
TOTAL	6006	6307	94·2	12 313	100

Source: computed from data in *Provisional estimates of fertility, mortality and population growth for Tanzania*, Central Statistics Bureau, Dar es Salaam, 1968

TABLE 52 Sex ratios of selected countries of Africa

Country	Year	Male sex ratio	Country	Year	Male sex ratio
Tanzania*	1967	95	Ghana	1960	102
Tanganyika	1957	93	Nigeria	1963	102
Tanganyika	1948	92	S. Africa	1960	102
Tanganyika	1931	94	Sierra Leone	1963	98
Kenya	1962	99	Senegal	1960/61	97
Uganda	1959	101	Dahomey	1960/61	96
Zambia	1963	98	Botswana	1964	95

* The sex ratio for Tanzania 1967 is for the total population; those for Tanganyika 1957, 1948 and 1931 are for the African population only

Sources: Tanganyika—*Census Reports*; others—*U.N. Demographic Yearbook*, 1967

TABLE 53 Selected sex ratios in Tanzania, 1967

1 NATIONAL

Tanzania	95
Mainland	95
Zanzibar	102

2 DISTRICTS

a. High		b. Low	
Pangani	123	Kibondo	80
Tanga	122	Kasulu	78
Mzizima	119	Njombe	81

3 DIVISIONS

a. High

Urban		Rural	
Dar es Salaam	123	Buzirayombo (Biharamulo)	117
Arusha	131	N. Iraqw (Mbulu)	112
Mtwara	120	Ismani (Iringa)	112
Tanga	119	Ulaya (Kilosa)	110

b. Low

Area	Ratio	Type
Buhoro	75	Northwest
Kinampanda	77	Central
Ukinga	80	Southwest
Njinjo	84	Coast
Mlalo	81	Mountain
Rombo South	84	Mountain

Source: Computed from data in *Tanzania: Preliminary results of the population census, August 1967*, Central Statistics Bureau, Dar es Salaam, 1967

TABLE 54 Growth of townships, 1948-67

Urban population		%	Rural population		%
1948	197 300	2·6	7 383 100		97·4
1957	364 100	4·1	8 424 400		95·9
1967	677 800	5·7	11 199 200		94·3

TABLE 55 Percentage of people living in townships

Region	Total pop. in '000s	% in towns & townships	Region	Total pop. in '000s	% in towns & townships
Coast	781	34·85	Mwanza	1057	3·67
Tanga	769	9·41	Iringa	683	3·21
Arusha	601	5·37	Mara	535	2·87
Morogoro	683	4·62	Mbeya	955	2·09
Kigoma	470	4·53	Singida	454	1·98
Dodoma	708	4·30	Ruvuma	392	1·37
Kilimanjaro	650	4·14	West Lake	658	1·24
Mtwara	1032	3·66	Shinyanga	888	0·91
Tabora	552	3·80			
(Ex. Zanzibar)			NATIONAL TOTAL	11 876	6·2

TABLE 56 Major existing land use in Dar es Salaam, 1966

Land use	Hectares within the 15 planning districts	Hectares outside planning districts (approximate)	Hectares Total
Residential	1 624	477	2 101
Mixed residential/ commercial	98	—	98
Commercial (other)	35	—	35
Industry, warehouse	326	159	485
Institutional	381	68	449
Education	213	18	231
University	—	372	372
Public open space	227	74	301
Private open space	68	—	68
Cemeteries	66	—	66
Airport	—	516	516
Vacant land subject to layout	1 718	881	2 599
Agriculture/cultivation vacant land	1 814	9 808	11 622
Military uses	40	439	479
TOTALS	6 610	12 812	19 422

TABLE 57 Mtwara: Imports and exports, 1967

Principal exports	Harbour ton	%	Principal imports	Harbour ton	%
Raw cashew nuts	47 749	42·8	Bulk oil	14 477	28·6
Cassava roots	30 001	26·8	General cargo	13 449	26·1
Sisal	12 881	11·5	Cement	10 234	19·8
Sesame seeds	4 013	3·6	Sugar	5 295	10·2
Copper	3 848	3·5	Milk	1 849	3·5
Tobacco	2 749	2·5	Sorghum	752	1·4
Timber	2 230	1·0	Corn meal	684	1·3
General cargo	1 934	1·7	Bitumen	638	1·2
Coffee	1 628	1·5	Lubricating oil	551	1·0
Groundnut oil/ cake	1 481	1·3			
SUB-TOTAL	108 514	96·2		47 929	93·1
Other	3 016	3·8		3 535	6·9
TOTAL	111 530	100·0		51 464	100·0

TABLE 58 Categories of services for service centres

Variety of services	High (3 pts)	Level Medium (2 pts)	Low (1 pt)	Max. pts
ADMINISTRATION				
Administration	Regional office	District office	Divisional office	3
Legal	High court	Resident magistrate	District magistrate	3
Finance	—	Senior revenue officer	Revenue clerk	2
Security	Regional hdq.	District hdq.	Police post	3
				11
TRANSPORTATION				
Telephone	Exchange with 24 hrs service	Service over limited time	Limited service	3
Postal	—	Full service	Limited service	2
Air Service	Daily	1–4 times weekly	Airstrip	3
Rail	—	Daily service	Limited service	2
Road	150 buses per week	25 buses per week	10 buses per week	3
		Major road junction	—	2
Petrol	—	Service station	Petrol outlet	2
Port	—	Lake and ocean ports with 10 or more departures	—	2
				19
COMMERCIAL				
Retail Trade	100 shops	Townships	Trading centres	3
Banking	—	National Bank of Commerce	—	2
Co-operatives	—	—	Co-operative Union	1
State Trading Corporation	—	—	State Trading Corporation	1
				7
SOCIAL				
Education	Post secondary school	Secondary school	—	2
Health	Fully equipped hospital	—	Bedded dispensary	3
Accommodation	—	Tourist hotel	Rest house	2
Others (1 pt each)	—	—	Library, Advocate, Piped water, Electricity, Private doctor, Cinema	6
				13
			GRAND TOTAL	50

TABLE 59　Tanga: imports and exports, 1967

Exports	Tons		Imports	Tons
Sisal	183 822		Fertilizers	6 094
Coffee	11 712		Maize meal	526
Tea	5 120		Salt	1 029
Wood flooring blocks	4 326		Bulk oils	16 988
Timber	2 647		Vehicles	4 953
Oil cakes	1 135		Tallow	2 352
Wattle	331		Cement in bulk	11 660
Castor seed	1 071		Cement	2 638
Cashew nuts	588		Beans	171
TOTAL EXPORTS APPROXIMATELY	230 770		TOTAL IMPORTS APPROXIMATELY	81 290

Key to diagram on p. 73

INTRATA	International Trading and Credit Company of Tanganyika Ltd
COSATA	Co-operative Supply Association of Tanganyika Ltd
NAPB	National Agricultural Products Board
TTB	Tanganyika Tobacco Board
BAT	British American Tobacco
TFCA	Tanganyika Farmers' Cooperative Association Ltd
NWB	National Wheat Board
NSB	National Sugar Board
LSMB	Lint and Seed Marketing Board
TCB	Tanganyika Coffee Board
TANITA	Tanita Co Ltd (Cashew Nuts)
TECO	Tanganyika Extract Co Ltd
TPB	Tanganyika Pyrethrum Board

Type 1　Tobacco, sugar, flour
　　　2　Oilseed, cashew, coffee, cotton, maize
　　　3　Pyrethrum and wattles

TABLE 60　Value and balance of trade (in millions of shillings)

	Imports			Exports			Total trade	Balance of trade
	Foreign	E. Africa	Total	Foreign	E. Africa	Total		
1947	240	30	270	209	13	227	497	−43
1957	785	155	940	820	40	861	1801	−79
1961	888	219	1107	1034	50	1131	2238	+24
1962	885	242	1127	1076	65	1193	2320	+66
1963	895	258	1153	1305	72	1419	2572	+266
1964	939	320	1259	1456	107	1597	2856	+338
1965	1068	337	1405	1313	121	1465	2870	+60
1966	1359	332	1691	1668	98	1878	3598	+187
1967	1345	280	1625	1645	83	1760	3385	+135

* Adjusted to include re-exports

TABLE 61　Value of domestic exports (in millions of shillings)

	1961	1962	1963	1964	1965	1966	1967
Coffee	135	132	137	221	172	301	237
Cotton	136	148	214	198	244	250	251
Sisal	281	315	453	437	286	235	201
Diamonds	116	109	99	136	147	186	223
Cashew nuts	36	47	40	66	83	100	92
Meat and meat preparations	41	46	39	43	38	57	48
Cloves	48	42	61	43	46	74	90
Oil seeds, nuts and kernels	51	46	80	61	57	53	45
Tea	27	32	31	31	29	45	43
Hides and skins	35	30	33	26	30	43	29
Gold	25	25	26	23	23	15	—
Others	103	104	132	171	163	203	387

DATE DUE

ÉCHÉANCE